Endorsements for *Strong Patronage, Weak Parties: The Case for Electoral System Redesign in the Philippines*

This book is a timely contribution to current debates on charter change, political reform and greater democratization in the Philippines. Moving the discussion beyond the usual debates about appropriate forms and systems of government, the authors have focused instead on electoral system redesign as an option that can possibly bring major changes to Philippine politics by addressing the problems of patronage systems and weak political parties. Drawing lessons from other experiences around the world, the book is a valuable resource for decision-makers as well as students of comparative and Philippine politics alike.

– MARIA ELA L. ATIENZA
Professor and Chair, Department of Political Science,
University of the Philippines-Diliman

In the on-going national debate on the shift to a federal system, we have always maintained that political and electoral reform are necessary ingredients to ensure the success of the change in the system of government. In this volume on electoral system redesign, Paul Hutchcroft and his colleagues have made a significant contribution to an evidence-based discussion on issues of constitutional reform. The 1987 constitution is far from "perfect," as some would claim. This book makes the case that the current Philippine charter needs to be revisited and that there are other viable alternatives we must explore and consider.

– JONATHAN E. MALAYA
Department of the Interior and Local Government Assistant Secretary-in-charge,
Inter-Agency Task Force on Federalism and Constitutional Reform

While there is much talk today of federalism as a possible answer against longstanding issues such as corruption, poverty and overconcentration of both wealth and political power in so-called "imperial Manila," it is critically important to recognize not simply the returns but also the potential risks related to such an overarching reform. This volume describes less risky, but no less impactful, alternatives to bring about fundamental change. Hopefully, it will trigger a real debate on what options offer our country the greatest chance of success with the fewest unintended negative consequences.

— RONALD U. MENDOZA
Dean, Ateneo School of Government

For any democracy, electoral rules are some of the most critical choices in constitutional design. Paul Hutchcroft and authors are building a strong case for prioritizing electoral reform in order to begin to redress two major ills of Philippine politics, namely patronage and weak political parties. As this book persuasively argues, electoral system reform can have a profound effect on the future political life of the Philippines, enabling the emergence not only of more inclusive representation but also of better policies and development outcomes.

— LEENA RIKKILÄ TAMANG
Director for Asia and the Pacific,
International Institute for Democracy and Electoral Assistance (IDEA)

STRONG PATRONAGE, WEAK PARTIES

The Case for Electoral System Redesign in the Philippines

Paul D. Hutchcroft
editor

Published by

World Scientific Publishing Co. Pte. Ltd.
5 Toh Tuck Link, Singapore 596224
USA office: 27 Warren Street, Suite 401-402, Hackensack, NJ 07601
UK office: 57 Shelton Street, Covent Garden, London WC2H 9HE

and

Anvil Publishing, Inc.
7th Floor Quad Alpha Centrum
125 Pioneer Street
Mandaluyong City 1550, Philippines

Library of Congress Cataloging-in-Publication Data
Names: Hutchcroft, Paul D. (Paul David), editor.
Title: Strong patronage, weak parties : the case for electoral system redesign in the Philippines /
  Paul Hutchcroft, editor.
Description: Singapore ; Hackensack, NJ : World Scientific Publishing Co. Ltd. ;
  Mandaluyong City, Philippines : Anvil Publishing, Inc., [2020] |
  Includes bibliographical references and index.
Identifiers: LCCN 2019044565 | ISBN 9789811212598 (hardback) |
  ISBN 9789811213601 (paperback)
Subjects: LCSH: Elections--Philippines. | Election law--Philippines. |
  Patronage, Political--Philippines. | Political parties--Philippines.
Classification: LCC JQ1418 .S78 2020 | DDC 324.609599--dc23
LC record available at https://lccn.loc.gov/2019044565

British Library Cataloguing-in-Publication Data
A catalogue record for this book is available from the British Library.

Copyright © 2020 by Anvil Publishing, Inc.
All rights reserved.

For any available supplementary material, please visit
https://www.worldscientific.com/worldscibooks/10.1142/11616#t=suppl

Desk Editor: Sylvia Koh

CONTENTS

A FOREWORD FROM THE ASIA FOUNDATION — vii

Chapter One
Electoral System Redesign: An Opportunity
for Effective Political Reform in the Philippines — 1
Paul D. Hutchcroft

Chapter Two
Why (and How) Electoral Systems Shape Development Outcomes — 27
Allen Hicken

Chapter Three
Designing and Reforming Electoral Systems in Southeast Asia — 43
Benjamin Reilly

Chapter Four
When Does Electoral System Reform Occur? — 59
Allen Hicken

Chapter Five
Gender and the Electoral System: What Works for Women — 77
Socorro L. Reyes

Chapter Six
Lessons from a Neighbor: The Negative
Consequences of Indonesia's Shift to the Open List — 93
Edward Aspinall

Chapter Seven
The Political Party Development Bill: Strengthening Parties
Toward the Goal of Strengthening Philippine Democracy — 111
Ramon C. Casiple

Chapter Eight
Patronage Politics and Parties in the Philippines:
Insights from the 2016 Elections — 133
Meredith L. Weiss

Chapter Nine
Untangling the Party List System — 151
Julio C. Teehankee

CHAPTER TEN
The Multi-Member Plurality System in the Philippines and its Implications — 169
Nico Ravanilla

BIBLIOGRAPHY — 188

CONTRIBUTORS — 201

INDEX — 203

LIST OF FIGURES AND TABLES

List of Abbreviations	viii
Political Parties	viii
Figure 3.1: The Four Major Electoral System Families	44
Figure 4.1: Necessary Conditions for Reform Initiation	74
Figure 4.2: Inter- and Intra-Party Dimensions of Electoral Systems	75
Table 2.1: Party-centric vs Candidate-centric Systems (in a nutshell)	38
Table 3.1: Electoral System Changes in Southeast Asia	54
Table 5.1: Electoral Systems and Women's Representation	80
Table 5.2: Top Countries with Voluntary Party Quotas	85
Table 5.3: Comparative Statistics of Women and Men Voters, Candidates and Winners	89
Table 7.1: Timeline of Political Party of Development Bill	(insert)
Table 9.1: Majoritarian and Proportional Representation Electoral Systems	153
Table 9.2: Types of Mixed Electoral Systems	154
Table 9.3: Philippine Party-List Elections: 1998–2016	157
Table 9.4: Seat Allocations Under the Philippine Party List System	159
Table 10.1: 2016 Senatorial Candidates and Their Bases of National Followings	172-73
Table 10.2: Parties Represented by Candidates for the Senate Elections, 1995–2016	174
Table 10.3: Parties Represented by Elected Members of the Senate, 1995–2016	175
Table 10.4: Number of Party/coalitions and Independent Candidates by Office, For election years 2001, 2004, and 2007	177
Table 10.5: Incidence of Party Switching of Candidates for City and Municipal Councils across Election Years 2001, 2004, and 2007	178
Table 10.6a: Voter Preferences across Parties, Part I	179
Table 10.6b: Voter Preferences across Parties, Part II	180
Table 10.7: Candidate Vote-shares and Probability of Winning, by Office	181

A FOREWORD FROM THE ASIA FOUNDATION

The Philippines has a hard-earned and proud history of democracy. Within the citizenry of Asia's oldest democracy, support for this system of government has not waned: a recent poll says 60 percent of the population prefers democracy over any other form of government (Social Weather Stations, March 2018).

In 2016, The Asia Foundation and the Australian Embassy supported a constructive discussion on electoral systems, gathering prominent scholars and interest groups to talk about the influence of electoral systems with respect to development outcomes here in the Philippines and other countries.

With this volume, we continue to nurture a healthy discussion on these critical issues. Authored by leading Philippine and international experts, including its editor, Dr. Paul Hutchcroft, the book explores options for tackling the electoral system challenges of the Philippines: improving the effectiveness of political parties, creating more space for women's representation, reforming the party list system, and considering alternative means of electing the Senate as well as local legislative councils, among others.

The book commendably offers a unique balance of perspectives: a wide lens, looking at other countries' electoral system design and experiences, and a lens that zooms in on the distinctiveness of the Philippine electoral system and suggestions for reform. The book, while directed towards Filipinos who want to keep abreast of politics and electoral processes, should also be an informative read for scholars and policymakers outside the Philippines. We are happy to support this publication, but at the same time want to emphasize that the views expressed here are those of the authors and are not the perspective of The Asia Foundation.

Any decisions on changing the current system of "converting votes to seats" are clearly for Filipinos to decide upon. However, we believe that offering a range of perspectives on electoral systems–making it less abstract to readers–is worthwhile. The Asia Foundation's more than 60 years of development experience in the Philippines, particularly in supporting fair elections and democratic political processes, and in strengthening governance, are guided by our recognition that a thriving democracy is sustained by an informed and engaged citizenry.

Sam Chittick
Country Representative, Philippines
The Asia Foundation

LIST OF ABBREVIATIONS

AV	alternative vote (or preferential voting, "instant runoff voting")
CDA	Constitutional Drafting Assembly (Thailand)
CEDAW	United Nations 1979 Convention on the Elimination of All Forms of Discrimination Against Women
CER	Consortium on Electoral Reforms
CLPR	closed-list proportional representation
COA	Commission on Audit
COMELEC	Commission on Elections
CPPR	Consortium on Political Party Reforms
DPR	People's Representative Council (*Dewan Perwakilan Rakyat*) (Indonesia)
EDSA	People Power Revolution of 1986 (Epifanio de los Santos Avenue)
FPTP	first past the post (SMDP)
IBP	*Interim Batasan Pambansa* or Interim National Assembly
INC	*Iglesia ni Cristo* or Church of Christ
IPD	Institute for Popular Democracy
IPER	Institute for Political and Electoral Reform
MES	mixed electoral system
MMD	multi-member district
MMM	mixed-member majoritarian system (parallel system)
MMP	mixed-member proportional system (compensatory system)
MPR	*Majelis Permusyawaratan Rakyat* or People's Consultative Assembly (Indonesia)
MPS	multi-member plurality system
NCR	National Capital Region
NIPS	National Institute for Policy Studies
OLPR	open-list proportional representation
PLS	party list system
PR	proportional representation
SMD	single-member district
SMDP	single-member district plurality
SNTV	single non-transferable vote
SOCE	Statement of Contributions and Expenditures
TRS	two-round system
TWP	"thinking and working politically"
WEF	Women's Empowerment Fund

POLITICAL PARTIES

BP	*Bangon Pilipinas,* or Arise Philippines
CDP	Centrist Democratic Party
CMD	Christian-Muslim Democrats
DPP	Democratic Party of the Philippines
GAD	Grand Alliance for Democracy

IBID	*Isang Bansa, Isang Diwa* or One Nation, One Spirit
K-4	*Koalisyon ng Katapatan at Karanasan sa Kinabukasan* or Coalition of Truth and Experience for Tomorrow
KAMPI	*Kabalikat ng Malayang Pilipino* or Partnership of Free Filipinos
KBL	*Kilusang Bagong Lipunan* or New Society Movement
KNP	*Koalisyon ng Nagkakaisang Pilipino* or United Filipino Coalition
KPPP	*Kilusan para sa Pambansang Pagpapanibago* or Movement fo National Change
LABAN	*Lakas ng Bayan* or Strength of the Nation
Lakas-CMD	*Lakas ng Tao*, National Union of Christian Democrats or Strength of the People, and Christian-Muslim Democrats. At certain points, *Lakas ng Tao* was also known as Lakas ng EDSA.
Lakas-NUCD	*Lakas ng Tao*, National Union of Christian Democrats or Strength of the People, and National Union of Christian Democrats. At certain points, *Lakas ng Tao* was also known as *Lakas ng EDSA.*
LAMMP	*Laban ng Makabayang Masang Pilipino* (renamed LAMP) or Fight of the Nationalist Filipino Masses
LAMP	*Lapian ng Masang Pilipino* or Party of the Filipino Masses
LDP	*Laban ng Demokratikong Pilipino* or Fight of the Democratic Filipino
LDP	Liberal Democratic Party (Japan)
LP	Liberal Party (Philippines)
LM	*Lapiang Manggagawa* or Workers Party
NP	Nacionalista Party or Nationalist Party
NPC	Nationalist People's Coalition
NUP	National Unity Party
PDI-P	*Partai Demokrasi Indonesia – Perjuangan*, Indonesian Democracy Party – Struggle
PDP	*Partido Demokratiko Pilipino* or Philippine Democratic Party
PDP-LABAN	*Partido Demokratiko Pilipino-Lakas ng Bayan*
PDSP	*Partido Demokratiko Sosyalista ng Pilipinas* or Democratic Socialist Party of the Philippines
PGRP	Philippine Green Republican Party
PIBID	*Partido Isang Bansa, Isang Diwa* or Party of One Nation, One Spirit
PKS	*Partai Keadilan Sejahtera*, Prosperous Justice Party (Indonesia)
PMM	*Partido ng Manggagawa at Magsasaka*
PMP	*Partido ng Masang Pilipino* or Party of the Filipino Masses
PNI	*Partai Nasional Indonesia*, Indonesian National Party
PROMDI	*Probinsya Muna Development Initiative* or Province First Development Initiative
PRP	People's Reform Party
Reporma	*Partido para sa Demokratikong Reporma* or Party for Democratic Reforms
UNA	United Nationalist Alliance
UNIDO	United Democratic Opposition
UNO	United Opposition
VNP	*Bagumbayan*–Volunteers for a New Philippines

Thumbs down to political patronage: revelations over pork barrel abuses in the previous administration brought forth large protests in Manila and other cities in late August 2013. Despite the protests, Philippine politics continues to be heavily driven by patronage and pork to the detriment of a focus on policies and programs.

Photo by Ted Aljibe, Agence France-Presse. Reprinted with the permission of Agence France-Presse.

CHAPTER ONE
ELECTORAL SYSTEM REDESIGN: AN OPPORTUNITY FOR EFFECTIVE POLITICAL REFORM IN THE PHILIPPINES

PAUL D. HUTCHCROFT

> "A good electoral system can give you a glimpse of Heaven, but a
> bad electoral system can give you a quick trip to Hell."[1]

Electoral systems help to shape incentives, and incentives help to shape behavior. If designed well, as the epigraph above suggests, electoral systems can help nurture polities that are more likely to be oriented toward positive collective political outcomes. Where these systems are not well designed, one should anticipate far more negative outcomes.

While there is no such thing as a magic bullet in the realm of political reform, the choice of electoral system can nevertheless have profound implications for both development and democracy. In many settings around the world, development outcomes are undermined by weakly institutionalized political systems that privilege patronage over policy; skew service delivery to narrow electoral considerations rather than broader development objectives; and feature election campaigns centered around vote-buying and gift-giving rather than policy choices. At the same time, the quality of democracy can be undermined by the weakness of political parties, and hence the lack of clear structure to political competition. This is particularly disadvantageous to poor and marginalized citizens, who are especially reliant on collective action to promote their interests in the policy realm.[2] Two overarching and enduring characteristics of Philippine politics, as captured in the title of this volume and discussed further below, are

---

1 Andrew Reynolds, University of North Carolina, speaking to a forum on electoral system reform of the International Forum for Electoral Systems and the Institute for Autonomy and Governance, Notre Dame University, Cotabato City, 23 February 2014.

2 As Gabriella Montinola explains, "Meaningful social change has been inhibited because political parties have failed to structure political competition to allow for the representation of interests of the poor and marginalized sectors. . . . Quality of choice depends on political parties, the main organizations that structure political competition" (1999, 133).

strong patronage systems and weak political parties. Well-designed electoral reform can strengthen political parties, and thereby begin to shift a political system toward a greater focus on policies and programs while reducing the relative importance of patronage and pork.

Over the past half century, the Philippines has on occasion had intensive discussions about the advantages and disadvantages of undertaking major changes to its political structures. In both 1973 and 1987, under what were very distinct circumstances, new constitutions instituting fundamental changes to the political system were put in place. On other occasions (most importantly 1997–98 and 2003–2009), extensive debates did not lead to constitutional revision. Since 2016, there have been further discussions about thoroughgoing political reform that have animated countless public forums throughout the archipelago, leading into the 2018 convening of a "Consultative Committee to Review the 1987 Constitution." As this volume goes to press, it is too early to assess whether this process will ultimately lead to substantial constitutional change.[3]

In general, the focus of these episodic national conversations on political reform via constitutional revision has been on shifts to new types of representational structures (from the longstanding presidential system, first put in place in the 1935 Constitution, to either semi-presidential or parliamentary systems) as well as—more recently—the character of territorial structures of governance (with proposals to move from the current unitary system to a federal system of government). Through this long history, however, it has been quite rare for significant attention to be given to a third major type of political reform, namely the redesign of the electoral system (most elements of which also require constitutional change). This makes the Philippines a bit of an outlier, relative to its neighbors, some of which (particularly those to the north, in East Asia) have used electoral system redesign as a potent tool for positive political reform.

This volume makes the case for why electoral system redesign deserves careful attention as a means of bringing major changes to the way in which politics is done in the Philippines. Any process of electoral system redesign must begin with a clear sense of what national goal (or goals) it is that one is seeking to promote. In the Philippines, political reformers have often voiced the need for measures that help both to undermine systems of patronage and to promote stronger political parties. To highlight a core observation at the outset, *the current combination of electoral systems in the Philippines pretty much guarantees*

---

3 On the latest state of play, see Malcolm Cook, "Philippine Federalism's Fortunate Falter," *ISEAS Perspective*, 13 September 2018 (Singapore: Institute for Southeast Asian Studies), at https://www.iseas. edu.sg/images/pdf/ISEAS_Perspective_2018_55@50.pdf.

the perpetuation of weak and incoherent political parties. As long as parties are weak and lacking in coherence, the primary focus of political contention is much more likely to be on patronage and pork than on policies and programs. *To fix these fundamental ills of the Philippine polity, there is no better reform option than a well-constructed set of changes to the electoral system.*

ELECTORAL SYSTEMS: WHAT IT MEANS

What do we mean when we speak of electoral systems? It involves, first of all, the formulas used to convert votes to seats. Ben Reilly's Chapter Three provides a fuller overview of the range of systems used around the world, but key types of particular significance include the following:

1. Plurality systems
   - The most common type of plurality system, found in many countries, is *first past the post* (FPTP), also known as a *single-member district plurality* (SMDP) system. In this system, one member of the legislature is elected from a district, and whoever gets the most votes (i.e., a plurality) wins the seat. As those who do not obtain a plurality are left with nothing, this is also called a *winner takes all* system. This is used in the election of the bulk of the members of the Philippine House of Representatives.

   - Another variant of this system—found in far fewer countries around the world—is the *multi-member plurality system* (MPS), described in Nico Ravanilla's Chapter Ten. Although not common internationally, this system plays a prevalent role in the Philippines as it is used to elect a whopping 80 percent of candidates: from the Senate to the ARMM Regional Assembly to the councils of the country's 81 provinces, 145 cities, and 1489 municipalities.[4] Voters are given as many votes as there are seats to be filled, and whichever candidates win the highest number of votes are elected to the legislative body.

2. *Proportional representation* (PR) systems, of different varieties as explained in Chapter Three, where the number of votes received by a party should

---

4 http://www.dilg.gov.ph/facts-and-figures/Regional-and-Provincial-Summary-Number-of-Provinces-Cities-Municipalities-and-Barangays/32

translate as closely as possible into the number of seats that the members of that party will obtain in the legislature.

- One variant, *closed-list PR* (CLPR), is often put in place with the goal of building stronger political parties. In CLPR, parties choose and rank the candidates on their party list. This enables parties to exercise considerable discipline over the candidates that are put on the list. It might be best thought of as *the party-centric type of PR*.

- A second variant, *open-list PR* (OLPR), has the virtue of sounding more democratic. The "open" element of the system is that while parties choose the candidates on their party list, it is the voters who determine their rank. While this increases voter choice, it at the same time undermines party discipline. As such, this system might best be thought of as *candidate-centric PR*. In Edward Aspinall's Chapter Six, he chronicles the negative consequences of Indonesia's shift from a closed- to an open-list arrangement.

3. The *party list system* (PLS), unique to the Philippines, where voters have one vote to deploy across a wide range of party-list groups that appear on the ballot. But in this peculiar system, no party (regardless of its vote total) is allowed to gain more than three seats in the House of Representatives. As such, it is not at all proportional in the outcomes it produces (and also, as explained in Julio Teehankee's Chapter Nine, has other features that distinguish it sharply from a standard PR system).

4. Various *mixed systems or hybrids*, which in many countries involve some element of SMDP (to ensure the representation of geographical interests) combined with closed-list PR (to foster the growth of stronger political parties).

In addition, when we speak of electoral systems we are referring as well to other arrangements that—as with the formulas surveyed above—are capable of critically shaping political outcomes. These include:

1. *Arrangements to elect national and local executives*, including

   a. Whether plurality (as is used, e.g., in the Philippines, the United States, and elsewhere) or majority-inducing run-off systems (as used, e.g., in France, Indonesia, and other countries). In the latter system, also known as a *two-round system* (TRS), a run-off election is held in the event that no candidate receives 50 percent of the vote in the first-round election.[5]

    b. Whether the president and vice president (as well governors and vice governors, mayors and vice mayors) are elected separately or as part of a joint ticket.

2. *District magnitude,* or the number of seats that are elected per district. In general, as explained in Allen Hicken's Chapter Two, larger district magnitudes are "associated with legislative seats going to many small parties" while smaller district magnitudes are likely to produce the opposite: "relatively fewer and larger political parties winning legislative seats."

Along with this description of what electoral systems *are,* it is also important to emphasize what electoral systems *are not.* When we speak of electoral systems, we are not referring to the following: electoral administration, electoral adjudication, voter education, and international election monitoring. All of these are important matters for understanding how elections are run, and elections cannot succeed without effective institutions of electoral administration (as such, these institutions need to be established with care, and their integrity needs to be carefully guarded across the decades). But as critical "rules of the game," electoral systems have the potential to change basic incentives and hence basic behavior. This means that electoral system reform has particularly strong potential for underlying transformative change of a political system—for good or for ill, depending on how the reform has been designed. Most importantly, in the Philippine context, well-considered electoral system redesign has the potential to bring greater institutionalization of politics by nurturing stronger political parties.[6]

---

5 See Ben Reilly, "Electing a President: Picked by Some, Rejected by Many," Rappler, 11 March 2016, at https://www.rappler.com/nation/politics/elections/2016/125133-reilly-presidential-elections-run-off

6 While the term "rules of the game" comes from North 2010, the analysis of this chapter relies instead on the institutionalist foundations of Huntington 1968 and in particular his focus on the capacity of strong political parties to structure political competition. The limitations of a Northian framework relative to a Huntingtonian framework are examined in Hutchcroft and Kuhonta 2018.

ELECTORAL SYSTEM REDESIGN IN THE CONTEXT OF OTHER TYPES OF POLITICAL REFORM

When reformers set out to change the structure of a democratic political system, there are three basic decisions that must be considered. While it is quite common for the three decisions to be confused with each other, they should in fact be treated as distinct.[7]

The first decision is about the *representational structures of the government*, and here one finds three major options:

1. *Presidentialism*. Should the linkages between the citizens and their elected representatives be via a presidential system, with the direct election of the president by the people and clear divisions of power and "checks and balances" among three branches of government? On the negative side of the ledger, a common danger of presidentialism is the excessive power that may come to reside in the country's chief executive. This can be counterbalanced by measures seeking to prevent presidential dominance over other branches of government as well as over constitutionally established commissions.

2. *Parliamentarism*. Or should these linkages be via a parliamentary system, in which the voters elect the members of a legislature (known as a parliament) who in turn elect a prime minister? In other words, within a parliamentary system executive authority arises out of the parliament rather than being directly elected by the people. This process necessarily requires that strong and cohesive political parties *already* be in place; without this critical precondition, the parliament will be challenged to bring forth stable executive authority. This risks frequent turnover of power from one prime minister to another.

3. *Semi-presidentialism*. A further option is a semi-presidential system, which contains features of both presidentialism and parliamentarism. Some view this as an attractive option since it "splits the difference" between the two more standard systems. Others warn that semi-presidentialism is "easy to choose" but "difficult to operate" (Wu 2007, 201); where it is not well designed, one should anticipate the potential for high levels of contention between the two leaders—president and prime minister— who share executive authority.

---

7 This discussion draws on Hutchcroft 2017.

Second, reformers have choices to make about *the type of relationship that is to be established between the central government and subnational levels of government* (regions, provinces, cities, municipalities, etc.). The core decision here is between a unitary system and a federal system, but it is critical to emphasize the huge variation that exists *within* each category. Some unitary systems are relatively more centralized while others more decentralized; likewise, some federal systems are relatively more centralized while others more decentralized. Neither should be viewed as a set package that can be taken off the shelf and simply "plugged in" to a country. Rather, each requires major collective deliberation as to how—within each system—relations among the different levels of government are not just to be defined *at the outset* but also implemented and enforced *over time*.

The third major decision to be made is *the type(s) of electoral system to be adopted*. Over the past half century in the Philippines, as noted above, it has generally been given far less attention than the other two major types of reform. This is particularly striking given how other countries in Asia and the Pacific have used electoral system reform as a way of seeking to bring change to the political system.[8] A key purpose of this volume is to highlight the promising opportunities that *well-designed* changes to the electoral system present for effective political reform in the Philippines.

These three basic decisions are critical foundations of a democratic political system, and a survey of democracies reveals that they are mixed and matched around the world in many diverse ways. While these decisions may be closely interrelated (e.g., reformers could choose to nurture stronger political parties through electoral system redesign *prior* to instituting parliamentarism), it is important to view them as three distinct components of political reform.

POLITICAL REFORM IN THE PHILIPPINES: MULTIPLE PURSUITS, TWO EPISODES OF CHANGE

As noted at the outset of this chapter, the Philippines has on numerous occasions engaged in intensive consideration of political reform. A Constitutional Convention began serious deliberations in 1971, only to be cut off by the declaration of martial

---

8 On the successful reform experiences in Japan and New Zealand, see Hicken's Chapter Four. This includes analysis of electoral system reforms in the 1997 Thai constitution that have subsequently been reversed by military governments. Further analysis of Japan and Thailand is found in Ravanilla's Chapter Ten. The broader (and decidedly mixed) picture of Southeast Asian reform experience is discussed in Reilly's Chapter Three, while Aspinall's Chapter Six focuses specific attention on lessons (largely but not entirely negative) from Indonesia.

law by President Ferdinand E. Marcos in 1972. This produced the authoritarian constitution of 1973, ratified by so-called "Citizens' Assemblies" carefully overseen by the newly installed authoritarian regime. The fall of Marcos in 1986 led directly into the 1986 Constitutional Convention, convened by President Corazon C. Aquino, which promulgated a new charter that was overwhelmingly ratified by popular referendum the following year. This was a constitution defined by its anti-authoritarian and human rights provisions, and its framers were intent on putting in place a political system that could not be manipulated in the future for authoritarian ends.[9]

Among the subsequent five presidents of the post-Marcos Philippines, three have given a great deal of attention to constitutional revision while only two have not. Fidel V. Ramos (1992–98) tried to extend his term and institute an authoritarian version of parliamentary government, but the effort failed in the face of strong popular opposition. Joseph Estrada (1998–2001), on the other hand, had quite fleeting interest in charter change and was, in any case, removed from office amidst the "People Power II" uprising of early 2001. During the tenure of Gloria Macapagal-Arroyo (2001–2010) talk of constitutional revision—toward not only a parliamentary but also a federal republic—was a valuable means of diverting attention from allegations that she had padded the results of the 2004 general election. The diversion was seemingly helpful as she successfully fended off impeachment challenges and maintained herself in power until the 2010 elections, but actual constitutional change was not to be. Benigno S. Aquino III (2010–2016), always keen to differentiate himself from his predecessor, expressed adamant opposition to altering the constitution that his mother had put into place. Most recently, under the presidency of Rodrigo Duterte (2016–present), the Philippines has once again shifted its attention to the prospect of major political reform. Unlike in previous years, however, the focus this time around is primarily on federalism and only secondarily on other variants of political reform.

In late 2014 and early 2015, well in advance of the 2016 election, Mayor Rodrigo Duterte of Davao talked up federalism in his initial forays around the country. The formal campaign in 2016 was primarily dominated by other issues—namely crime, corruption, and drugs—but since his inauguration on 30 June 2016 there has been frequent (although less than consistent) attention to the stated goal of moving the country to a federal system. In December 2016, Duterte signed an Executive Order announcing plans to name a "Consultative Committee to Review the 1987 Constitution." It was not until late January 2018, however, that the members of the committee were actually named, after which they were given precious little time to craft a constitutional draft in advance of the President's annual State of the Nation Address in late July.

---

9 See Wurfel 1988, 310 and Abinales and Amoroso 2017, 234.

Given the circumstances in which it was named, it came as no surprise that the Committee's centerpiece element of reform has been a proposed shift to federalism—albeit combined with significant attention to electoral system redesign.[10] From the standpoint of the reform goals focused upon in this book, namely curbing patronage and building stronger parties, federalism would have little if any efficacy. More likely, in fact, it is likely to nurture new playgrounds for patronage—most obviously in the new federal states that are to be created across the archipelago.[11] One can also predict new stresses on the already weak political party system, as regional bosses may become tempted at the prospect of building regional political parties. This would have enormously negative consequences on the capacity of the political system to deliver nationally oriented public goods.[12] More generally, one must anticipate the huge risk of unintended consequences that would be posed by such a major restructuring of the country's territorial structures. A shift to federalism, paradoxically, requires a strong and capable central government able to enforce the rules by which authority is being devolved to the subnational level. Given the ongoing weakness of the Philippine state, at the national and more especially the subnational level, the only thing that is safely predictable is unpredictability: it is extremely difficult to know what kind of polity might emerge at the end of the process.

---

10 The draft constitution submitted by the Consultative Committee to President Duterte includes a very positive change in the system used to elect members of the House of Representatives. The current party-list system (PLS), used to elect 20 percent of the body, would be replaced by closed-list proportional representation (CLPR) for the election of 40 percent of the body (with the remaining 60 percent to be chosen by single-member district plurality or first past the post). Parties would be subjected to a very significant 5 percent electoral threshold. Perhaps in an effort to assuage concerns from participants in the current PLS, the highly problematic focus on "sectoral representation" remains partially in place for the first three terms of a new legislature (one-half of the CLPR seats will initially be "reserved for labor, peasant, urban poor, indigenous peoples, and fisherfolk groups, provided that they organize themselves as parties or coalitions of parties"). The electoral system chosen for the Senate was entirely uncreative, essentially mimicking that of the United States (two seats per federal state). The full draft of the new constitution can be found at https://www.scribd.com/document/384009529/ConCom-Draft-Constitution-Final-Copy-July-17-2018#fullscreen&from_embed.

The committee also considered changes to representational structures, but rejected both parliamentary and semi-presidential systems in favor of retaining presidentialism. See http://newsinfo.inquirer.net/971782/consultative-committee-con-com-duterte-constitution-federal-presidential-government-system-federalism. The ultimate fate of the committee's draft will be decided in subsequent phases of deliberation over constitutional revision; this could be through the eventual convening of a Constituent Assembly jointly composed of the Senate and the House of Representatives.

11 Within the Philippines' patronage-oriented polity, the introduction of political contention to a new level of the system creates a new playground of patronage politics—whether with the election of provincial governors in 1902 (see Hutchcroft 2000b) or the establishment of barrio councils in the 1950s (see Hutchcroft 2014a).

12 For all the hefty criticism that is justly heaped on Philippine political parties, it must also be acknowledged that they have one major virtue in that they are generally national rather than regional in scope (a point made as far back as Landé 1965). On the dangers of regional parties, see Hicken's Chapter Two.

ELECTORAL SYSTEM REDESIGN:
FEWER RISKS COMBINED WITH HIGH EFFICACY

Electoral system redesign, by contrast, carries far fewer risks of unintended consequences. Based on comparative experience, political scientists can hazard a pretty good guess as to what is likely to happen if you introduce System X into Country Y. This is not to suggest that electoral system redesign is some kind of magic bullet, to reiterate a point emphasized at the outset, as it can take time for electoral system reform to overcome entrenched practices (e.g., it was some years after Japan's 1994 electoral system reforms that deeply rooted factionalism in the dominant Liberal Democratic Party began to subside[13]). There are always going to be particular characteristics of Country Y that need to be taken into account. At the same time, however, electoral system redesign has repeatedly shown itself to be capable of changing the way that politics is done across varying political contexts.[14]

While any attempt at instituting political reform poses some risk of unintended consequences, this also needs to be balanced against *the very substantial risk of maintaining the current set of electoral arrangements as put in place by the 1987 Constitution.* While it was certainly not the intent of the framers when they drafted that charter more than three decades ago, they did in the end manage (willy-nilly) to choose a set of electoral system arrangements that quite effectively ensure the perpetuation of weak and incoherent political parties. The specifics are found in the chapters of this volume, but three key examples deserve attention here.

1. The *multi-member plurality system* (MPS), used (as noted above) to elect four out of five elected officials in the Philippines, guarantees a high level of intraparty competition—which is a sure way of building a candidate-centric rather than a party-centric polity. As Ravanilla explains in Chapter Ten, "Given that MPS fosters competitions among co-partisans, and winning elections is all about building a personalized network of support, candidates have very little incentive to coordinate campaigns and policy stances along party-lines." He further notes that MPS "produces multiple

---

13 Even if the results of electoral system reform in Japan were gradual, they were nonetheless decisive. As Greg Noble explains, the new system "greatly decreased intra-party competition and reliance on delivery of pork barrel spending as a way for candidates to differentiate themselves. Party leaders gained more effective control over nominations. The role of factions declined, while party labels, ideology, and programmatic intentions grew more important, symbolized by the increasingly large role played by party manifestos" (2010, 260).

14 As highlighted, in particular, by the chapters of Hicken, Reilly, Reyes, Aspinall, and Ravanilla. The most comprehensive overview of electoral systems around the world is Reynolds, Reilly, and Ellis 2005.

short-lived coalitions" and "weakens the incentives of politicians to respond to broad constituencies." Not surprisingly, there has been a world-wide trend (including in nearby Japan and Taiwan[15]) to move away from multi-member systems that foster high levels of intraparty competition.

2. *The president and vice president (as well as governors/vice governors and mayors/ vice mayors) are elected separately rather than as part of a joint ticket.*[16] This is a very rare system, internationally, as it enhances the likelihood (frequently realized) that the two top officials of the land (as well as the province, city, and municipality) will come from different political parties. This produces a high degree of incoherence at the top, not to mention (as explained in Ramon Casiple's Chapter Seven) competition between the "official" tandem of party-mates and new "unofficial" tandems in which some political entrepreneurs have begun to build shadow campaigns for a presidential candidate of one party and a vice-presidential candidate of another. Once again, this fosters a candidate-centric rather than a party-centric polity.

3. Perhaps the oddest component of the current Philippine electoral system is the *party-list system* (PLS). Its three-seat ceiling not only violates the principle of proportionality, as explained above, but also leads to a high number of small and ineffectual parties. "As it generates dozens of tiny parties," Teehankee explains in Chapter Nine, "the PLS contributes to the weakness and incoherence of the Philippine party system. Whereas political parties are meant to *aggregate* societal interests, the PLS *splinters* them instead." This is exacerbated by provisions that were initially intended to limit the system to "marginalized sectors," the interpretation of which has led to a great deal of subsequent confusion.[17]

Thus we can point very directly to the existing "rules of the game" if we want to understand the weakness of Philippine political parties. These are the

---

15 See Lin 2006.

16 See Ben Reilly and Ramon C. Casiple, "Single Ticket: How About Voting for President and VP Together?," *Rappler*, March 23, 2016, at https://www.rappler.com/nation/politics/elections/2016/126795-single-ticket-president-vice-president

17 This confusion is extensively chronicled in the Teehankee chapter. Samuel Huntington, who assesses the strength of political institutions according to four characteristics—autonomy, adaptability, coherence, and complexity—notes that a "political party…that expresses the interests of only one group in society—whether labor, business, or farmers—is less autonomous than one that articulates and aggregates the interests of several social groups" (1968, 20). By encouraging such a narrow basis of representation, therefore, the Philippine party list system ensures the weakness of the party-list organizations that participate within it.

incentives that shape the relationship of candidates to parties, and in the current system parties are structurally challenged to exert discipline over their members. This core conclusion runs directly counter to those who might want to suggest—and one does occasionally hear this in Philippine political discourse—that some sort of innate cultural traits explain the weakness of the country's political parties. This could not be further from the truth. In a study undertaken of the historical development of Philippine political parties, co-author Joel Rocamora and I trace the strength of patronage structures and the weakness of Philippine political parties back to institutional innovations put in place in the early American colonial era. Since that time, the incentives emerging from the electoral system have helped to perpetuate the "strong patronage and weak parties" highlighted in the title of this volume. "Because institutional deficiencies bear the bulk of the blame for the many historical shortcomings of Philippine democracy," we argue, "it is through institutional reform that the country can best begin to construct a democracy with benefits for all" (Hutchcroft and Rocamora 2012). *In sum, the weakness of Philippine political parties does not derive from some supposed set of national cultural barriers to the fostering and maintenance of stronger and more coherent political parties. By changing the underlying incentives, through electoral system redesign, we can anticipate changes in how politics is done.*

This point is perhaps best illustrated by the comparative experience of countries that have used electoral system redesign to try to promote greater women's participation in the political process, specifically through the election of larger percentages of women to legislatures. As Socorro Reyes explains in Chapter Five, the adoption of specific measures[18] has achieved striking success in giving women more seats in legislatures across a wide range of different political, social, and cultural contexts: "from northern Europe (Sweden, Finland, and Norway) to Latin America (Nicaragua, Costa Rica, and Mexico) to Africa (Rwanda, Namibia, South Africa, and Mozambique)." If similar electoral system reforms have similar degrees of success across such a wide range of cultural contexts, it is pretty safe to presume that imagined cultural propensities do not doom the Philippines to a future of either weak political parties—or, as Reyes highlights in Chapter Five, less-than-stellar performance in achieving gender balance in its national and subnational legislative bodies.

---

18 The optimal means of bringing more women into the legislature, she emphasizes, is *closed-list proportional representation* with a *zipper system*. In this system, as explained further in Chapters Three and Five, parties choose and rank the candidates on their party list and must alternate the names of women and men throughout the list.

IDENTIFYING THE PROBLEMS TO BE SOLVED: A CRITICAL FIRST STEP OF ELECTORAL SYSTEM REDESIGN

Before embarking on any process of political reform, it is important first to specify the problems that are to be resolved. By studying and understanding pre-existing conditions, it is possible to embark on a *problem-driven process of political reform*: first identifying the major problems to be addressed and then (and only then) working out what would be the proper solutions to resolving those problems.[19] This is in contrast to an inherently flawed *solution-driven process of political reform*, in which one proposes a solution and then works backwards to justify the solution that has already been chosen.[20]

So what are the problems to be solved by electoral system redesign? This volume takes its cue from longstanding frustration in the Philippines over the strength of patronage systems and the weakness of political parties. This is a problem with deep historical roots, traceable as already noted to the institutional innovations of the American colonial era. Historical roots aside, we know that patronage remains alive and well today throughout the Philippines. In Chapter Eight, Meredith Weiss makes the following observations based on an extensive collaborative research effort that examined 2016 elections in 45 localities throughout the archipelago—from northern Luzon to the Visayas to Mindanao:

> Overall, our research concludes that—at least at the local level—money matters in Philippine elections as much as if not more than ever. This salience manifests in the "retail politics" form of payments for votes (to some extent signaling a patron's sincerity, wherewithal, and generosity, and to some extent simply buying favor); in the form of project-based contracts and concessions to be awarded post-polls, at least partly contingent on votes (with project

---

19 As explained in Hutchcroft 2017, this *examination of pre-existing conditions, combined with an identification of the problems to be solved*, is the first of three basic principles of political reform. The second is to *understand the nature and capacity of underlying political institutions—especially the two critical institutions of the bureaucracy and political parties*. And the third, already touched on above, is the need to *anticipate unintended consequences*. As a corollary, one must anticipate that the bigger the reform package the bigger the risk of unintended consequences.

20 An example of the latter might begin something like this: "Hey, I have a great solution and it's called federalism!" Proceeding from that assertion, the next step (backward) is to come up with specific reasons as to why there should be a shift to a federal system. The inherent flaws of a solution-driven process of reform were expressed most succinctly in the rather cynically framed title of a September 2016 forum organized by the University of the Philippines School of Economics: *If Federalism is the Answer, What is the Question?*

proceeds funding subsequent contests); and in the form of national programs, association with which intensifies incumbent advantage and continues to lure legislators to the president's fold.

The Philippines is well known, internationally, for its extraordinarily high number of elective posts: every three years, roughly 45,000 candidates seek election to the more than 18,000 elective posts that are contested across national, provincial, city, and municipal levels.[21] At one level, this could be viewed as an indication of the vibrancy of Philippine democracy. Indeed, the Philippines is also known internationally for the great exuberance that goes into electoral contests—often likened to a grand fiesta, with levels of voter turnout (averaging nearly 76 percent of registered voters[22]) that would be the envy of many other countries. At the same time, the appeals to voters—especially at the local level—are far more oriented to the dispensation of pork and patronage than to policies and programs.[23] As voters often struggle to detect substantive policy differences among those who are listed on the ballot, it is no surprise that their choices are instead often heavily influenced by the material resources that are doled out at election time. For ordinary citizens, explains economist Emmanuel S. de Dios, "government is an abstraction, an alienated entity, whose only palpable dimension is the episodic patronage dispensed by bosses and politicians, which merely reinforces the poor's real condition of dependence" (de Dios and Hutchcroft 2002). While entirely rational from the perspective of the individual voter, the impact on democratic accountability is quite damaging. When voters have already received material benefits from an official at election time, their capacity to follow up with that official on policy matters after the election has been diminished. The democratic contract has been undermined.

Patronage thrives within a polity in which candidates are strong and parties are weak. Given that here are some 45,000 candidates running for office every three years, one might hope that they would be organized relatively coherently into parties. One might further hope that their affiliation with a party would provide voters with clear signals as to policy preferences along the lines of "if I vote for Juana de la Cruz, a member of Party Z, I can be confident that she will vote for measures intended both to build a stronger and more effective national

---

21 Based on figures for the 2016 election, found at https://www.rappler.com/newsbreak/iq/130157-statistics-2016-elections-candidates

22 See https://www.rappler.com/newsbreak/in-depth/131521-voter-turnout-philippines-trend-asia-world

23 Holmes 2019 carefully documents how, in comparative perspective, Philippine politics has long been greased by an extraordinarily high level of pork barrel resources—not only through congressional slush funds and earmarks but also through a wildly creative array of pork and "quasi-pork" dispensed by the executive branch.

health care system as well as to promote better vocational training opportunities through the Department of Education. Why? Because I read about these goals in the platform of her political party."

In fact, as we know, Philippine political parties rarely pay much attention to their platforms (if in fact they even bother to write them up) and membership in a political party provides few clues as to what policies candidates may choose to pursue once they are in office. The large number of candidates for elective office in the Philippines are not well organized within parties, as most parties (with a very few exceptions[24]) are woefully lacking in coherence and programmatic orientation. This accords with Nathan Quimpo's colorful and oft-quoted description of contemporary Philippine political parties: "Far from being stable, programmatic entities," he explains, "they have proved to be not much more than convenient vehicles of patronage that can be set up, merged with others, split, resurrected, regurgitated, reconstituted, renamed, repackaged, recycled, or flushed down the toilet at any time" (2005: 4–5).

Thanks in large part to the electoral system put in place in the 1987 Constitution, along with the single term limit imposed on the president,[25] there has been a massive proliferation of parties in the post-Marcos Philippines. It is, without exaggeration, a complete free-for-all. From the presidential race to the Senate to the House to mayoral posts, the Philippines has an extraordinarily fractured party system:

- Presidency: Across the five elections of the post-Marcos Philippines (1992, 1998, 2004, 2010, and 2016), there were a staggering total of 18 parties or coalitions of parties that put up candidates as well as three additional candidates that ran as independents. Only one political party—the Liberal Party—can be said to have had a consistent presence, as its candidates contested four out of the five elections. (Casiple, Chapter Seven)

- Senate: "Nineteen of the current 24 members of the upper house are dispersed across eight parties, with the remaining five declaring themselves to be independent of any party affiliation." (Ravanilla, Chapter Ten)

---

24 The exceptions include parties on the left of the ideological spectrum: Akbayan Citizens' Action Party and the multi-member Makabayan bloc (composed of many distinct party-list parties, which are collectively incentivized to circumvent the highly restrictive three-seat ceiling of the party list system by splintering or disaggregating themselves into multiple entities). Among the mainstream parties, the Liberal Party (LP) has at certain points been an exception to the rule. Strangely enough, however, it became less powerful organizationally across the six years in which LP member Benigno S. Aquino III was in the presidential palace. Since the assumption of Rodrigo R. Duterte to the presidency in 2016, the LP has been reduced to a mere shadow of its former strength.

25 See Hicken, Chapter 2.

- House party-list parties: "Between 1998 (when the party-list system was put into operation) and 2016, an average of 104 party list organizations participated in the party list elections and the average number of winning parties exceeded 25." (Teehankee, Chapter Nine)

- Mayoral posts: In just three election years (2001, 2004, and 2007), candidates for city or town mayor ran under a total of 202 party banners while those elected to the post represented a still quite remarkable 101 political parties. (Ravanilla, Chapter Ten)

The numbers above, each deserving their own multiple exclamation points, strikingly demonstrate why the Philippines is regularly referred to as a candidate-centric polity. With some significant degree of hyperbole, one could say that it is almost as common for candidates to put up parties as it is for parties to put up candidates.

THE CASE FOR ELECTORAL SYSTEM REDESIGN: KEY ARGUMENTS AND INSIGHTS

As the twin problems of "strong patronage and weak parties" continue to drag down the democratic ideal in the Philippines, and demands for political reform endure, it would be wise to give careful consideration to the opportunities for transformative change that could come through well-designed electoral system redesign. Collectively, the remaining nine chapters of this volume make the case for such reforms. They are briefly summarized below.

Chapter Two: *Why (and How) Electoral Systems Shape Development Outcomes.* If the comments above focus largely on the impact of electoral systems on the quality of Philippine democracy, Allen Hicken provides rigorous analysis of how "electoral systems influence the level and pattern of development"—and does not find a positive linkage in the Philippines. He is interested, in particular, in the capacity of polities to provide 1) decisiveness, as well as adaptability to challenges and opportunities; 2) credibility and stability; and 3) responsiveness to broad interests. Party-centric systems, relative to candidate-centric systems, are likely to nurture policy environments that are more oriented to national issues (albeit not to the exclusion of local issues). In addition, they have longer time horizons, better capacity to enforce party discipline, and less orientation to clientelism and patronage. As he concludes, "the current Philippine electoral system has nurtured an environment that generally hampers the capacity and incentives of policy makers to pass and implement the kinds of policies that promote development."

Chapter Three: *Designing and Reforming Electoral Systems in Southeast Asia.* Ben Reilly's chapter has two major objectives. First, it provides a basic primer of major "electoral system families," setting aside the more esoteric arrangements found around the world and concentrating on a subset of most relevance to current debates in the Philippines. This feeds into the second part of the chapter, which examines the diversity of electoral system design in Southeast Asia. His survey of recent electoral system reform in Southeast Asia concludes that the "new systems…have not produced dramatic improvements in terms of either democratic accountability or party strengthening," thus highlighting "the need for careful consideration of goals, and careful selection of means, when undertaking electoral system redesign."

Chapter Four: *When Does Electoral System Reform Occur?* The volume benefits again from the insights of Allen Hicken, who begins by posing the following basic puzzle: "Given that politicians are generally loath to change the rules under which they themselves were elected, why would electoral reform ever get on the political agenda in the first place?" Drawing on comparative experience, the dynamics of which are carefully illustrated, he elucidates three conditions that together need to be present "if politicians are going to be motivated to begin a reform process." These are what he calls "systematic failure, a catalytic event, and change in incumbents' preference."

Chapter Five: *Gender and the Electoral System: What Works for Women.* Socorro Reyes examines the capacity of electoral system redesign to enhance the prospects of women who are running for seats in the legislature. She begins by looking at goals that were set internationally, through the United Nations 1979 Convention on the Elimination of All Forms of Discrimination Against Women (CEDAW), as well as domestically through a 2009 law known as the Magna Carta of Women. In each case, the targets established for women's political participation have not been met. Reyes highlights the particular potential of CLPR with a zipper system, while at the same time emphasizing the positive impact of other sorts of quota arrangements. The current national focus on constitutional revision, she concludes, "presents an opportunity to shift from the traditional plurality system, known to limit women's prospects of winning, to more creative systems that work for women."

Chapter Six: *Lessons from a Neighbor: The Negative Consequences of Indonesia's Shift to the Open List.* Lest anyone get the impression that electoral system reform brings good outcomes, Edward Aspinall explains the negative consequences that have come forth in Indonesia since its shift from the closed-list (party-centric) variety of PR to the open-list (candidate-centric) variety: less party coherence, an expansion and deepening of patronage politics, and more expensive elections. This "has thus fuelled a vicious cycle in which electoral patronage fuels corruption which in turn erodes the faith of Indonesian voters in their parties and elected representatives, making·them ever more susceptible to patronage politics." While some may argue that this demonstrates a kind of "Philippinization" of Indonesian politics, Aspinall instead enumerates "four features of Indonesia's institutional design [that] have prevented dissolution of the party system." These include restrictions on independent candidacies; strict registration requirements for political parties (including the capacity to demonstrate broad geographic scope); prohibitions on party switching by sitting legislators; and thresholds meant to reduce the proliferation of small parties. These four features might thus be viewed as positive lessons that can be garnered from the Indonesian experience.

Chapter Seven: *The Political Party Development Bill: Strengthening Political Parties Toward the Goal of Strengthening Philippine Democracy.* Ramon Casiple, a veteran of efforts to promote stronger political parties in the Philippines, provides an analysis of the more than fifteen-year effort to bring the passage of a proposed Political Party Development Act. In essence, the various versions of the bill focus upon (1) upholding party loyalty and adherence to ideological principles, platforms, and programs by penalizing turncoatism; (2) reducing cases of graft and corruption by regulating campaign financing through transparent mechanisms to level the playing field; and (3) professionalizing political parties through state subsidy, thus supporting them to become effective agents of democracy. Those advocating for the bill labor on, in the current Congress, but the long-term story is that advocacy for the bill has been "a tortuous road, littered with broken promises, half-hearted support from its direct beneficiaries, and misplaced opposition from opinion makers and the general public."

Chapter Eight: *Patronage Politics and Parties in the Philippines: Insights from the 2016 Elections.* Meredith Weiss brings in valuable comparative insights from a "money politics" project that examined electoral dynamics across three countries in recent years: Malaysia (with a focus on the 2013 elections), Indonesia (with a focus on the 2014 elections), and the Philippines (with a focus on the 2016 elections). In each of these elections, roughly 45–60 researchers observed national elections from different localities across the respective three countries. Based on the findings of this research, Weiss is able not only to provide a well-evidenced assessment of the ongoing dominance of patronage politics at the local level in the Philippines but also to compare patterns of patronage politics in the Philippines with those in Malaysia and Indonesia.

Chapter Nine: *Untangling the Party List System.* In this chapter, Julio Teehankee carefully analyzes the many dysfunctional elements of the current party list system (PLS), as well as the substantial legal contention that it has generated since its introduction in 2009. He concludes that the solution moving forward is not to abolish it *"but rather to reform and strengthen it by instituting the features of a closed-list proportional representation (CLPR) system as generally practiced in other parts of the world* (emphasis in original). *"* This would bring forth a system that is truly proportional, able to promote the political participation of "marginalized and underrepresented groups." The ultimate goal is "to strengthen not only parties but the party system as a whole."

Chapter Ten: *The Multi-Member Plurality System in the Philippines and Its Implications.* Nico Ravanilla closes out the volume by examining the electoral system that is most prevalent in the Philippines. His analysis of its dysfunctional consequences is already summarized above, to which must be added his forceful assertion of its broader impact: "Given that MPS is the system used in the selection of over 14,000 of the country's some 18,000 elected officials, it is safe to conclude that the deficiencies of MPS translate quite directly into deficiencies of Philippine democracy more generally." After surveying electoral reform experiences in Japan and Thailand, he suggests that "shifting to closed-list PR while maintaining the multi-member nature of districts might offer some traction and prove successful in improving democratic outcomes in the Philippines." Through the use of CLPR for elections to the Senate, party members would "now have the incentive to coordinate amongst each other, so that campaign strategies tend to be more party-centered." Such a shift is not without risk, he further emphasizes, as "without clear laws governing the conduct of political parties, the system is prone to capture by the 'list maker(s)' within the party—those controlling who gets to be included in the party slate and how they are to be ranked." Having acknowledged these risks, he nonetheless concludes by advocating an end to the current highly dysfunctional system: "If the overarching goal is to facilitate democratic accountability and consolidation, develop well-functioning political parties, improve representation, and shift campaign strategies as well as governance styles from personalistic to programmatic, then electoral system reform is a critical first step."

BACKGROUND TO THE STUDY AND ACKNOWLEDGEMENTS

This volume comes forth from the "Electoral Systems Redesign for Development" project, supported by the partnership in the Philippines between the Australian Embassy and The Asia Foundation (TAF). The core motivation, from the start, was to identify ways in which the reform of the electoral system could enhance development outcomes in the Philippines. Within the development world, often shackled in the past to technical solutions that paid little attention to political context, there has in recent years been a very belated recognition of the centrality of "thinking and working politically"—now known throughout the business as TWP. This is a paradigm shift that is utilizing important new approaches to enhance the quality of overseas development assistance. Strikingly, however, there is a tendency within TWP to view political structures essentially as a given. Some might view them as too hard to change, others might mistakenly adopt a culturalist explanation (e.g., perhaps linking high levels of patronage in Pacific Island nations to what are viewed as primordial "gift-giving" practices). As a result, TWP has incorporated deeper analysis of political context but rarely if ever pushed forward to what might be called Political Reform for Development (which may someday even acquire its own three-letter acronym: PRD). As Hicken argues so effectively in Chapter Two, the achievement of the best development outcomes will not come about by accepting electoral systems as they are; rather, it is important to identify specific reforms in electoral structures that have the potential to promote better development outcomes. As long as there is a candidate-centric political system, Hicken demonstrates, one should not expect to see the emergence of the types of policy environments "most conducive to long-term growth and development."

To take that one step further, there are ample opportunities for overseas aid agencies to work with like-minded local partners wanting to improve development prospects in their country. The goal should not be to impose specific solutions from the outside, but rather to set out a range of options based on comparative experience. That is the approach taken in this book, where one can see that the international experts (Hicken, Reilly, Weiss, and Aspinall) tend to focus more on providing comparative insights. The Philippine experts, on the other hand, tend to combine close attention to comparative experience with more explicit and finely tuned prescriptions as to how the electoral system might be reformed. Reyes, for example, first draws on her years of work with United Nations women's organizations to demonstrate how certain countries around the world have managed to perform better than the Philippines in enhancing women's political participation. She then provides specific reform solutions for how the Philippines can itself do a better job. Casiple adds temporal comparisons, from the perspective of an inside player who has for years been championing the cause of stronger political parties in the Philippines. Teehankee combines his knowledge of Philippine politics and comparative politics (including comparative electoral systems) with a specific plan for how to fix the major problems with the country's very distinctive party list system. And Ravanilla combines data-rich insights on the dynamics of Senate and local elections with analysis of recent electoral reform experiences in Japan and Thailand before proceeding to offer clear prescriptions for the Philippines. His very explicit goal is to enhance the overall quality of democracy in his country.

This project began in late 2015, long before anyone could anticipate the results of the May 2016 presidential election. No one knew who was going to win, let alone whether the winner might be amenable to constitutional revision—and, if so, with what specific priorities. We began in October 2015 with a scoping visit of Ben Reilly, who shared his broad expertise on international electoral systems with the House committee that considers issues of electoral reform, staff from its Senate counterpart, key officials from the Commission on Elections, and a range of other local stakeholders. The original plan was to hold off on any project activities until after the May 2016 elections, but in the course of Reilly's visit it became clear how little awareness there was of global and regional experiences in the realm of electoral system reform. There was, moreover, a tendency for the focus to be on electoral administration to the exclusion of electoral systems (and even, on occasion, to conflate these two very distinct realms). That led to a small public education campaign in advance of the May 2016 elections, published as seven informational articles (with accompanying videos) in a leading online news source under the banner "Elections: What PH can learn from the world."[26] After the election, in July 2016, the project organized a workshop in Manila that brought together international and domestic resource persons (whose papers now appear as chapters in this volume) with a wide group of stakeholders and potential stakeholders. This included then-incoming Senate President Aquilino "Koko" Pimentel III as well as then-Chairman Andres Bautista of the Commission on Elections and party-list pioneers from the Makabayan bloc and Akbayan Citizens' Action Party.

From the start, the project was put in place by a small core group composed of myself (then Lead Governance Specialist with the Australian aid program in Manila), Steve Rood (then Country Representative for TAF in the Philippines), Socorro Reyes from the Center for Legislative Development, Ramon Casiple of the Institute for Political and Electoral Reform, and Ona Caritos of the Lawyers Network for Truthful Elections (LENTE). We are very grateful to the Australian embassy for its generous support of this project through its partnership in the Philippines with TAF. Within the embassy, David Dutton and Geoff King took an early interest in

---

26 The seven articles can be found at Rappler, https://www.rappler.com. Five were authored by Reilly, one by Reilly and Casiple, and one by Reilly and Reyes.

the project and enabled it to get off the ground in late 2015 and early 2016; more recently, ongoing support has been provided by Mat Kimberley, Kerrie Anderson, and Pablo Lucero. We are also very grateful for the support provided by colleagues at TAF, including Sam Chittick, Chris Bantug, Quintin Atienza, Chrys Pablo, Marikit Castillo, and Patricia Taglay. Particular thanks go to Jowil Plecerda, who organized the July 2016 workshop in Manila and handled administrative arrangements leading into the publication of key findings.

This volume builds on insights from earlier elements of the project, and we thus want to thank those who hosted us at the House, Senate, and Commission of Elections in 2015; to Rappler for facilitating the publication of the articles in early 2016; and of course to all those who participated in the 2016 workshop. Sincere thanks to Maxine McArthur of the ANU Department of Political and Social Change for her skillful copyediting and indexing as well as to the team at Anvil—Andrea Pasion-Flores, Ani Habúlan, and Isa Lorenzo—for (once again) producing a beautiful volume. As always, the editor is deeply grateful to Edna Labra Hutchcroft both for her loving support and for her ever-wise counsel on the intricacies of Philippine politics.

CONCLUSION: ENVISAGING STRONGER AND MORE COHESIVE POLITICAL PARTIES IN THE PHILIPPINES

The core purpose of this volume, as explained at the outset, is to demonstrate how electoral system redesign has the potential to bring fundamental changes to the way in which politics is done in the Philippines. Of all the political reforms being considered amidst the latest round of national discussions on constitutional revision, electoral system reform is arguably the one that would bring *the highest degree of efficacy* with *the lowest risk of unintended consequences*.

Just as importantly, electoral system redesign places far fewer demands on the institutional capacity of a polity that has long been known for the weakness of its political institutions. Let us compare the three major reforms. *A shift to federalism* would require a much higher level of administrative capacity, not only across the newly created federal states but also at the center (in order to implement, and enforce over time, the rules by which authority is being devolved to the subnational level). This is a huge challenge given the ongoing weakness of the Philippine state at the national and subnational levels. *A shift to a parliamentary system* would require the prior existence of strong and cohesive political parties (in order to ensure an orderly process of building the coalitions from which executive authority can emerge). *Electoral system redesign*, on the other hand, would make no such major demands on the limited institutional capacity of the Philippines, as the new "rules of the game" could quite readily be put in place without putting unreasonable demands on the administrative wherewithal of the Commission of Elections. *Unlike the other two major types of political reform, therefore, electoral system redesign can readily be accommodated within existing levels of bureaucratic capacity.*

Once in place, moreover, electoral system redesign presents yet another enormous advantage relative to other forms of political reform: *by nurturing stronger political parties, it has the very substantial potential to enhance the overall capacity of Philippine political institutions.* In other words, the effective implementation of a well-designed package of electoral system reform is not challenged by the weak institutional capacity of the Philippines; very much to the contrary, it is able to begin to address this weakness by helping to nurture the emergence of stronger political parties.

This would bring myriad benefits relative to the current system, which continually throws up an enormous number of political parties that are generally lacking in any substantial degree of internal cohesion while also exhibiting little capacity to endure over time. As explained in Hicken's Chapter Two, the more actors there are in a given political system the harder it is (all other things equal) for a country as a whole to be decisive and to adapt policies to changing needs and opportunities. The multiplicity of actors in the Philippines is evidenced across at least three key dimensions. First and most obviously, more political parties means more political actors. Second, when political parties are lacking in cohesion one can conclude that there are, in effect, an even larger number of political actors in the system as a whole. (The nominal leader of a party may claim to speak for his or her party, but in actuality not be able to do so given the range of factions within.) Third, when political parties lack staying power there are a greater number of actors across time. This, quite obviously, is disadvantageous when reform packages require long-term commitment and follow through.

The Philippine political system is highly candidate-centric, as opposed to party-centric, and this brings all of the negative tendencies that are highlighted in Hicken's Chapter Two. As he explains, candidate-centric polities tend to a) focus on narrow particularistic interests at the expense of the delivery of broader public goods; b) have shorter rather than longer time horizons; c) be associated with weaker rather than stronger party discipline; and d) exhibit stronger and deeper patterns of clientelism and patronage politics.

The central question, therefore, is how to build stronger and more cohesive political parties and thus begin to shift the Philippine political system toward a greater focus on parties as opposed to candidates. This has been identified as a crucial goal by political reformers in the Philippines across recent decades, leading many to push for a political party development act that adopts a largely regulatory approach toward the achievement of the goal. In effect, the proposed law decrees to political parties that *thou shalt* develop programmatic platforms and *thou shalt not* spend above certain limits on campaigns—and then complements these decrees with state subsidies intended to build stronger parties. Well-intentioned though this reform effort has been, it fails to address the question of whether the Philippine state actually has the regulatory capacity to enforce the proposed decrees. In any case, as carefully chronicled in Casiple's Chapter Seven, fifteen years of hard effort have yet to bring successful passage of the proposed act.

One can find proposed within this volume a very different approach, based not on state regulatory capacity but rather on the introduction of an entirely new set of incentives through electoral system redesign. Among the huge range of electoral system options that one can find internationally, comparative experience suggests that the gold standard for party strengthening is the use of a closed-list proportional representation (CLPR) system in the election of at least some substantial portion of a legislature. This is the solution proposed by Reyes in Chapter Five (toward the goal of enhancing women's participation in the political system), Teehankee in Chapter Nine (to "untangle" the dysfunctional party list system) and Ravanilla in Chapter Ten (to curtail the intra-party competition that is inherent in the current multi-member plurality system). By binding candidates to parties and requiring voters to cast votes for parties rather than candidates, CLPR is an excellent means by which to ensure higher levels of party cohesion.[27] When accompanied by laws mandating a "zipper system"—alternating women and men on parties' lists of candidates—CLPR has shown itself to be highly effective in promoting greater gender equality. The party list can be similarly engineered to ensure diversity across regions, or across sectors of society, and thus ensure the fuller representation of those who have historically felt themselves to be marginalized from the larger national community. This could include neglected regions or such marginalized societal sectors as the urban poor, lowland peasants, or upland peoples.

---

27 In crafting a CLPR system, it is important to select a district magnitude—i.e., determine the number of seats per district—that is appropriate to reform goals. The smaller the district magnitude, the less proportional it will be. In addition, as Socorro Reyes argues in Chapter Five, women may be less likely to be chosen for party lists when districts only have a small number of seats. Excessively large district magnitude, on the other hand, risks the fragmentation of a party system because parties can win seats with only a tiny fraction of the vote.

This volume is dedicated to those who seek to improve the quality of democracy in the Philippines. As is the case anywhere in the world, building better democracy is always a work in progress, and it is an ongoing challenge to ensure that democratic rhetoric is translated into actual democratic substance of value to those—at the bottom of society—who most need to have their voices heard in the halls of power. The strengthening of institutional foundations is a critical first step to ensuring that democratic systems can become more responsive to the citizenry as a whole. In the Philippine context, such a process of institutionalization has the major advantage of building on the wonderfully exuberant spirit that Filipinos have long brought to the practice of democracy.

Candidate-centric systems generate strong incentives to cultivate a personal vote, such that "public" works are commonly branded with the goal of promoting the prospects of individual candidates. Years after he had left office, the name of a former governor remained etched into the side of a pedestrian overpass in the province of Camarines Sur.

Photo by Paul D. Hutchcroft

CHAPTER TWO
WHY (AND HOW) ELECTORAL SYSTEMS SHAPE DEVELOPMENT OUTCOMES[1]

ALLEN HICKEN

INTRODUCTION

According to Dani Rodrik, institutions are "the fundamental determinant[s] of long run growth…" (Rodrik 2007, 8). While scholars may debate the relative importance of institutions versus other determinants of growth (e.g. geography or factor endowments), or disagree about which particular institutions merit attention, there is wide consensus that institutions have profound and predictable consequences for growth and development (North 1990; 1997; Rodrik 2007; Acemoglu 2009; Acemoglu and Robinson 2012). Included among such institutions are the institutions that make up an electoral system.[2] In this paper I explore some of the ways in which electoral systems influence the level and pattern of development by focusing on how the electoral system can shape the capacities and incentives of key actors and decision makers.

Electoral systems are made up of multiple components. The components most relevant for our purposes are the electoral formula (the way in which votes are translated into seats), district magnitude (the number of seats per electoral constituency), and ballot structure (whether voters cast a vote for a party, single candidate, multiple candidates or some combination).

Electoral Formula: This is the most widely recognized feature that distinguishes one electoral system from another. As surveyed in greater detail in the next chapter, the primary distinction is between plurality/majoritarian systems, where the candidates or parties with the most votes win, and proportional representation (PR) systems where parties are awarded seats in rough proportion to the number of votes they receive.

---

1 This review draws heavily on my "Party Systems and the Politics of Development," 2016.
2 Among the institutions that receive the most attention are rule of law and property rights regimes. As important as electoral institutions may be, if there is no rule of law and property rights are insecure the choice of electoral regime will be of little consequence for growth.

- Plurality/majoritarian systems are winner-take-all, and within this category single-member district plurality (SMDP) is the most common formula. SMDP is widely used around the world: from the United Kingdom to India to the United States. In the Philippines, it is the formula used to elect the bulk of the seats in the Philippine House of Representatives.

- PR, by contrast, allows even losing contestants to secure some representation. It is also widely used around the world—including in the Netherlands, Portugal, Israel, and Argentina.

- Mixed systems combine features of both systems, allowing voters to select representatives through both plurality/majoritarian and proportional rules. This system has long been used in some countries (for example in Germany) and has gained widespread popularity in recent decades through its adoption in, for example, Japan, South Korea, New Zealand, and post-conflict Nepal.

District Magnitude: The number of seats allocated per constituency/district can range from one, in single-seat plurality elections, to 120 for the Israeli Knesset. District magnitude can be overlooked by institutional engineers but it has a powerful effect on representation and the number of parties. As explained further below:

- Large district magnitude (many seats per district) is associated with legislative seats going to many small parties.

- Small district magnitude (fewer seats per district) is associated with relatively fewer and larger political parties winning legislative seats.

Ballot Structure: Ballot structure refers to the options the ballot presents voters in the polling booth. The two primary features of ballot structure I will focus on are: a) whether voters cast a vote for a political party or candidate, and b) whether or not the system pits co-partisans against each other (intra-party competition). Together these help shape the degree to which the electoral system is candidate- or party-centered.

These features of electoral systems have profound implications for policy making and development. Specifically, electoral systems help shape the interests of policy makers (influencing who they respond to) as well as their capacity to pursue those interests. In the remainder of this paper I explore each of these implications and their connection with the political economy of development. In the next section I sketch out the characteristics of policy environments that are the most conducive to long-term growth and development. I then show how the electoral system shapes the policy environment through its effect on the interests and capabilities of policy makers.

POLICY ENVIRONMENTS CONDUCIVE TO DEVELOPMENT

To make the case that electoral systems matter for development we must first assume that state policies can affect economic development. This is a rather uncontroversial assumption. Even those who view meddling in the economy by political actors as ineffectual at best, and inimical to development at worst, still recognize that the policy environment can be more or less conducive to economic development (see Hill 1997). If we accept that public policies can affect development, what kinds of policies produce environments that are the most conducive to long-term growth and development?

DECISIVENESS

First, policy environments that can respond to challenges and opportunities in a timely manner are more likely to promote economic development than those that are indecisive. Economic development requires a certain amount of decisiveness and adaptability on the part of policy makers (Cox and McCubbins 2001; van de Walle and Rius 2005; Tommasi 2006). Economic shocks may batter the economy, policies that once worked well may begin to fail, and new opportunities for growth and investment may emerge. Governments that can respond to such developments with the needed reforms will be at an advantage over those who cannot.

CREDIBILITY

Second, policy environments that are stable and credible are more likely to lead to economic development than are policy environments that are unstable and unpredictable (see Rodrik 1991; Dixit 1994; Feng 2001; Jensen 2008; Canes-Wrone and Ponce de Leon 2014; Kang et al. 2014). The effects of policy initiatives on development outcomes depend on more than just the content of those policies. In fact, expert judgment over which policies are most conducive to growth and development varies across time and across experts (Tommasi 2006). But while economists and policy makers may argue about the pros and cons of financial liberalization, for example, one thing is certain; the effect of any policy on development outcomes is contingent on the actions and reactions of economic and social agents to those policies (Tommasi 2006, 3). In other words, the *credibility* of a policy in the eyes of economic decision makers, whether foreign investors, local businesses, or consumers, is a *necessary* condition for development.

Take, for example, trade policy. Rodrik points to the critical role of credibility in connecting trade reforms to positive development outcomes.

> [I]t is not trade liberalization per se, but credible trade liberalization that is the source of efficiency benefits. The predictability of the incentives created by a trade regime, or lack thereof, is generally of much greater importance than the structure of these incentives. In other words, a distorted, but stable set of incentives does much less damage to economic performance than an uncertain and unstable set of incentives generated by a process of trade reform lacking credibility (Rodrik 1989, 2).

In short, we know that actors, while they have preferences over policy content, also care about the credibility of policy. All other things being equal, uncertainty about the policy environment will tend to reduce the incentives of those actors to respond favorably to policy initiatives.

RESPONSIVENESS TO BROAD INTERESTS

Third, policy environments that respond to the broad public interest by promoting investment in national/public goods and services are more likely to produce economic development than are those that reflect narrower special interests (Olson 1993; Besley and Ghatak 2006). Every political system provides politicians with different incentives and capabilities to provide broad public policies. These are policies that a) bring long-term benefits but short-term costs, and/or b) benefit society as a whole, but may impose concentrated costs on some groups. For purposes of this paper I label these long-term, broadly beneficial types of policies as "national policies" or "national goods."[3] There is a large literature that links the supply of these kinds of national policies with greater/more rapid economic development (for example, Olson 1993; Bardhan 2005; Doner 2009; Acemoglu and Robinson 2012).

Each of these three characteristics—decisiveness, credibility, and responsiveness to broad interests—is necessary for development to occur. Sound national policies

---

3 National policies can include classic public goods (such as defense) as well as collective goods or policies that might not meet the strict public goods definition of non-rivalrous consumption and non-excludability. In other words, non-rivalrous means that consumption of a public good by one actor does not disadvantage the consumption of the same good by another actor, while non-excludability means that no one can be excluded from consuming the good. Examples include secure private property rights regime or a national primary education policy.

have little effect if they are never adopted or if actors are uncertain of their credibility, either because they anticipate the policies will never be implemented or they are worried the policies will be reversed. Likewise, decisiveness, stability and predictability are only virtues so long as they undergird favorable policies. A kleptocracy is unlikely to produce development, even where decisiveness is high and the patterns of extraction are stable and predictable. So how does the electoral system shape the ability of governments to provide needed national policies in a timely and credible manner? In the following section I review how the electoral system shapes the incentives and capabilities of policy makers to provide the national policies necessary for development. I examine both the *direct effect* of the electoral system on the policy-making environment and, just as importantly, the *indirect effect* of electoral systems through the nurturing (or not) of a strong party system.

ELECTORAL SYSTEMS AND THE POLITICAL ECONOMY OF DEVELOPMENT

DECISIVENESS, CREDIBILITY AND THE ELECTORAL SYSTEM

Decisiveness and credibility are both essential, but there is at the same time tension between them. An environment with few constraints empowers policy makers to act decisively (Tsebelis 1995; 2002; Mainwaring and Shugart 1997; Cox and McCubbins 2001; Shugart and Haggard 2001; Henisz 2002). However, the lack of checks against attempts to change the status quo—that is, excessive arbitrariness—also tends to reduce the credibility of policy (ibid). This tension between decisiveness and credibility is one which governments can resolve in a variety of ways, but governments that find themselves at the extremes of the decisiveness–credibility continuum tend to perform poorly (MacIntyre 2002).

The electoral system has its most direct impact on decisiveness and credibility via its effect on the party system—specifically on the number and nature of political parties. To begin with, there is a clear, positive (though not one-to-one) relationship between the number of political parties and the number of actors (or veto players) involved in the policy process. The more parties there are in a given party system, the more actors there are likely to be in the policy-making process. Thus, all other things equal, the harder it will be to change existing policies or adopt new ones.[4]

---

4 Tsebelis (1995) and Cox and McCubbins (2001) refer to these actors as veto players. To precisely determine the number of veto players in the policy process, we need to know not just the number of actors with power to block changes to the status quo but also whether those actors have preferences/ ideal points that are distinct from one another (Tsebelis 1995; 2002).

So, what kinds of electoral systems tend to produce large numbers of parties? Permissive electoral systems—those that combine proportional representation with large district magnitudes—allow smaller parties to secure representation and are associated with more parties winning seats in the legislature as well as multi-party coalition governments. By contrast, electoral systems that feature plurality/majoritarian rules or low district magnitude are more likely to produce near-majority or majority governments where only the largest parties win seats.

In addition to the number of parties, the strength of political parties (what is sometimes called the degree of party institutionalization) also has an important impact on the number of actors. Where parties are strong, or institutionalized, parties are meaningful, valuable organizations to both candidates and voters and parties tend to have high levels of cohesiveness. Where parties are weakly institutionalized, they tend to be thinly organized temporary alliances of convenience that are either factionalized or atomized. Because of the factionalized or atomized nature of political parties in under-institutionalized systems, they will tend to produce more actors, at the cost of policy decisiveness, than their institutionalized counterparts, all else being equal.

The electoral system can either promote or undermine incentives to build and invest in strong, cohesive, institutionalized parties. Specifically, electoral systems that require a candidate to belong to a political party, and that require voters to vote for political parties (rather than candidates) are associated with stronger, more cohesive parties. In addition, the more the fortunes of candidates are tied to the fortunes of their co-partisans, the stronger we expect parties to be. Parties should be the most cohesive under a closed-list proportional representation (CLPR) system, where voters vote for a single party list and party leaders determine the order of the candidates on that list. Under CLPR a candidate's success depends entirely on the fortune of the party—the better the party does, and the more he or she is preferred by party leaders, the better their chances at winning office. By contrast, under rules that encourage or require voters to vote for candidates rather than parties, the investment in party building and attachments to parties tends to be less. This is the case in many plurality/majoritarian systems, but can also occur under open-list PR (OLPR) where voters are allowed to vote for individual candidates and thus determine the order in which candidates are elected from the party list. Where such intraparty competition between candidates occurs it is associated with lower levels of party cohesion and higher levels of party factionalism or atomization.

To summarize, either through its effect on the number of parties, or on party cohesion, the electoral system shapes the number of actors who have a say in the policy process. Where the electoral system produces multiple actors whose joint agreement is necessary to change policies, credibility is higher, but at the cost of some degree of decisiveness.

But let's examine additional ways the electoral system can influence policy credibility other than through its effects on the number of actors. The concept of credibility, while intuitively simple (do I believe what you say you are going to do?), is analytically more complex. The distrust of government policies may arise for a large number of reasons, but I want to focus here on two broad categories of concerns that, when present, undermine policy credibility and ultimately, prospects for development.

The first is what we might term *reversal risk*. Namely, the chance that the policies the government announces today may be nullified, reversed, or superseded tomorrow. Electoral systems affect reversal risk through their effect on party and party system institutionalization. Party-centered electoral systems encourage parties to stake out distinct, identifiable policy positions, while investing in and defending the collective reputation of the party. This has important implications for reversal risk. Where party labels matter, once parties have made a major policy commitment (for example, to an international cooperative agreement, or to a particular set of macroeconomic policies) it will be costly for them to change their position. Thus, where electoral systems encourage more institutionalized parties we should observe less frequent policy reversals within governments as well as more continuity across governments of the same party, *all other things being equal.* By contrast, in candidate-centered electoral systems the collective reputational costs of a policy reversal by sitting governments are much less, and policy continuity from one government to another is far from assured, even when the same party is at the helm. In addition, where electoral systems encourage weak parties the chance of maverick outsiders coming to power, unfettered by past policy commitments, is much greater (Mainwaring and Torcal 2006).[5]

The second category of risk is *implementation risk*, specifically, the risk that the policies a government adopts formally and legally will not be the policies in practice. It is not hard to imagine how characteristics of the electoral and party systems might affect an actor's calculation of implementation risk. We know, for example, that certain features of the political system are associated with higher levels of government instability (for example, high levels of partisan fragmentation and low levels of party cohesion). Short-lived cabinets will have a much more difficult time fully implementing new policies. In Thailand, for example, during the turbulent 1980s

---

5 Although, as Geddes (1995) and van de Walle and Rius (2005) point out, where outsiders are reform-minded this may not be such a bad thing. However, the very features of the party system that allow outsiders to come to power (lack of institutionalization and a concomitant lack of party cohesion and discipline) may also hinder their ability to govern effectively.

and 1990s the electoral system produced large, multi-party coalitional governments that were notoriously unstable. In a system where the average cabinet duration was around eighteen months the Thai bureaucracy was famous for scuttling attempts at policy reform by dragging its feet until the inevitable change in government brought about change in political principals and policy priorities.

We should also expect a government's implementation capacity to vary with the extent to which electoral systems encourage strong, cohesive parties. In party-centered electoral systems, party cohesion should be higher. There should consequently be a stronger correspondence between what is passed by party leaders and what is implemented by lower-level party functionaries and bureaucrats. By contrast, where the electoral system produces parties that are highly factionalized and where party members have few shared policy preferences, party functionaries and bureaucrats are likely to be less-than-perfect implementing agents and the correspondence between what is promised and what is delivered should be lower.

In summary, the electoral system has an important impact on government decisiveness and credibility. Where the electoral system produces a large number of parties and/or weakly institutionalized political parties we tend to see more potential veto players and hence a less decisive, but more credible, policy-making environment. Additionally, party systems with low levels of institutionalization should suffer from lower levels of credibility due to the greater risk for policy reversal and failed/partial policy implementation.

HOW ELECTORAL SYSTEMS SHAPE PARTY-CENTRIC VERSUS CANDIDATE-CENTRIC INCENTIVES

As important as decisiveness and credibility are, they will not move a state along the path towards greater economic development if they are not paired with appropriate policies. Earlier, I discussed the important link between what I labeled "national policies" and development. The two key characteristics of these types of policies is that 1) they privilege the interests of broad over narrow groups and 2) they balance long-term interests and opportunities with shorter-term exigencies. One of the key challenges related to development is insulating decision makers against "the ravages of short-run pork barrel politics" (Bardhan 1990, 5). *In other words, for development to occur policymakers must be more public-regarding than private-regarding* (Cox and McCubbins 2001).

The electoral system helps shape actors' incentives to provide public-regarding national policies. One key dimension of variation among electoral systems is between party-centered and candidate-centered electoral systems.[6] In other words, different electoral systems provide distinct incentives for cultivating a party versus a candidate vote. I will proceed to examine these incentives across four major dimensions: 1) degree of focus on national issues; 2) time horizons; 3) party discipline; and 4) linkages to clientelism and patronage.

DEGREE OF FOCUS ON NATIONAL ISSUES: PARTY-CENTRIC V. CANDIDATE-CENTRIC SYSTEMS

In systems where politicians have fixed geographic constituencies, and/or where the electoral system induces politicians and voters to privilege person over party, the incentives to provide national policies are weak at best. Party-centered electoral systems are more apt to give rise to cohesive parties with stable support bases. These types of parties are much more likely to be responsive to broad constituencies than are the more factionalized, locally focused parties in candidate-centered vote systems (Hankla 2006b). The nature of competition is also different across party-centered and candidate-centered systems. Party-centered electoral rules makes it more likely that parties will pursue programmatic strategies—meaning that parties will compete with each other and voters will assign accountability primarily based on policy platforms and policy performance (Jones 2005). By contrast, where the electoral rules generate strong incentives to cultivate a personal vote candidates are more concerned with directing targeted benefits to their narrow group of supporters and have very little interest in broader public issues (Aspinall 2014).

Regionally based parties pose particularly grave challenges to the goal of promoting attention to broad national interests. When political competition at the national level occurs between parties that represent narrow subnational constituencies, then the outcomes of policy debates and conflicts lead to two potentially damaging kinds of public policy outcomes: (a) an oversupply of pork-barrel policies, resulting from logrolls across politicians and regions, which

---

6 A second strand of literature considers the difference between PR and plurality, with three broad findings. First, where class is a salient partisan division PR is associated with greater levels of redistribution compared to plurality (Iverson and Soskice 2006). Second, where parties are meaningful PR is associated with greater benefits and protections for producers while plurality is associated with more consumer-friendly policies (Chang et al. 2011). Finally, compared to plurality, PR is associated with more, but also less efficient public spending by politicians (Persson and Tabellini 2003). These distinctions are of less relevance in the Philippines, where a) class is not a strong partisan division; b) political parties lack programmatic coherence; and c) the weakness of the bureaucracy presents major underlying challenges to the efficiency of public spending.

benefit certain constituencies but at a cost in terms of efficiency and general welfare, and (b) an undersupply of nationally focused public goods. Some countries (including Indonesia, as explained in Edward Aspinall's Chapter Six) therefore impose strict regulations to ensure that parties engaging in national-level competition must demonstrate a strong national—or at least significantly cross-regional—breadth of political support.

TIME HORIZONS: PARTY-CENTRIC V. CANDIDATE-CENTRIC SYSTEMS

Politicians in party vote systems also tend to have longer time horizons than party leaders in candidate-centered systems. They have a strong incentive to protect the party brand as a valuable cue for voters and mobilization tool for politicians (Jones 2005). Protecting and investing in the party label means balancing the narrowly focused short-sighted preferences of individual politicians, worried about their next election, with the broader, longer-term interests of the party as a whole. Shorter time horizons can also flow from the lack of a stable, predictable basis of support within less institutionalized parties. This lack of a stable support base means that politicians must be more responsive to immediate electoral prospects even if that means sacrificing medium and long-term opportunities. We can think of a concrete example in the area of trade policy. A party with ephemeral supporters is much less likely to bear the substantial upfront costs of liberalizing trade than a party that has a stable constituency and which expects to be around to reap the rewards of trade openness in the future (Hankla 2006a). Reaching and enforcing these types of inter-temporal agreements are crucial for development, as Tommasi argues:

> In political environments that facilitate such agreements, public policies tend to be higher in quality, less sensitive to political shocks, and more adaptable to changing economic and social conditions. In settings that hinder cooperation, policies are either too unstable (subject to political swings) or too inflexible (unable to adapt to socioeconomic shocks). They tend to be poorly coordinated, and investments in state capabilities tend to be lower. (2006, 7)

PARTY DISCIPLINE: PARTY-CENTRIC V. CANDIDATE-CENTRIC SYSTEMS

The electoral system also affects the ability of party leaders to mobilize and discipline their co-partisans in support of national policies. National party leaders tend to have a broader (and longer-term) focus than the average member of the party.[7] In party-centered systems national party leaders are more likely to have the incentives and the capacity to push through policies crafted with a focus on broad, national constituencies (Olson 1982; McGillivray 1997; Nielson 2003; Hallerberg and Marier 2004; Hankla 2006a). By contrast, in candidate-centered systems, where party labels are ephemeral and party organizations anemic, national party leaders may lack the leverage to compel party members to sacrifice short-term, locally focused policy preferences (for example, preferences for pork) in favor of broader, public-regarding policies. Instead, we are likely to get legislative or partisan logrolls, where each narrowly focused politician secures some particularistic benefit for his or her constituency, while broader public goods are undersupplied (McGillvray 1997; Nielson 2003; Hicken and Simmons 2008).

LINKAGES TO CLIENTELISM AND PATRONAGE: PARTY-CENTRIC V. CANDIDATE-CENTRIC SYSTEMS

Finally, candidate-centered electoral systems and weak, under-institutionalized parties are also strongly linked with clientelism—though the correspondence is not perfect (see, for example, Mainwaring 1999; Van Cott 2000; Randall and Svåsand 2002; Roberts 2002; Mainwaring and Torcal 2006). If the ties that link voters to politicians and parties are not ideological/programmatic then a common alternative form of linkage is clientelism with a focus on patronage. Likewise, if shared ideological or programmatic goals do not bring co-partisans together, then clientelist cords are likely to be the ties that bind parties together.

To the extent that candidate-centered electoral systems and clientelism do go together, candidate-centered systems will be subject to the many policy challenges outlined in the large literature on clientelism. This includes higher levels of rent-seeking and particularism, larger public sectors and public sector deficits, and public sector inefficiencies (Calvo & Murillo, 2004; Gimpelson & Treisman 2002; O'Dwyer 2006; Grzymala-Busse 2008), and a general under-supply of the national public goods and policies that are crucial for development (Keefer 2006; Keefer 2007; Hicken and Simmons 2008; Hicken 2011). Politicians who are the chief beneficiaries of clientelist arrangements also represent the primary source of opposition to needed economic reforms in many countries (van de Walle and Rius 2005).

---

7 This is not always the case. See Stokes 1999.

TABLE 2.1 PARTY-CENTRIC V. CANDIDATE-CENTRIC SYSTEMS (IN A NUTSHELL)

	Party-centric	Candidate-centric
Capacity to focus on national public goods	*Higher capacity to address broad programmatic interests*	*Greater tendency to focus on particularistic interests*
Time horizons	*Tend to be longer*	*Tend to be shorter*
Party discipline	*Stronger*	*Weaker*
Patronage and clientelism	*Less common*	*More common*

CONCLUSION

One cannot understand the politics of development in democratic settings without taking the electoral system into account. The electoral system helps shape the capacity and incentives of policy makers to pass and implement the kinds of policies that promote development. Through its influence on the number of actors the electoral system shapes the capacity of governments to act in response to new opportunities and challenges. The electoral system can also bolster or undercut the credibility of government attempts to promote development. Perhaps more fundamentally, the electoral system helps shape the incentives of policy makers to pursue needed national policies in the first place. In general, party-centered systems tend to produce policy makers who have longer time horizons and who are responsive to broader constituencies than is the case in personalized, candidate-centered systems. But where does the Philippines currently sit on these dimensions?

DECISIVENESS AND CREDIBILITY IN THE PHILIPPINES

Let us begin by examining decisiveness and credibility. With the exception of the party list elections, the Philippines uses plurality/majoritarian electoral rules to elect its politicians. Single-member district plurality is used for all executive contests (president, governor, and mayor) and for most of the House of Representatives. The multi-member plurality system is used for the Senate, provincial boards, city and municipal boards, and barangay (village) elections. The result of these rules is a modest number of parties, as we would expect. If we exclude the party-list parties, the House of Representatives has had between three and four "effective number of parties" over the last three elections.[8] If we include

---

8 Within political science, the effective number of parties statistic is a common way to measure the number of parties. In effect, it weights parties by their size.

the party-list parties then the number increases to more than six effective parties. However, the well-known pattern in the Philippines is the massive switching to the president's party or coalition in the wake of an election, which almost always leaves the president with a majority in the House of Representatives, and often a majority in the Senate as well. This might suggest a high level of decisiveness, with presidents being able to enact their policy agenda with the support of their legislative coalition. However, the Philippines' electoral system also contributes to the well-documented weakness of Philippine political parties.

Four features of the Philippine electoral system tend to undermine the strength and cohesion of political parties in the Philippines. First, as discussed by Nico Ravanilla in Chapter Ten, the use of the multi-member plurality system for the Senate and provincial municipal and local boards pits co-partisans against one another. This encourages candidates to develop personal networks of support that are distinct from parties, and encourages voters to discount party label as a guide to voting. Second, separate elections for executive and vice-executive positions undermines the value of parties for voters and candidates. Together, these first two features of the electoral system encourage candidates to eschew party strategies in favor of personal strategies. Elections are first and foremost personality contests and candidates generally possess little in the way of party loyalty. Multiple votes also allow voters to split their votes between candidates from different parties—something that Filipino voters frequently take advantage of (Hicken 2014). Third, the peculiar features of the Philippines party-list electoral system limits the influence of more party-centered strategies and effectively ghettoizes smaller, more programmatic parties. And finally, the presence of term limits—in an environment where parties are already weak—undermines incentives for incumbents to invest in party building. This is particularly true of the presidency, where term limits have contributed to "less party discipline, more factionalism, and to a larger number of short-lived parties" (Hicken 2014, 322).

To summarize, the Philippines electoral system contributes to anemic political parties and this has important implications for decisiveness and credibility. Because of the factionalization of political parties in the Philippines, there tend to be a lot of actors involved in the policy-making process. This has obvious costs in terms of policy decisiveness. While presidents may control nominal legislative majorities, the low levels of discipline within parties and coalitions means that in reality those majorities are very brittle. Presidents cannot count on the loyalty of their co-partisans and therefore must regularly cobble together ad hoc legislative coalitions, which can be costly both in terms of decisiveness, but also in terms of the pork and other benefits that must be doled out to purchase loyalty. On the other hand, weak parties mean that majority of the presidents have to deal with more veto players than we might otherwise expect, which could in some circumstances make it harder to change the status quo (MacIntyre 2002). But because of the candidate-centered nature of the Philippine electoral system (more on this below), the collective reputational costs of policy reversal by sitting governments are much less, undermining policy continuity and credibility.

PARTY-CENTRIC V. CANDIDATE-CENTRIC INCENTIVES IN THE PHILIPPINES

The Philippine electoral system is extremely candidate-centered, generating strong incentives to cultivate a personal vote. This has contributed to perennially weak political parties. This has several consequences. First, the type of environment required for the fostering of national policies has been chronically undersupplied. Philippine policy makers are generally unable to transcend powerful economic interests that have long dominated Philippine politics (Hutchcroft 1998). As a result, public policy caters to the interests of narrow elites at the expense of broader national interests (de Dios and Hutchcroft 2003). Second, weak parties have also meant that Philippine politicians operate with very short time horizons (Lim and Pascual 2001, Hutchcroft and Rocamora 2003), yielding chronic under investment or inefficient investment in public services, human capital and physical infrastructure. Third, the Philippine electoral system promotes low levels of party discipline. Weak parties, often the vehicles of powerful personalities, are unable to constrain party leaders, particularly presidents. Hence, Philippine policy has been dependent on the peculiar preferences and personalities of individuals, which, in turn, undermines the predictability and credibility of policy (Balisacan and Hill 2003; de Dios and Esfahani 2001; Hutchcroft 2000a). Fourth, as one would expect in a candidate-centered electoral system with weak, under-institutionalized parties, the Philippines exhibits high levels of patronage and clientelism (Hicken, Aspinall, and Weiss 2019). Finally, the failure of parties to adequately respond to broader societal interests has meant that pressures for reform often take "extra-parliamentary—and even extra-legal—forms..." (Hutchinson 2001, 57), resulting in periodic eruptions of political instability and a concomitant erosion of investor confidence.

In short, the current Philippine electoral system has nurtured an environment that generally hampers the capacity and incentives of policy makers to pass and implement the kinds of policies that promote development. The chapters that follow explore opportunities for the Philippines to move toward a more party-centered system, oriented (all other things equal) to more promising long-term development outcomes.

The 1987 Constitution sets forth the current electoral system of the Philippines. The charter was drafted by a Constitutional Commission that met from June to October 1986; soon thereafter, it was overwhelmingly ratified in a February 1987 plebiscite.

Photograph from Official Gazette, Republic of the Philippines.

CHAPTER THREE
DESIGNING AND REFORMING ELECTORAL SYSTEMS IN SOUTHEAST ASIA

BENJAMIN REILLY

A SIMPLIFIED PRIMER OF ELECTORAL SYSTEMS

An electoral system is designed to do three main jobs. First, it determines how votes cast are translated either into seats won in a legislature (or other representative body) or into the election of a president (or other chief executive, including governors and mayors). Second, electoral systems act as the conduit through which the people can hold their elected representatives accountable, allowing more direct or more distant channels of accountability based on their design. Third, different electoral systems give incentives for those competing for power to couch their appeals to the electorate in distinct ways (Reynolds, Reilly and Ellis 2005). Viewed from the perspective of the Philippines, the redesign of the electoral system is one of the most promising means for beginning the long-term process of curbing patronage practices and strengthening political parties.

A standard approach to the description and categorization of electoral systems is to group them according to how proportional they are: that is, how closely the ratio of votes to seats is observed in electoral outcomes. One such classification gives four broad families: plurality systems; majority systems; proportional representation (PR) systems; and mixed/hybrid systems. These constitute the vast bulk of the electoral systems used for elections in the world today. Figure 3.1 provides an overview of these four major families.[1]

---

1 There are in fact many other types of electoral systems, but the focus here is a simplified description of the four major families. Readers seeking further detail are urged to consult International IDEA's handbook on electoral system design, which describes the wide range of systems used throughout the globe (Reynolds, Reilly and Ellis 2005).

FIGURE 3.1: THE FOUR MAJOR ELECTORAL SYSTEM FAMILIES

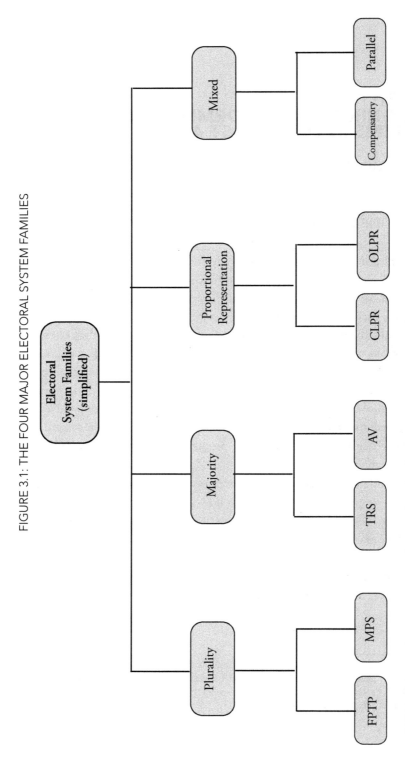

FPTP: first past the post; MPS: multi-member plurality system; TRS: two-round system; AV: alternative vote; CLPR: closed-list proportional representation; OLPR: open-list proportional representation

PLURALITY SYSTEMS

Plurality systems are won by those who gain a plurality of the vote (i.e., more than any other candidate), and can be contrasted with majority systems, which are structured so as to ensure that the winning candidate gains an absolute majority (i.e., more than 50 percent) of eligible votes. The two types of plurality systems are first past the post (FPTP) and the multi-member plurality system (MPS).

- Under *first past the post*, the winner is the candidate who gains the most votes, but not necessarily an absolute majority of the votes, in single-member districts—hence its other name, *single-member district plurality* (SMDP). Such elections are typically presented as a contest among candidates, rather than parties. Voters choose their favored candidate with a tick or a cross on the ballot paper, and the winner is simply the candidate who gains more votes than any other. This is the world's most commonly used electoral system, and (as described further in Teehankee's Chapter Nine) is used to elect the bulk of the members of the Philippine House of Representatives.

- The *multi-member plurality system* (often known internationally as the "block vote"[2]) is the application of plurality rules in multi-member rather than single-member electoral districts. Voters have as many votes as there are seats to be filled,[3] and the highest-polling candidates fill positions sequentially regardless of the percentage of the vote they actually achieve. This is a much less commonly used system globally, but plays a dominant role in Philippine elections. As explained in Ravanilla's Chapter Ten, roughly 80 percent of the 18,000 elective posts in Philippines elections are decided by this system: from the 12 senators elected at the national level to the 24 members of the regional assembly of the Autonomous Region in Muslim Mindanao to nearly 800 provincial board members and over 13,000 city and municipal councilors.

MAJORITY SYSTEMS

There are two primary types of majority systems, the two-round system (TRS) and the alternative vote (AV), both of which are applied only in single-member electoral districts.

---

2 In the International IDEA handbook, my co-authors and I refer to this system as the "block vote." In the Philippine context, however, "block vote" commonly refers to straight-party voting. For this reason, the term used in this volume is "multi-member plurality system" or MPS.

3 Variations on the MPS, not examined in this chapter, include the Limited Vote (if voters have fewer votes than there are seats), or the Single Non-Transferable Vote (if they have only one vote).

- The most common form of majority system, the *two-round system*, takes place in two rounds of voting, often a week or two apart. The first round is conducted in the same way as a normal plurality election. If a candidate receives an absolute majority of the vote, then he or she is elected outright, with no need for a second ballot. If, however, no candidate has an absolute majority, then a second round of voting is conducted, usually as a runoff between the two highest polling candidates from the first round, and the winner of this round is declared elected. This system is often used for the election of executives (presidents, governors, and mayors) but can also be used for single-member legislative seats.

- Another majority system is the *alternative vote,* or preferential voting, as used, for example, to elect the Australian House. In this system, voters number their second and later preferences among candidates, and these preferences come into play in the event that a voter's first choice does not win. As such, the system is sometimes called "instant runoff voting."

PROPORTIONAL REPRESENTATION (PR) SYSTEMS

The rationale underpinning all PR systems is the direct translation of each party's or candidate's share of the votes at an election into a corresponding proportion of seats in an elected body. For instance, a party that wins 20 percent of the votes should gain about 20 percent of the seats under a PR system, whereas the same vote total under most plurality or majority systems would result in no seats at all. Thus, if plurality and majority systems are often characterized as "winner takes all," with no benefits possible for the loser, PR systems ensure that all parties which gain a certain minimum threshold of votes will also win a proportionate number of seats.[4]

All PR systems require the use of electoral districts with more than one member: it is not possible to divide a single seat elected on a single occasion proportionally. As a result, multi-member electorates are essential to any PR model. This highlights the particular importance of "district magnitude" in

---

4 The technical process, in brief, is as follows. PR elections start by determining the "quota" of votes needed to win a seat. This is typically calculated by taking the total number of votes gained by all parties in the election and dividing this number by one more than the number of seats to be elected. For example, if there are 100,000 votes for 99 seats of the legislature the quota would be 100,000 divided by 100 seats = a quota of 1000. Seats are allocated sequentially, with the process repeated until all seats are filled; in this example, a party will receive a seat as soon as it obtains its first 1000 votes. Usually, any remaining seats are allocated to the parties with the highest leftover vote less than a full quota.

analysis of PR systems, defined as the number of seats per electorate or district. As explained by Hicken in Chapter Two, "[l]arge district magnitude (many seats per district) is associated with legislative seats going to many small parties" while "[s]mall district magnitude (fewer seats per district) is associated with relatively fewer and larger political parties winning legislative seats."

In most PR systems, voters choose among parties, not candidates. [5] In such systems, there are two major variants—closed list and open list.

- *Closed-list PR*, the most common type of proportional representation system, requires each party to present a list of candidates to the electorate. Electors vote for a party or list rather than for individual candidates; parties receive seats in proportion to their overall share of the national vote. Winning candidates are taken from the lists in the order set by the party itself, and voters are unable to express a preference for a particular candidate.

- *Open-list PR*, by contrast, allows voters to choose not just a party but also a particular candidate from a party list or, in some cases, more than one list. This removes the power of parties to control places on the list.

Open- and closed-list PR may seem similar at first glance, but can bring forth sharply contrasting types of electoral appeals. Open-list PR is much more a contest for personal popularity and yields candidate-centric contests. In closed-list systems, parties both choose candidates and determine the ranking of those candidates (i.e., they make the decisions about which candidates are placed in winnable positions). This yields a much more party-centric system, with all of the advantages highlighted in Hicken's Chapter Two. Conversely, in Chapter Six, Aspinall examines how Indonesia's shift from a closed- to an open-list has brought forth the negative consequences of a more candidate-centric system.

Another major advantage of the closed-list system is its capacity to advance goals of gender equality. As explained in Reyes's Chapter Five, this occurs most specifically through the so-called "zipper system," whereby a party's list of

---

5 There is a third type of proportional representation that involves voting for individual candidates: the *single transferable vote* (STV) form of proportional representation, used to elect the Australian Senate and also found in Ireland and Malta. The system requires voters to rank order the candidates, and allows both for the reallocation of preferences from those candidates who do not meet a basic quota of votes as well as the reallocation of the "surplus" of those candidates elected with more than a full quota.

candidates alternates between women and men. For the zipper system to have the greatest positive impact on women's political representation, she further notes, the closed-list system needs to be constructed on the basis of relatively large district magnitudes.

MIXED SYSTEMS

Mixed electoral systems attempt to combine the positive attributes of both plurality/majority and proportional electoral systems. In a mixed system, these two electoral formulae run alongside each other. Votes are cast by the same voters and contribute to the election of representatives under both systems: typically, a plurality system, often utilizing single-member districts, and a proportional list, often elected on a national basis.

Mixed systems have been a feature of electoral system choice in recent decades, and have been a particularly popular choice in transitional democracies— perhaps because, on the face of it, they appear to combine the benefits of local representation with more equitable allocation of seats, offering "the best of both worlds" (Shugart and Wattenburg 2001). Mixed systems can be divided into two broad categories, compensatory and parallel systems.

- *Compensatory* systems are designed so that part of the parliament (often one-half) is elected from single-member districts, while the remainder is elected from PR lists. Voters can be given a separate vote for each or only one vote. As the name suggests, compensatory systems use the PR list seats to compensate for any disproportionality produced by the district seat results. Such systems deliver truly proportional election results and are thus often categorized as a form of PR. Germany, New Zealand, and Mexico are examples.[6]

- *Parallel* systems, by contrast, use both PR party lists and local districts running side-by-side, but with no compensatory provisions. Part of the assembly is elected by proportional representation, part by some type of plurality or majority method.[7] Japan, Taiwan, and South Korea are examples of parallel systems.

---

6 In the political science literature, these compensatory systems are known as "mixed-member proportional" (MMP) systems—thus highlighting the high degree of proportionality that they deliver.

7 In the political science literature, these parallel systems are known as "mixed-member majoritarian" (MMM) systems, with "majoritarian" being a term that (rather confusingly) encompasses *both* majority *and* plurality systems.

THE DIVERSITY OF ELECTORAL SYSTEM DESIGN IN SOUTHEAST ASIA

As discussed below, many of the electoral reforms in Southeast Asia in recent years have led to the development of new electoral systems.[8] As a result, the region has become something of a showcase for the diversity of electoral system design. Southeast Asia today not only provides clear examples from each of the four main families of electoral systems—plurality, majority, proportional, and mixed models—but also from most of the main electoral sub-types: plurality first past the post (Myanmar, Malaysia, Philippines), multi-member plurality (Philippines, Singapore), two-round systems (presidential elections in Timor Leste), open-list PR (Indonesia), and closed-list PR (Cambodia, Timor Leste).[9] In addition, the region provides several distinctive examples of electoral system design such as Singapore's party-block system (as described below), Indonesia's "distributional" presidential electoral formulae,[10] and the mixed models found in Thailand (which have repeatedly been altered over time) and the Philippines (since the promulgation of the 1987 constitution).

The Philippines was the instigator of Asia's trend towards mixed systems: its 1987 Constitution provides that up to fifty-two legislative seats (20 percent of the legislature) be chosen from a national list representing "sectoral interests" and marginalized groups such as youth, labour, the urban poor, farmers, fishermen and women, with the remaining 80 percent of seats chosen from single-member districts. Plagued by problems of design and implementation, the Philippine Supreme Court subsequently opened up party-list seats to others beyond this initial list of "marginalized" groups (Torres-Pilapil 2015). The system is not in fact proportional, as I have explained elsewhere, in part because of its three-seat ceiling on the number of seats that can be won by any single political party.[11] This lack of proportionality is further highlighted in Chapter Nine by Teehankee, who argues strongly for the Philippines to move to a more standard closed-list PR system.

Thailand, after experimenting with a variety of different electoral system models, also chose a mixed system as part of its 1997 political reforms: its lower house was composed of 400 members elected by plurality from single-member districts and another 100 chosen by closed-list PR from a national list (but with the idea, since abandoned, that list seats would be the preserve not of under-

---

8 I discuss this in detail in Reilly 2015.
9 For more on these classifications, see Reynolds, Reilly and Ellis 2005.
10 As explained in Chapter Six by Aspinall, winning presidential candidates in Indonesia must garner "at least 20 percent of the votes in at least one half of the country's thirty-four provinces."
11 See Reilly 2016.

represented minorities but of elites, providing a pathway to office for potential cabinet ministers) (Hicken 2007). In the unstable period of coups and military rule since then, Thailand has tried other variants of mixed systems, combining PR with both single-member and (in 2007) multi-member plurality. It remains to be seen what system will be used for Thailand's next election, now scheduled for early 2019.

Singapore uses a different mixture of electoral models again, combining single-member and multi-member electoral districts as part of a party-block system in which the winning party claims every seat in a district. This creates an exceptionally majoritarian electoral system, but one which can in theory assist minority representation by ensuring that at least one member elected from each "Group Representation Constituency" must hail from a minority (e.g., Malay, Indian) community. In an additional twist, Singapore also has Nominated Members of Parliament, whereby up to nine non-elected MPs with expertise and ability can be added to parliament. In practice, these have also tended towards functional representation for labor, women's, and environmental groups (Rodan 2005).

Unlike many mixed systems in other world regions, Asian mixed-member systems tend to be weighted in favor of the districts and run the list component of elections separately, with no compensatory interchange between the two. This makes them less proportional in their operation than most similar models elsewhere. Indeed, the shift towards less broadly representative and more majority-centric electoral models can be considered a hallmark of an "Asian model" of democracy (Reilly 2007).

Elsewhere, the region's proportional electoral systems have also become increasingly contested. After experimenting with several different models, Indonesia today uses an "open list" PR system with relatively small district magnitude, which in some provinces results in two or three-member districts. This limits the proportionality of the system's operation (see Aspinall's Chapter Six on the broader implications of the shift to open-list PR). In authoritarian Cambodia, electoral arrangements also break the standard rules of PR, as a third of all seats are chosen from single-member districts—thus giving incumbents a marked structural advantage in what is already a heavily biased system which favors the governing Cambodian People's Party. At the other extreme lies East Timor: having used a mixed system for its founding 2002 elections, East Timor now uses a closed-list PR model, with the whole country forming one constituency.

Only Malaysia and Myanmar today rely exclusively on the kind of standard single-member plurality system familiar to British or American practice. But there too the impact of electoral systems has heightened in recent years, with what appears to be a process of "electorally led" democratization taking place. While the idea of "democratization by elections" as a distinctive mode of transition (Lindberg 2009) has not seriously been applied to Asia, recent political openings may provide an example of the way in which flawed but partially competitive elections can themselves lead to greater democratization. The electorally led transitions that occurred in both Myanmar in 2015 and in Malaysia in 2018 represent the first changes of government in many decades in both countries, raising hopes that they may usher in a return to genuine electoral democracy.

STRONGER PARTIES

A frequent but by no means consistent reform aim in Southeast Asia has been to strengthen ruling political parties and party systems, many of which have long been seen as deficient. Thailand's 1997 Constitution, for instance, aimed to promote stronger parties and more stable governments. Alongside the mixed system described above, in which 20 percent of seats were chosen through closed-list PR, election rules for the House included a 5 percent list threshold (to weed out splinter parties). This was accompanied by a strengthened prime minister's office and mandatory party membership for all MPs (to reduce pre-election party-hopping). However, in what has been a pattern of Thailand's reforms, the aim of strengthening of parties was undermined by the creation of a non-partisan Senate, chosen by the single non-transferable vote—an electoral system formerly used in Japan that is notorious for promoting personalistic competition.[12]

Political scientists often laud the role of institutionalized political parties as "a crucial pillar in the functioning and consolidation of emerging democracies," seeing them as the "missing link" in the quest for democratic consolidation across the region (Hicken and Kuhonta 2011, 573). From the standpoint of promoting stronger development outcomes, Hicken's Chapter Two forcefully argues the advantages of a party-centric relative to a candidate-centric polity. Building stronger parties comes primarily through the choice of electoral system, but also through the legal framework through which parties are to be organized. Indonesia, the world's most populous emerging democracy, has gone the farthest in regulating its political parties, requiring parties to establish

---

12 On Japan's SNTV, see Ravanilla's Chapter Ten.

an organizational network across the archipelago and also giving them a direct role in the nomination of candidates for president. By effectively banning local parties, Indonesia has created putatively national parties with a cross-regional organisational basis by fiat, as parties must satisfy these branch-structure requirements before they can compete in elections.[13]

The interaction between different electoral and party systems creates divergent incentives for public goods delivery. Selway (2015) argues that closed-list PR rules are better for public goods provision in homogenous states such as Japan, or states which do not display strong market inequalities between groups such as Switzerland.

> PR in such countries tends to produce parties with geographically dispersed bases of support, making it difficult to selectively target resources. In addition, the list feature of PR gives candidates strong incentives to be loyal to the central party leadership who are more concerned with the party's overall success and thus the least responsive to narrow demands. We thus see less success in catering to narrow constituencies with particularistic goods because it is simply more cost-effective to distribute government resources broadly (Selway 2015, 14).

He uses the example of health care and hospital construction in Thailand following the decision in 1997 to add a closed-list PR tier in a single national district to the electoral system. This reform led to a change in the party system, from a fractionalized system of narrowly oriented parties based around local strongmen to a more nationalized two-party system. These new parties developed their own independent policy platforms to a much greater extent than had previously been the case as they sought to distinguish themselves in a national electoral contest. Health was a prominent campaign issue. In power, both the main parties made significant reforms: "whereas the pre-1997 era was characterised by building of hospitals and the over-purchasing of expensive medical equipment, and rampant corruption, the post-1997 era witnessed a much broader distribution of health resources. Specifically, access to health resources was extended to a much larger proportion of the population" via rural health clinics and the 30-baht health card. In sum, pre-reform health policy was focused on expensive hospital and equipment directed to strongman's

---

13 An exception to this rule applies in Aceh, and was a key part of the 2005 peace agreement there. See Hillman 2012.

local districts; post-reform policy was much more focussed on delivering goods throughout the country based on population size (Selway 2011).

However, despite their public-goods enhancement, Thailand's reforms have been characterized as a case of "be careful what you wish for" (Kuhonta 2008): so many incentives for cohesive parties and strong government were put in place that they unbalanced the political landscape and helped facilitate the rise of Thaksin Shinawatra and his Thai Rak Thai party. In other words, the system produced a range of unintended consequences. Following the 2006 coup, many of these incentives for strong parties and stable government were revoked, in a direct response to the Thaksin years, which continue to echo through Thailand's contemporary politics. Given the ongoing strength of rural support for Thai Rak Thai's successor parties, particularly in the northeast, the post-2014 military regime has demonstrated a desire to fragment the party system and thus make it harder for any one party to win government.

The strategic nature of electoral system choice is also important. Incumbent regimes and opposition movements face different incentives over institutional choices depending on their electoral prospects. Established parties or those who think they will be able to secure a clear plurality of the vote have an incentive to choose winner-take-all models such as first past the post to maximize the seat bonuses that such systems typically provide to the largest party. Hence the support for such systems by parties like Golkar in Indonesia in 1999 or the National League for Democracy in Myanmar today. By contrast, declining governing parties or challengers less sure of their vote totals are better off choosing PR, to protect themselves from an electoral wipeout and to guarantee a fair share of seats (hence the late push for a shift to PR in 2015 by the now-opposition Union Solidarity and Development Party in Myanmar). Mixed systems present a good compromise solution in situations of electoral uncertainty, one reason for their popularity in transitional cases. In short, rational calculations of future electoral support are important strategic considerations for system choice.

Table 3.1 sets out recent changes in electoral systems across Southeast Asia. In almost all cases, electoral reforms have seen the introduction of new systems which have not produced dramatic improvements in terms of either democratic accountability or party strengthening. This points to the need for careful consideration of goals, and careful selection of means, when undertaking electoral system redesign.

TABLE 3.1: ELECTORAL SYSTEM CHANGES IN SOUTHEAST ASIA

Country	Former Electoral System	New Electoral System
Indonesia	Closed-list PR, with large districts (1999/2004)	Open-List PR, with smaller districts (2009/14)
Philippines	Plurality (FPTP and MPS) (pre-1986)	Mixed Plurality (FPTP and MPS) and Party List System (PLS), the latter with three-seat limit (1987 and 1998)
Thailand	MPS (pre-1997)	Mixed Plurality-PR (1997, 2001, 2004); MPS-PR (2007); Plurality-PR (2011)
Singapore	Plurality in mostly single-member districts (pre-1988)	Party Block in mostly multi-member districts (post-1988)

CHALLENGES

Attempts at electoral system redesign have not been without problems. Many electoral changes have been adopted in a piecemeal fashion and appear uncoordinated with other reforms. Indonesia's open list model, for instance, in theory promotes greater accountability to individual candidates but in practice weakens party cohesion by encouraging members of the same party to compete directly with each other for votes. The 2009 and 2014 legislative elections were thus very much a contest between candidates rather than party brands, and featured (predictably) high levels of intra-party contestation as electoral success became dependent on a candidate's personal vote total rather than the party vote. This move, the result of a Constitutional Court decision, increased intra-party competition and undermined other efforts aimed at building stronger parties in Indonesia (Dressel and Mietzner 2012).

In the Philippines, the courts have also been influential, limiting party list group representation to a maximum of three seats and restricting the ability of larger parties to compete for them. The effect of these rulings appears to have been widespread confusion, and the party-list seats have been dogged by problems, with less than half the winning list of candidates taking up their seats in the first four elections after the system was introduced in 1998 (see Teehankee's Chapter Ten). In the absence of clear legal guidance, established parties have also colonized the party list seats with front organizations, to the point where some scholars argue that the party list seats have exacerbated, not ameliorated, the Philippines' "democratic deficit" (Hutchcroft and Rocamora 2003).

Another challenge is the tension inherent in different institutional reform packages, some of which appear to work at cross-purposes. Thus the dominance of single-member districts in Thailand—as found in the mixed systems put in place in 1997 and 2011—were made with an expectation that they would, over time, improve political accountability by forging closer links between individual politicians and voters. However, this may simultaneously retard another often desired aim—the development of more nationally focused and programmatic political parties—as district-based systems are generally considered to be less effective at promoting nationally cohesive parties than PR. In the same manner, Indonesia's use of open list voting in 2009, introduced to build greater links between individual candidates and the electorate, has created internal pressures on party cohesion as members of the same party compete for votes. Initial reforms in both Indonesia and Thailand also saw party strengthening in lower house elections undercut by the design of "non-party" upper houses (Rich 2012).

Many of the region's reforms thus appear to lack coherence when viewed from a comparative perspective. The Philippines provides a good illustration of this incoherent approach to political engineering. Numerous aspects of the electoral process—limited public funding, a candidate-centered ballot, and frequent party switching—have undermined broader goals of political consolidation. Party-list seats have brought new groups into Philippine electoral politics, but have also encouraged a proliferation of organizations representing (or purporting to represent) underprivileged groups. A low electoral threshold opens the floodgates to a large number of players within the party list system (an average of more than 100 parties per election, explains Teehankee in Chapter Nine), while the three-seat ceiling has further undermined the push for more coherent party politics (Reilly 2016).

CONCLUSION

Across Southeast Asia as well as neighboring East Asia, electoral reforms to promote political stability have been linked to broader ideas of governance and development (Reilly 2006; Rock 2013). Motivations have included a reaction to former authoritarian structures (as in the 1987 Philippine Constitution) or an antidote to scenarios of national disintegration (as in Indonesia after the fall of Suharto in 1998). In part because of a widespread elite consensus on the need for "pro-development" policies, there has been an active effort to promote more programmatic party politics, either via electoral system change (as in Japan in 1994 or Taiwan in 2005), as part of a new constitution (as in Thailand 1997), directly via political party laws (as in Indonesia in 1999), or combinations of all three. While distinct, most of these reforms have at their heart the quest for stronger and more cohesive party politics which could aggregate social cleavages and, in theory, deliver more stable and effective governance.

This approach to electoral system design does not assume that governments have suddenly become angels, devoid of self-interest. Rather, winning electoral strategies for governing parties have shifted as party systems have changed. Parties which aspire to nationwide electoral dominance and to claim government outright rather than in coalition with others need national electoral strategies. Under such circumstances, it is too costly and insufficiently electorally rewarding to try to deliver private or club goods to localized bases of voter support. Rather, a more efficient strategy is to deliver broad-based public goods—in the shape of policy, not pork—to broad social groups as a means of securing voter support (Keefer 2011).

In Asia, as in most developing countries, one of the largest potential groups which can be targeted in this way are poorer voters, who often constitute a sizeable proportion of all electors. These voters constitute an important potential vote bank for any party willing and able to deliver benefits to them in a credible way. The health reforms sponsored by Thai Rak Thai in Thailand in the early 2000s, which prioritized the building of rural health clinics, cheap health cards and other benefits for poor rural populations, is an example of this trend. Other examples include the program of direct cash transfers to 20 million low income households championed by Indonesian President Susilo Bambang Yudhoyono in Indonesia, on the back of his victory at the 2009 elections, and similar reforms in India to target cash transfers directly to poor recipients rather than though third parties.

However, elections do not guarantee such pro-poor outcomes. While electoral democracy may now be institutionalized in Indonesia, East Timor, and the Philippines, the persistence of low-quality governance in such democracies has given rise to increasing pressures for further electoral reform. Reforms which push towards more "centripetal" political outcomes are worth greater investigation (Reilly 2011). These may include, in the case of the Philippines:

- Joint tickets for presidential and vice-presidential candidates

- Majority-rule requirements for presidential and/or congressional elections, e.g., via a two-round or instant-runoff system

- Stronger political party laws following, for instance, the Indonesian example

- Amendments to the party list to make it a truly nationwide contest, e.g., by instituting a standard closed-list PR model and thus removing the three-seat ceiling on the number of seats a party can gain

- More ambitious reforms for Congress, e.g., introducing proportional representation in the Senate

- Regional distribution requirements for presidents, along the Indonesian model

Comparative experience suggests that all of these reform options offer some potential advantages in terms of democratic development and should be placed on the agenda in the current round of political reform discussions. Some of these reforms (e.g., distribution requirements for presidential elections, revised electoral arrangements for the Senate) would also be compatible with the current push for federalism, and would help to enhance the operational viability of a federal political structure.

The front page of the *Asahi Shimbun* after the Japanese Diet passed a landmark 1994 electoral system reform (with 300 members to be elected via first past the post and 200 via closed-list proportional representation). At the center of the photo is Prime Minister Morihiro Hosokawa, whose election the previous year had ended the 38-year dominance of the Japanese Liberal Democratic Party.

Photograph by Maxine McArthur, with thanks to Menzies Library, Australian National University. Used with the permission of *Asahi Shimbun*.

CHAPTER FOUR
WHEN DOES ELECTORAL SYSTEM REFORM OCCUR?

ALLEN HICKEN

Major electoral reforms are generally rare events. While politicians and election management bodies regularly tinker with minor reforms (redrawing districts, changing ballot structures, etc.) wholesale reforms of electoral systems are much less common. This isn't surprising. Incumbent politicians are understandably reluctant to change the rules under which they themselves have been successful. In addition, the hurdles required to reform the electoral system can be daunting—going well beyond normal policy-making procedures. These can include amending the constitution or submitting proposed changes to a public referendum. And yet, despite these obstacles, countries can and do reform their electoral systems. This suggests a puzzle and a question. First, why would political actors choose to reform the rules under which they have come to power? Second, when (that is, under what conditions) do these efforts succeed and when do they not? In this paper I focus very briefly on the puzzle of "why reform?" before focusing my primary attention on the closely related question of "when reform"?

Why reform? Given that politicians are generally loath to change the rules under which they themselves were elected, why would electoral reform ever get on the political agenda in the first place? Reform proposals circulate like seeds in the wind in most political systems. What does it take for those seeds to take root? What circumstances are necessary in order for politicians to begin considering reform? Most reform efforts fail to get on the public agenda. This leads into more careful attention to the required conditions for reform initiation (Shugart 2008).

When reform? If electoral reform is going to be initiated in the Philippines what needs to occur? Drawing on comparative reform experiences and the political science literature I propose three conditions for reform initiation: systemic failure, a catalytic event, and change in incumbents' preferences. Each of these is necessary if politicians are going to be motivated to begin a reform process (see Figure 4.1).

- *Systemic failure* occurs when the current electoral system fails to meet the normative expectations of the public—namely, it fails to produce governments that are responsive, accountable and effective. Systemic failure may exist for some time within a political system.

- A *catalytic event*, generally a crisis of some kind, is usually necessary to draw the connection between political and/or economic woes and the electoral system and thus generate demand for reform.

- Finally, if reform is to proceed, *incumbent politicians must come to feel they have something to gain by pursuing reform (or at least not opposing it)*. They may come to prefer reform because—as explained further below—they believe they or their party will achieve better long-term electoral outcomes under a different set of rules (referred to in the literature as "outcome motivation") or because they expect short-term electoral benefits from taking a stance as a reformer (known as "act motivation").

After examining the why and when of reform, I proceed briefly to venture into the question of *how*. More specifically, I discuss how delegative reform institutions—even those set up with cynical motives—can themselves become catalysts for electoral reform.[1]

In conclusion, I apply this framework—most of all the why and the when of reform—to the Philippines.

SYSTEMIC FAILURE

The first condition necessary in order to initiate reform is failure of the electoral system. Absent a judgement that the existing system has failed in some way, demand for reform is likely to be too low and the costs prohibitively high. A systemic failure exists when the electoral system is unable to deliver on one or more of the normative goals that the system is designed to achieve. Without that diagnosis of systemic failure—that the electoral system has fundamentally failed in some way—electoral reform cannot proceed.

What does systemic failure look like in practice? Precisely how electoral systems fail, and which failings trigger reform attempts, vary by case. However,

---

1 Note that I give little attention to *"what reform?,"* i.e., the question of why politicians choose a particular type of reform over another. In other words, I focus primarily on the catalyst behind reform attempts, rather than on the creation and content of the reforms themselves.

there are some common patterns in how and where systemic failures emerge. It is helpful to start by dividing electoral systems along two dimensions—*interparty* and *intraparty* (Shugart 2001). Electoral systems, like all institutions, embody trade-offs. Along the *interparty* dimension is the trade-off between what we might call plurality/majoritarian visions of democracy versus proportional visions of democracy.

- *Plurality/majoritarian systems* place great value on decisiveness and effectiveness—governments being able to pass policies quickly and efficiently. They also value identifiability (voters being able to vote directly on who they want to control government) and accountability and clarity of responsibility (being able to assign clear credit or blame to policy makers in order to hold them accountable). This corresponds with a preference for a small number of large parties—ideally two parties or party blocks—one of which will likely gain full control of the government.

- The *proportional vision* (also called the power-sharing or consensus vision), by contrast, values giving voice and representation to lots of groups and interests. A variety of interests should have seats at the table. The proportional vision values power-sharing, inclusiveness and consensus over majority rule, and policy stability/credibility over decisiveness. This corresponds to a preference for lots of parties and large, multiparty coalition governments.

A trade-off exists between these two visions. Moving in a plurality/majoritarian direction can come at the cost of representation and policy stability, while moving in a proportional direction sacrifices some decisiveness and clarity of responsibility.

Along the second, *intraparty* dimension we have a trade-off between personalistic and party-centered politics.

- *Personalized systems* value close ties between individual politicians and local voters/constituents. They want politicians with whom voters can personally interact and to whom they can go for help. The focus, under this vision, is on responding to local needs and local interests. This corresponds with a preference for candidate-centered electoral systems and weaker, decentralized parties.

- The *party-centered vision*, by contrast, privileges close ties between politicians and their national party. Politicians' primary loyalty should be to party leaders and the package of policies the party label represents. The focus of party-centered systems is on national policies and on responding to broad national constituencies as defined by party leaders. This is reflected in a preference for strong, party-centered electoral systems and strong, centralized parties.

Again, there is a trade-off here. As we move toward more personalized systems, we sacrifice collective partisan accountability and a broader, national focus, while movement in the opposite direction comes at a cost of connections between politicians and local constituencies/voters.

The bottom line is that there is no ideal system, as different societies will place different weights on these competing values. However, we know that as polities approach the extremes of these dimensions they are more likely to experience systemic failure—what Shugart (2001) calls electoral system pathologies or inefficiencies. Figure 4.2 presents these two extremes across the two dimensions, interparty and intraparty.

- *Interparty dimension (horizontal axis).* At the two extremes of this dimension we get hyper-representativeness, where a large number of parties contributes to government instability, policy deadlock, and low identifiability and accountability, and pluralitarianism where the electoral system produces governments representing well under a majority of the electorate (Shugart 2001).

- *Intraparty dimension (vertical axis).* Turning our attention to the *intraparty dimension*, at one extreme we have hyper-personalism (or hyper-particularalism), where narrow political interests completely swamp collective party and national interests. In hyper-personalized systems we see resources flowing to narrow interests while broader, collective interests are neglected. At the other extreme we have hyper-partisanship, where the connection between individual legislators and voters/local constituents is completely broken. Politicians are focused solely on pleasing the party leadership and are not responsive at all to local constituents and their interests (ibid).

Aside from providing a visual representation of the conceptual framework, Figure 4.2 also shows some prominent examples of where countries were located prior to their reform efforts. New Zealand's system regularly produced manufactured majorities—governments headed by single parties that had the support of less than half of the electorate. At the other extreme, the Italian and Israeli electoral systems produced multi-party governments that were unstable and ineffective. Japan's SNTV electoral system was the epitome of a hyper-personalized electoral system, and Venezuela's hyper-partisan electoral system contributed to an acute representation and accountability crisis in that country. Finally, Thailand's pre-reform system scored high both in terms of hyper-personalism and in terms of hyper-representativeness. Each of these cases is discussed in more detail below, and in the conclusion I will discuss the situation of the Philippines.

CATALYSTS AND CRISES

Never let a good crisis go to waste.
–Winston Churchill

Systemic failures can exist for years and never trigger a serious reform attempt. What does it take to translate failure into a demand for electoral reform? Typically what is needed is a catalytic event—usually a crisis of some sort—that focuses public attention on the need for political reform and draws attention to the systemic failures of the electoral system specifically. This kind of event goes beyond economic crises, run-of-the-mill corruption scandals, or normal political crises. A catalytic event results in the political and/or economic ills being explicitly tied to fundamental failings in the electoral system—namely, the inability of the electoral system to produce governments that are responsive, accountable and effective.

As the quote from Winston Churchill suggests, crises create opportunities for would-be reform entrepreneurs. These might be individual politicians, political parties who seek an electoral advantage by advocating reform (more below), or societal groups. The key is that these entrepreneurs take advantage of the crisis to tie political, social, or economic ills to the systemic failure of the electoral system. Without this explicit linkage electoral reform can be eclipsed by less specific calls for combatting corruption or improving governance.

The kind of event that triggers reform demands varies across contexts, but it is usually directly related to the features of the existing electoral system. The more direct the connection between the event and the existing electoral system the easier it is for reformers to make the case for electoral reform. Here are a few illustrative examples:

Israel. By the late 1980s the feeling that the Israeli political system was dysfunctional was widely shared. Governments were indecisive and ineffectual. The grand coalitions that made up governments were often held hostage by their more radical members (Rahat 2001, 133). Much of the blame for this state of affairs can be attributed to the country's hyper-representative electoral system. However, the catalyst for reform was a political crisis in 1990. After the collapse of one government, political parties in the Knesset were unable to reach an agreement on a new government for three months, during which time ultra-orthodox religious parties leveraged their positions to extract unpopular concessions from potential coalition partners. Known as the "Stinky Trick" period, this crisis galvanized support for electoral reform on the part of the public and many of the members of mainline political parties as a way to improve political stability and reduce the influence of small, radical religious parties (Rahat 2001, 135). In the wake of Stinky Trick, the Knesset began debate of electoral reforms culminating in a 1992 reform law.

Italy. For decades many of Italy's governance ills had been laid at the feet of the electoral system. The electoral system was blamed for "creating and maintaining the conditions of fragmentation, factionalism, incapacity, instability, and irresponsibility that afflicted the Italian polity" (Katz 2001, 96). However, the catalyst for electoral reform, which began via a referendum in 1993, was the rise of a new party (the Northern League) which backed reform, and a massive corruption scandal that grew to implicate the leaders of all of the established government parties, leaving those parties thoroughly discredited and willing to back reform as a way to salvage their political future.

Bolivia. By the late 1980s the Bolivian electoral system was under attack for undermining political responsiveness and accountability and fostering weak links between parties and voters. However, reform proposals went nowhere until a political crisis erupted in 1989 in the wake of that year's general election. The two parties that made up the governing coalition were found to have manipulated votes to artificially create a parliamentary majority. In the aftermath of the crisis, all major parties took up the task of electoral reform under enormous pressure from societal groups, including the Catholic Church, business groups, and organized labor. After intense bargaining a set of constitutional amendments were adopted in 1994 that reformed the electoral system (Mayorga 2001).

New Zealand and Great Britain. In both New Zealand and Great Britain the costs and benefits of a plurality electoral system were generally understood, and for decades, fairly non-controversial. A series of related events, however, highlighted for voters the existence of systemic failures, which produced high levels of voter distrust and dissatisfaction. These included pluralitarian outcomes where parties that came in second in the voting nonetheless captured a majority of the seats, and extremely high levels of disproportionality, where smaller parties were almost entirely unrepresented in parliament despite winning a significant number of votes. In New Zealand these electoral outcomes were reinforced by the pursuit of radical and unpopular economic policies by the two largest parties—policies which departed sharply from the policies the parties had campaigned on and highlighted how unaccountable to voters parties had become (Denemark 2001). Both countries initiated electoral reforms in the wake of these events, with reform ultimately succeeding in New Zealand, and failing in Great Britain.

Japan. As in most of the other cases of reform discussed so far, the feeling that the Japanese political system was broken had existed for decades. Japanese political history was littered with failed reform attempts stretching back 40 years. So why, finally, did the Japanese Diet pass a law in 1994 that overhauled the electoral system? Again, crises served as catalysts, spurring public demand for some kind of change. To begin with, a 1988 scandal implicated most senior leaders of the ruling LDP party. In response, the prime minister set up a special committee that did not contain any Diet members, and that committee came back with a recommendation for electoral reform in 1990. However, the resulting bill failed to find enough support in the Diet. Opposition parties were divided over the best electoral alternative, and a significant portion of LDP members also opposed the draft. Reform might have once again faded into the background were it not for another major scandal that broke in 1992, again implicating senior members of the LDP. Public outrage over the crisis obliged the LDP prime minister to once again take up the subject of reform. Opinion polls showed that while the public was fed up with the political system and demanding change, they did not have strong feelings about the Japanese electoral system. They simply wanted political reform. However, the opposition united behind an alternative electoral system and soon electoral reform became a symbol of politicians' willingness to reform (Reed and Thies 2001). (The fact that the LDP proposed electoral reforms that would clearly have advantaged the LDP also helped the opposition's cause.) Indeed, reformers succeeded in tying the political scandals to the propensity of the Japanese electoral system to promote hyper-personalized politics, factionalized parties, and close ties between politicians and financial contributors. When the LDP tried to force its preferred plan through parliament this triggered a vote of no-confidence, and, after members of the LDP defected to the opposition, the LDP government fell. The ensuing election brought a new government to power, which for the first time did not include the LDP. With a mandate for reform and the LDP in the opposition the government quickly adopted a new electoral system.

Finally, note that there are two specific kinds of political events that can serve as catalysts for reforms: transitions to and from democracy, and the election of political outsiders/populists.

First, when autocracies come to an end we often see the new democratic actors rewriting the electoral rules of the game (if elections were held under authoritarian auspices), or introducing elections and electoral rules for the first time. Where the outgoing authoritarian regime is defeated and discredited the new democratic actors bargain among themselves over what the new rules should look like. Actor preferences over the new rules are informed by both their view of which democratic goals should be prioritized (for example, representation or decisiveness) and their beliefs about which system is likely to bring them the most electoral success. The 1987 constitutional reforms in the Philippines would fall into this category. Where the end of autocracy is negotiated between the autocrat and democratic forces, then the autocrat presses for reforms that will allow the autocrat to retain some power and influence while opening up political competition to the democratic opposition. This opposition, meanwhile, presses for rules that would give them the upper hand. The outcome is a result of bargaining between the two sides. The early electoral systems in post-communist Eastern Europe often reflected such bargaining. Democratic reversals can also trigger electoral reform. For example, the 2006 and 2014 Thai coups were each accompanied by electoral reform designed to reshape the country's party system and advantage parties allied with Thailand's conservative forces.

Second, the electoral victory of former political outsiders can serve as a catalytic event. When actors who perceive themselves to be disadvantaged by the current rules manage to win power, then they often have an incentive to leverage their victory to push for reform of those rules. The Italian and Japanese reforms both came about only after formerly dominant parties were turned out of power and replaced by parties formerly in the opposition. Similarly, and more worryingly from a democratic perspective, populist politicians have often used their electoral mandates to push for constitutional and electoral reform. Venezuela's Hugo Chavez, Turkey's Recep Erdogan, Bolivia's Evo Morales, and Russia's Vladimir Putin, all capitalized on their popularity and power to remake electoral rules in their favor once in office.

ALIGNING INCUMBENT PREFERENCES

Systemic failure and catalytic events help establish a demand for reform, but in order for reform to proceed, political incumbents must choose to initiate the reform process. Successors to autocratic governments and political outsiders have clear incentives for reform. But why would political incumbents support reform of the rules under which they have previously been successful? There are two reasons why incumbent preferences might align in favor of initiating reform. *First*, the governing coalition may come to believe that it will do better under new rules. *Second*, incumbents may come to believe that initiating reforms will boost their popularity among voters (or that failing to initiate reform will bring punishment by voters). The former is called *outcome motivation*, and the latter is called *act motivation* (see Figure 4.1) (Reed and Thies 2001; Shugart and Watenberg 2001; Shugart, Moreno and Fajardo 2007). Let me talk about each of these in more detail.

Outcome motivation. This puts the focus on long-term electoral advantage under new rules. *A majority of incumbents may come to believe that they would achieve better electoral outcomes under the new rules.* Perhaps voting patterns have changed or new groups have entered the electorate. Incumbents may calculate that they would be better off under new rules (for example: they may garner more seats, get elected more easily or at lower cost). For example, the switch to PR in parts of Europe was supported by some ruling conservative parties as a way to limit their losses in the face of the growing threat from parties on the Left (see Boix 1999, Cusack et al. 2004). Conservative parties came to feel it was to their long-term advantage to switch away from a winner-take-all system to one in which winners would be obliged to share power. More recent examples of such calculations include the French reforms in 1981 and 1986, and the 2006 Italian reforms (Chang et al. 2011). In these cases governments that expected to lose electoral support in the next election changed the electoral rules so as to minimize those losses. Similarly, the Democrat-led government in Thailand altered the electoral system in the run up to the 2011 government under the (mistaken) belief that the new electoral system would boost their electoral prospects.

A number of scholars hold the view that outcome motivations are the primary drivers of reform (Benoit 2001; Remmer 2006; Boix 1999; Colomer 2005; Cusack et al. 2004).[2] But rarely are outcome motivations enough to bring about

---

2 Where this is the case reforms should follow electoral trends (Remmer 2006). For example, where we see an increase in party system fragmentation these scholars would expect electoral reforms in the direction of more proportional, permissive electoral systems. By contrast, where fragmentation has declined and a few large parties have emerged, they would expect reform in the opposite direction.

reform. First, politicians are risk averse, and even if electoral gains seem likely, they are apt to discount those gains where there is a degree of uncertainty. And even if *some* parties/politicians would be better off under reform it must be the case that a *majority* would be better off. Second, while incumbents may perceive advantages from electoral reform, they are wary of being punished by voters for behaving in an overtly opportunistic manner. Third, outcome motivations can't explain cases where politicians back reforms that they expect will actually harm their (or their party's) long-term electoral prospects. Thus, in addition to outcome motivations, a second major type of motivation—oriented to shorter term response to public demand—needs to be given emphasis.

Act motivation. This puts the focus on the act of reforming a system that much of the public views as urgently in need of reform. Most reform comes about when politicians, who are otherwise opposed to reform, come to realize that it is in their short-term best interest to support it. They come to believe that *the act of supporting reform itself brings electoral benefits.* Typically, this calculation is driven by public anger over systemic failures and concomitant demands for reform. *Politicians realize that they can attract new supporters by taking up the reform mantle, or, alternatively, they fear that voters will punish them in the next election if they oppose reform.* Even if reforms risk long-term harm to the politician or party, such potential harm is less worrying than the real possibility that they could lose the next election. One strategy such reluctant reformers often adopt is setting up institutions tasked with studying reform and suggesting alternatives. It is to these delegative reform efforts that I now turn.

DELEGATIVE REFORM

A common first step in the reform process is for politicians to delegate power to institutions whose primary task is considering political reform. These institutions can come in a variety of forms—from independent commissions, to citizen assemblies, to specially created government agencies—and their level of independence from political incumbents varies. However, the setting up of a dedicated institution charged with proposing political or electoral reform "raises the profile of electoral reform (compared, for example, to a parliamentary committee or internal party study), thereby suggesting a level of seriousness about, minimally, putting the question on the public agenda" (Shugart 2008, 20).

Note that the setting up of delegative institutions can be driven by either of two conflicting motivations (Shugart 2008, 18). Politicians, under pressure from the public, might organize such bodies in an attempt to appear reformist while kicking the can down the road and reducing the chance that reform actually occurs. The hope is to use delegative institutions to derail or at least delay reforms that incumbents do not favor. Alternatively, politicians might opt for delegative institutions as a way to legitimize reforms that they favor, but fear will be seen as opportunistic (ibid). An independent consultative process, then, is a strategy to try and build broader support for their favored reforms.

Regardless of the motivation behind the setting up of delegative institutions, there is always a danger that, once set up, they will suggest reforms that incumbents oppose and/or raise the popular profile of reforms to such a degree that they become too costly for politicians to ignore. We see this happen time and again. Here are three examples:

New Zealand. In the face of the pressures discussed earlier, New Zealand's incumbent government set up a Royal Commission on the Electoral System in 1986 with the power to suggest an alternative electoral system. The choice to set up a royal commission by the Labour Party was an attempt to create the illusion of accommodating voters' demands for electoral reform while remaining staunchly opposed to such reform (Denemark 2001, 84). It was a sop to disenchanted voters and to a small number of reform crusaders within the party. The party believed that such a commission posed no threat and planned to exile the commission's findings to perpetual further study in a parliamentary committee. However, after two years of work and public consultation the Royal Commission was unanimous in its recommendation—a mixed-member proportional (MMP) system. While both major parties had every intention of "consigning the issue of electoral change to oblivion" (Denemark 2001, 88), the Royal Commission had succeeded in placing electoral reform firmly on the political agenda. In the end, while both parties were strongly opposed to electoral reform, public support for reform led each to back a referendum in a strategic attempt to gain an electoral advantage over the other. Both firmly believed that the status quo plurality system would prevail when put to a binding vote, which it was in 1993. To be sure, they worked to organize opposition to the change and worded the referendum in such a way as to advantage the status quo. Despite these hurdles, MMP won the referendum by a comfortable margin.

Venezuela. The 1980s and early 1990s were politically and economically turbulent in Venezuela. Electoral reform was proposed as a way to repair Venezuela's broken and unresponsive party system. Economic decline and unpopular government policies had produced political unrest, riots, and government repression. Public distrust of the country's political parties was substantial, and this was manifest in high levels of voter abstention (Crisp and Rey 2001). Public demand for reform was strong, but the focus was not necessarily on electoral reform. In 1984, in response to the growing calls for reform, the president created the Presidential Commission on Reform of the State. The commission was advisory, and tasked with considering a wide range of reforms. While the commission's recommendation was ultimately fairly modest, it drew attention to the possibility of electoral reform and succeeded in placing such reform on the political and public agenda. Once there, continued economic decline and political crises kept electoral reform on the agenda until a new electoral system was adopted in 1989 (ibid).

Thailand. The Thai case is illustrative of the conditions described thus far—the presence of systemic failure, a catalytic event, and alignment of incumbent preferences—as well as the agenda-setting potential of delegative institutions. Thailand's political system throughout the 1980s and 1990s was characterized by both hyper-representation and hyper-personalism. The electoral system produced a highly factionalized party system that gave rise to large, multi-party coalition governments that were notoriously short-lived (between 1978 and 2001 the average duration of government cabinets was just over eighteen months). Thailand's candidate-centered electoral system produced parties that were little more than ephemeral electoral alliances of convenience, and politicians that were focused on providing resources to narrow constituencies—with little attention or interest in broader public policy. The event that served as a catalyst for reform initiation was the 1991 military coup and subsequent attempt by the military to re-write the constitution to favor conservative forces over elected representatives. After the military was forced from power in 1992 there was a strong public demand for an extensive constitutional review process. When that constitutional reform failed to materialize, prime ministerial candidate Banharn Silpa-archa seized on constitutional reform as a winning electoral issue, and support for reform helped his party win the election and propel him into the premiership. While his government survived less than eighteen months, he did oversee the passage of a law which set up a Constitutional Drafting Assembly (CDA), charged with recommending constitutional reforms. The CDA consisted of indirectly elected representatives from each of the country's provinces alongside appointed experts in the fields of public law, political science, and public administration. By statute the CDA draft was subject only to an up or down vote in the legislature and could not be amended.[3] Within the CDA itself the majority of the work of constitutional design and drafting was delegated to a select committee of academics and technocrats with no clear partisan affiliations.

The CDA explicitly drew a link between Thailand's political and governance woes and its electoral system and proposed major electoral reforms. These reforms

---

3 In the event of a no vote the draft would then go before the people in the form of a referendum.

threatened the interests of many of Thailand's traditional power centers. It's not surprising then that support for the CDA draft constitution was greeted by most incumbents with wariness and even outright opposition. The political elite of many of the major political parties and factions, including the ruling NAP party, expressed strong reservations about the draft. The fact that most ultimately voted to adopt the draft constitution, despite their very serious misgivings, reflects the short-term political calculation that voting against the constitution would prove more costly than supporting the reforms to which they were sincerely opposed. The catalyst behind this calculation was the Asian Financial Crisis which began in Thailand in late June/early July 1997, just as the drafting process was wrapping up. It shone a spotlight on some of the shortcomings in the Thai political system (MacIntyre 2002) and effectively raised the stakes connected with passage or rejection of the draft. In the minds of many voters and investors the constitutional draft became a symbol of the government's commitment to difficult but needed political and economic reforms. Constitutional reform and the broader reform agenda became so linked, in fact, that the stock market and currency markets reacted quickly and noticeably to expressions of opposition or support by leading government officials. In the end the potential economic and political costs of a no vote outweighed the risks of reform and the draft was adopted by a vote of 518 to 16 (with 17 abstentions).

As these examples demonstrate, delegative institutions have the potential to place electoral reform on the agenda, even where incumbents are opposed to such reforms. This is most likely when a) the members of such institutions are independent from incumbent politicians, and b) their recommendations are required to be voted on by either the legislature or the public via referendum. But even when delegative institutions are only advisory they can set the terms of the debate, raise expectations, and thereby make it very costly for politicians to ignore calls for electoral reform.

CONCLUSION: THE PROSPECTS FOR POLITICAL REFORM IN THE PHILIPPINES

In this chapter I have reviewed three conditions that are necessary before electoral reform can occur: systemic failure, a catalytic event, and change in incumbents' preferences. Given these conditions, what are the prospects for electoral reform in the Philippines? The early 2018 convening of the Consultative Committee is a notable development, but are conditions conducive to electoral reform?

Let's start, first of all, with systemic failure. Systemic failure occurs when the current electoral system fails to meet the normative expectations of the public—

72

namely, it fails to produce governments that are responsive, accountable, and effective. In terms of Figure 4.2, where would we locate the Philippines?

- On the *intraparty dimension,* one can readily make the case that the Philippines is on the hyper-personalized (lower) side of the continuum. Politicians are almost entirely focused on cultivating their narrow political bailiwicks at the expense of party loyalty and a broader, national focus.

- On the *interparty dimension,* I would place the Philippines on the pluralitarian (right-hand) side of the continuum. After martial law the Philippines did not return to the pre-1972 system of two major national parties. With the introduction of the party list the party system further fragmented, producing legislatures with a large number of parties. At the same time, however, presidents are effectively assured (after what is commonly a rampant post-election process of party switching) of gaining a legislative majority. While it is hard to anticipate which of the many party-list parties will make it into Congress, the only mystery regarding the government coalition is which presidential candidate will end up leading it. Once the election is over, party switching to the winning candidate's party will typically give the president a large majority.

Thus, in my view, one can make the case for systemic failure in the Philippines in the form of hyper-personalism, and perhaps pluralitarianism. The first necessary reform condition is arguably met.

However, systemic failure is not enough to produce reform. In each of the countries examined above, the systematic challenges had been present for years, sometimes decades, before reform was initiated. This leads us to the second necessary condition, namely the existence of some catalytic event, generally a crisis of some kind, able to draw the connection between political and/or economic woes and the electoral system. Where does the Philippines stand? While the Philippines has had its fair share of political crises (for example, the so-called "People Power II" uprising in 2001, the "Hello Garci" electoral scandal of 2005, and the pork barrel scandal that started in 2013[4]), to date these have not served as catalytic events that focused public

---

4 In the "People Power" uprising of 2001, Joseph Estrada was forced from the presidential palace after corruption allegations and replaced by Gloria Macapagal-Arroyo. She was then re-elected in 2004, but came under fire in the following year based on allegations of electoral fraud backed up by tapes in which a voice sounding like that of President Arroyo is heard requesting favors from an election commissioner by the name of Virgilio Garciliano (hence "Hello Garci"). See Hutchcroft 2008, 145–46. The 2013 scandal involved allegations that pork barrel funds had earlier (during the Arroyo presidency, between 2007 and 2009) been funneled to fake non-government organizations. See Holmes 2016, 24.

attention on the systemic failures of the electoral system and the urgent need for electoral reform. Worth watching, however, is whether the rise of political outsider Rodrigo Duterte to the presidency will turn out to be such a sufficient catalytic event.[5] Thus far, however, the calls for reform from the president and his supporters have largely, but not entirely, neglected the electoral system. Most of the reform attention has instead been on center-periphery arrangements (unitary or federal) and secondarily on the nature of the representational structures (whether presidential, semi-presidential, or parliamentary).

What is still lacking in the current debate, then, is a recognition of how the underperformance of the existing electoral system—which nurtures and sustains generally weak and incoherent political parties—contributes in very fundamental ways to the country's longstanding governance problems. This is problematic. It is not an exaggeration to say that political reform is likely to fail and more likely produce unintended consequences if it fails to pay appropriate attention to the electoral and party systems. A simple analogy can help to make the point. Imagine I have a goal to become more healthy and my response is to change gyms and start using new exercise equipment. That may have some effect, but if I don't change my eating habits or increase my workout time, I am unlikely to get the benefits I am hoping for. Similarly, one can anticipate limited benefits from the current package of Philippine political reforms if they neglect the need for electoral system reform. As discussed in Chapter Two, it is through such reform that the country will be able to shift incentives from the current *candidate-centric* electoral system towards a *party-centric* electoral system. All other things equal, this would be an extremely positive change not only for development outcomes but also for the quality of Philippine democracy.

Finally, if reform is to proceed, the third condition is that incumbent politicians must come to feel they have something to gain by pursuing reform (or at least not opposing it). They may come to prefer reform because they believe they or their party will do better under a different set of rules (outcome-motivated) or because they expect short term electoral benefits from taking a stance as a reformer (act-motivated). Where do things stand in the Philippines? The establishment of a delegative institution in the form of the Consultative Committee is an indication that there is some political support for reform. But electoral system design, while given attention, was by no means front and center. Even if electoral reform does make it more firmly onto the reform agenda,

---

5 Based on comparative experiences discussed above, one additional point is worthy of emphasis: though populist reform efforts may channel public dissatisfaction over the status quo and thus help to overcome institutional constraints on reform, they also risk empowering populist leaders at the expense of democratic norms and institutions.

experience suggests that it is unlikely that a majority of politicians will conclude that they have a better chance at being elected under new rules. Political party leaders may come to recognize the virtue of electoral system reforms that can enhance party discipline, but under the old system it would likely be a challenge for them to marshal the votes for change (even under the slogan that "change is coming"). Hence, the best chance for reform is likely to be if the work of the Consultative Committee raises expectations of and demand for electoral reform among the public, making it costly for politicians to oppose reform. After all, as we know from comparative experience, once delegative bodies have been established they sometimes raise the popular profile of reforms to such a degree that politicians are forced to pay attention and respond accordingly.

FIGURE 4.1: NECESSARY CONDITIONS FOR REFORM INITIATION (ADAPTED FROM SHUGART 2008)

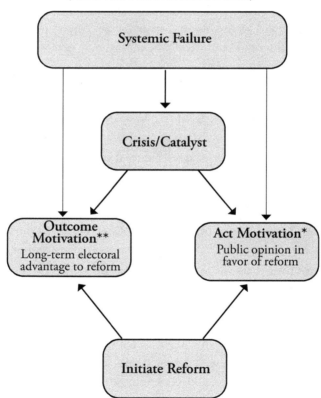

* Act Motivation: Incumbents are motivated to undertake reform by short-term concerns in response to strong public views on the urgent need for reform.

** Outcome Motivation: Incumbents are motivated to undertake reform by longer-term concerns as they believe they will achieve better electoral outcomes under the new rules.

FIGURE 4.2: INTER- AND INTRA-PARTY DIMENSIONS OF ELECTORAL SYSTEMS (ADAPTED FROM SHUGART 2001)

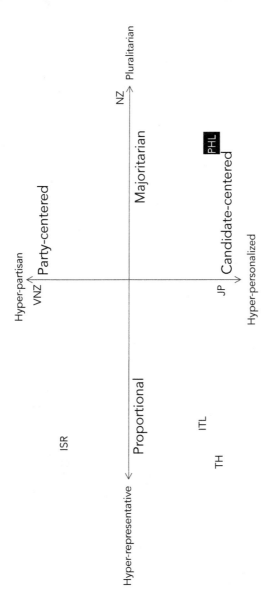

Notes: The figure presents the *pre-reform* positions of the following countries: pre-1992 Israel (ISR), pre-1989 Venezuela (VNZ), pre-1993 New Zealand (NZ), pre-1997 Thailand (TH), pre-1993 Italy (ITL), and pre-1994 Japan (JP)—all of which have fairly recently undertaken electoral reform. In addition, it includes the *current* position of the Philippines (PHL) as it is considering major political reforms.

Women comprise more than 60 percent of the national parliament in Rwanda—the highest proportion of any national legislature in the world. Its members are elected via closed-list proportional representation combined with the zipper system (an arrangement mandating that political parties' lists of ranked candidates for legislative seats alternate between women and men).

Photograph from *The New Times* (Kigali, Rwanda). Reprinted with the permission of *The New Times*.

CHAPTER FIVE
GENDER AND THE ELECTORAL SYSTEM: WHAT WORKS FOR WOMEN

SOCORRO L. REYES

INTRODUCTION

The electoral system is one of the key structural factors that limit or enhance the chances of women candidates to run and win seats in elective legislative bodies at the local, regional, or international levels. In the broad sense, electoral system refers to the entire electoral process, including provisions concerning electoral rights and election administration. In the narrow sense, as used in this volume, electoral systems regulate the means by which voters express their political preferences and how votes are translated into seats. This chapter will specifically address which electoral systems are most favorable to increasing women's representation based on global experience. It recognizes, however, that there are other structural factors that can hamper or facilitate this process, including the degree to which the internal governance mechanisms of political parties uphold or discourage the goal of gender equality. Equally important is the socio-cultural context, which can either recognize and respect or deny and violate women's right to participate equally with men in a society's political and public life.

As explained in Chapter Three, there are four basic types of electoral systems: proportional representation (PR), plurality systems, majoritarian systems, and mixed or combined systems. Studies show that countries with proportional representation have a significant increase in women's political representation while only modest advances have been made through plurality or majoritarian systems. Within PR, specific arrangements that support women's political representation are: 1) closed-list PR (CLPR), in which parties both choose and rank the list of candidates for legislative seats; 2) for these closed party lists, a zipper system that alternates between women and men candidates toward the goal of equal gender representation; 3) large district magnitude, meaning a large number of seats in the multi-member districts from which representatives are elected; and 4) high legal threshold, such that only parties able to demonstrate a basic level of electoral support are eligible to receive seats in the legislature.

This chapter begins by looking at the major international and national frameworks that have guided the advocacy for enhanced gender equality in political participation before proceeding in the next two sections to examine which types of electoral system reform work best for women. The optimal results can be achieved through CLPR with zipper systems, but a second (and sometimes complementary) avenue is the adoption of other types of gender quotas. The penultimate section of the chapter highlights the need to build political parties that are not only strong but also gender-sensitive, and the conclusion places the reform proposals within the context of the present discussion of constitutional revision in the Philippines.

LEGAL AND POLICY FRAMEWORKS

Several international and national legal and policy frameworks provide the basis for increasing women's political representation and participation through a review and reform of electoral systems, the introduction of quotas, and gender mainstreaming in political parties. Among these are the Convention on the Elimination of All Forms of Discrimination Against Women (CEDAW) of 1979, the Beijing Platform for Action of 1995, the UN General Assembly Resolution of 2011, and the Philippine Magna Carta of Women signed in 2009.

When adopted in 1979, CEDAW (also known as the international Bill of Women's Rights) was the first UN convention to endorse quotas to rectify gender imbalance in elective and appointive positions. As temporary special measures, "they shall be discontinued when the objectives of equality of opportunity and treatment have been achieved."[1] CEDAW set a target that women should hold at least 30 percent of all national parliamentarian posts by 2030.[2]

Sixteen years later, in 1995, the Beijing Platform for Action reiterated this when it called on states to "take measures to ensure women's equal access to and full participation in power structures and decision-making."[3] It also recommended that political parties include women's issues in their political agenda.

In 2011, when the global representation of women in parliaments was still falling way short of the 30 percent target enunciated by CEDAW, the UN General Assembly passed a resolution on "Women and Political Participation." It urged states to review, adjust and reform their electoral systems to improve women's political participation and representation in elective bodies.[4] Addressing political parties, the resolution

---

1 CEDAW, Article 4, par. 1
2 See https://unngls.org/index.php/un-ngls_news_archives/2012/361-un-celebrates-30th-anniversary-of-cedaw-with-a-focus-on-women-s-political-participation-and-leadership
3 Beijing Platform for Action, G.1.
4 UN General Assembly Resolution on "Women and Political Participation," 19 December 2011.

strongly recommended that they develop the capacity of women to analyze issues so they can participate fully and equally in making party decisions. Today, worldwide, women constitute only 23 percent of the members of both houses of Parliament.[5]

On the home front, the Philippine Congress passed the Magna Carta of Women in 2009, a comprehensive law that covered the social, economic, and political rights of women as human rights. Specifically, it provided that the state "shall undertake temporary special measures to accelerate the participation and equitable representation of women in all spheres of society, particularly in the decision-making and policy-making processes in government and private entities, to fully realize their role as agents and beneficiaries of development."[6] Had the Magna Carta been implemented, women should have been in 50 percent of the positions in the third level of the Civil Service in 2014, or five years after its enactment. They would also be in 40 percent of the development councils and planning bodies at the regional, provincial, city, municipal, district, and barangay levels. These goals have yet to be realized. While the Magna Carta sets ambitious targets, it has not unfortunately accompanied those targets with the imposition of mechanisms for enforcing quotas.

At the same time, the Magna Carta of Women did encourage the integration of women into the leadership, structures, and processes of political parties. It also provided that the state shall "provide incentives to political parties with a women's agenda."[7] Pursuant to this, Akbayan Representatives Barry Gutierrez and Walden Bello filed the "Women Participation and Representation in Political Parties Act of 2013" in the Sixteenth Congress. It provided for the creation of a "Women's Empowerment Fund" (WEF) to reward those political parties with a Gender and Development Agenda and Program as well as those in which women constitute 30 percent of the: 1) party leadership; 2) internal policy-making structures; and 3) official candidates of the party.[8] The amount political parties can access from the Fund was to be equal to the funds they reserved for their respective Women and Gender and Development Programs. During an election year, parties would be able to spend 60 percent of their share in WEF for the campaign expenditures of its women candidates. The bill did not prosper in the House for two reasons: 1) few political parties, aside from Akbayan, have Women and Gender and Development Programs; and 2) most of them, especially the big political parties with their multiple sources of huge funding, do not need WEF to support the campaign expenditures of their candidates, whether women or men.

---

5 IPU, "Women in National Parliaments," June 2016.

6 Magna Carta of Women, Section 11.

7 Magna Carta of Women, Section 11 (e).

8 Gutierrez, Ibarra and Bello, Walden. Women Participation and Representation in Political Parties Act of 1913.

WHAT WORKS FOR WOMEN, PART I: CLOSED-LIST PROPORTIONAL REPRESENTATION WITH A ZIPPER SYSTEM

Among the top fifteen parliaments in terms of women's representation, ten used the list proportional representation system, three adopted the mixed or combined system, one used the plurality system and one the two-round system.[9]

TABLE 5.1. ELECTORAL SYSTEMS[10] AND WOMEN'S REPRESENTATION[11]

Country	Number of Seats	Percentage of Women's Seats	Electoral System
1. Rwanda	80	61.3% (49)	CLPR with zipper system
2. Cuba	605	53.2% (322)	Two-Round System
3. Bolivia	130	53.1% (69)	Mixed (First Past The Post and List PR)
4. Grenada	15	46.7% (7)	Plurality (First Past the Post)
5. Namibia	104	46.2% (48)	CLPR with zipper system
6. Nicaragua	92	45.7% (42)	List PR
7. Costa Rica	57	45.6% (26)	List PR
8. Sweden	349	43.6% (152)	CLPR with zipper system
9. Mexico	500	42.6 % (213)	Mixed (List PR and Majoritarianism)
10. South Africa	394	42.4% (167)	CLPR with zipper system
11. Finland	200	42% (84)	CLPR with zipper system
12. Senegal	165	41.8% (69)	List PR
13. Norway	169	41.4% (70)	CLPR with zipper system
14. Mozambique	250	39.6% (99)	Mixed (FPTP and CLPR with zipper system)
15. Spain	350	39.1% (137)	List PR

---

9 Grenada, a southeastern Caribbean state with a population only slightly more than 100,000, uses the plurality or the first past the post system as it has a small legislature of only fifteen members. As explained in Chapter Three, the two-round system is a majoritarian system requiring that winning candidates receive at least 50 percent of the vote; should no candidate achieve this in the first round of elections, a second round pits the top two vote-getters against each other.

10 "Electoral Systems: Comparative Data," Electoral Knowledge Network http://aceproject.org/

11 "Women in National Parliaments," 1 April 2018 http://www.ipu.org/wmn-e/world.htm

The experience of most countries where women have high political representation tends to show that women have more chances to win in a system with at least some element of *list PR* than in a system with only plurality or majoritarian elements. Political parties have more leeway to include women in their list of candidates and voters have more opportunity to elect women candidates. Where single-member plurality systems are dominant, political parties tend to field those who they think are "winnable" or "more widely acceptable." In single ballot, single member, plurality systems, political parties tend to field those who they think are "winnable" or "more widely acceptable" and, in a patriarchal society, these tend to be mostly men.

But there are other factors to consider in a list PR to make it work for women. Among these are: 1) type of list; 2) district magnitude as well as the related concept of party magnitude; and 3) legal threshold.

PARTY LISTS

Party lists or the list of candidates fielded by a political party during an election are of several types: open, closed, and free lists.

- *Open lists* are those where voters can express their preference among the candidates, ranking them according to who are most and least favored. In effect, the parties choose the candidates while the voters rank them. Many list PR systems in Western Europe use the open list.

- In *closed-list arrangements*, political parties both choose and rank the candidates, and the voters cannot move them around based on who they like best and like least. When closed-lists are accompanied by the *zipper system*,[12] women and men will alternate in the list. Neither the political party nor the voters can tamper with the order once it is released for the election.

- *Free lists* are used in countries such as Ecuador, Luxembourg, and Switzerland where voters can choose their favored candidates not just from one party list but across other party lists as well.[13]

What will work best for women? The answer is clearly *closed party list, zipper style* within which, as noted, neither the party nor the voters can change the woman-man-woman-man-etc. alternation on the list. This means that

---

12 Also known, particularly in Africa, as the *zebra system.*

13 Krennerich, Michael. *Impact of Electoral Systems on Women's Representation in Politics.* Report: European Commission for Democracy Through Law. 23 February 2009.

the political party cannot move women down the list and move men up if it only receives a small percentage of the votes and consequently only a few seats. If it were not a closed zipper list, for example, a party that gets only four out of ten contested seats would be able to ignore the alternating of women and men candidates in the list. Instead of two seats each for women and men, it could hypothetically just award all four seats to men. Neither can the voters rearrange the order of the candidates in the list. There are strict ranking rules or placement mandates that both the parties and voters have to observe. Among the top fifteen countries in the number of women in national parliaments, as shown in Table 5.1, the following seven countries use the closed party list, zipper system: Rwanda, Namibia, Sweden, South Africa, Finland, Norway, and Mozambique.[14]

DISTRICT AND PARTY MAGNITUDE

Women have more chances to be included in the list of party candidates in *large multi-member districts* (MMDs) than in small, multi-member districts. In fact, studies show that small MMDs can be even worse than single-member districts (where, as noted above, men are commonly favored). The experience of Tunisia in its first election after the dramatic change of government in 2011 showed that small multi-member districts work against women, especially when a number of political parties contest the elections.[15] Similarly, small MMDs in Ireland and Chile are blamed for low levels of women's representation in their respective parliaments—especially in Chile, where until recently there were only two members elected out of a district. Political parties tend to include women candidates in large, multi-member districts to attract the support of women voters as well as constituents with diverse identities based on class, race, sexual orientation, etc.[16] It also gives them more opportunity to come up with a gender-balanced ticket.

Recent empirical studies of electoral system reform show that something called *party magnitude,* or the number of candidates that a political party fields in a district, can in some cases be more critical than district magnitude in deciding whether or not the party will include women in the list of candidates. In essence,

---

14 WEDO. "Getting the Balance Right in National Parliaments." 2008.

15 Benjamin Reilly and Socorro Reyes. "Zipper System: How to Get More Women Elected." Rappler, 2016. https://www.rappler.com/nation/politics/elections/2016/129938-zipper-system-get-more-women-elected-congress

16 As explained by Reilly and Reyes, "[s]ome countries also use zipper systems to ensure the representation of various minorities based on regional, ethnic, linguistic, or religious cleavages. Others in the LGBT community may someday choose to use zipper systems to promote not just gender equality but gender diversity. While the objectives differ, in each case the mandated alternation of positions on the party list is key."

political parties that have a history of winning seats in the district will most likely field more women than if it has a poor track record of victory.[17]

District magnitude and party magnitude are of course interrelated. The larger the district, the more likely a party will balance its ticket with women and men candidates.[18] The more candidates a party has, the greater chances for the party to win seats and increase its party magnitude.[19]

LEGAL THRESHOLD

Legal threshold refers to the minimum number of votes that a party must win in an election in order to qualify for a seat in parliament. It is argued that high threshold prevents the proliferation of small parties and thus avoids political fragmentation. Formal thresholds are provided in constitutional or legal provisions such as the case in Germany, New Zealand, and Russia, where political parties must obtain at least 5 percent of the votes cast to qualify for parliamentary representation.

What kind of legal threshold is good for women candidates? On the one hand, a lower threshold might favor women if their political affiliations are with small minority parties. On the other hand, higher thresholds and larger district magnitudes should enhance the chances for women to be included in the line-up of big political parties—and thus provide greater probability that they will win. For example, Sweden and Costa Rica both use high legal threshold and both have high percentages of women in parliament. In Sweden, there are 152 women in the 349-seat parliament (or 43.6 percent of the total) while in Costa Rica, 26 out of 57 seats (or 45.6 percent) are held by women.[20]

---

17 In Richard E. Matland's analysis of Norway, "party magnitude, the size of a party's district delegation, is a more powerful explanatory factor than district magnitude." But its influence can change over time and "appears to follow a cycle. Prior to demands for representation being raised, party magnitude has little effect. As women mobilize and representation demands are raised party magnitude plays a significant role, but once women are firmly entrenched as powerful players in party politics, party magnitude's effect decreases." See Matland 1993.

18 At the same time, as discussed by Allen Hicken in Chapter Two, large district magnitudes are also associated with "legislative seats going to many small parties"—with the Israeli Knesset an extreme example with 120 seats elected from a single district. Larger districts, as further explained by Julio Teehankee in Chapter Nine, favor proportionality at the expense of representativeness (i.e., the connection between legislators and their constituents). These are additional factors that need to be considered in deciding the optimal district magnitude and its interaction with other such measures as legal threshold.

19 Both district and party magnitudes are important to the election of women, explains Tracy-Ann Johnson-Myers. "If women and minorities are to win seats in parliament, parties have to win several seats, and it is only as the number of seats per district increases that parties will go further down their lists to help fill those seats." See T-A. Johnson-Myers, "The Impact of Electoral Systems on Women's Political Representation," in *The Mixed Member Proportional System: Providing Greater Representation for Women?* Springer Briefs in Political Science, https://www.researchgate.net/publication/310484134_ The_Impact_of_Electoral_Systems_on_Women%27s_Political_Representation.

20 "Women in National Parliaments," 1 April 2018 <http://www.ipu.org/wmn-e/world.htm>

WHAT WORKS FOR WOMEN, PART II: OTHER TYPES OF GENDER QUOTAS

While closed-list PR with zipper-style alternation has the greatest potential to work for women, it is not the only gender quota that can be used to increase women's political participation. Within other electoral systems, including "winner takes all" plurality arrangements, other types of quotas can also be effective. Stepping back, we can observe that there are three broad categories of quotas: reserved seats, legislated or mandated candidate quotas (including but not limited to zipper systems), and voluntary party quotas.[21]

- *Reserved seats* specify a number of seats that will be occupied by underrepresented sectors such as women, indigenous people, persons with disabilities, etc. There are twenty-three legislatures that reserve seats for women including Afghanistan, Bangladesh, and Pakistan.

- *Legislated or mandated candidate quotas* are provided for in national constitutions or electoral laws. Among the fifteen top countries in the percentage of women in parliament which have legislated or mandated quotas are: Rwanda, Bolivia, Senegal, Mexico, Nicaragua, and Spain. Global experience reveals not only zipper arrangements alternating strictly between women and men, but also a range of other variants as well.[22]

- *Voluntary party quotas* go above and beyond legislated measures, and may either be verbal commitments or written provisions in party statutes. Among the top fifteen countries with the largest percentages of women representatives, Table 5.2 lists those political parties that supplement legislative mandates—whether the zipper system or other types of quotas—with their own voluntary internal quotas. These voluntary quotas are used in developing the list of party candidates who will run for office. Legislated quotas, on the other hand, determine the percentage of seats to be occupied by women.

---

21 See https://www.idea.int/data-tools/data/gender-quotas/quotas.

22 As explained in Reilly and Reyes 2016, these other examples include a) a requirement that the top two candidates are not of the same sex (for example, in Belgium); b) a 40:60 ratio for every five posts on the list (similar to what Spain does); and c) one out of every group of three candidates must be a woman (as practiced in Albania, Argentina, Indonesia, Serbia, and Timor-Leste).

TABLE 5.2: TOP COUNTRIES[23] WITH VOLUNTARY PARTY QUOTAS[24]

Country	Percentage of Women in Parliament	Political Parties with Quotas for Women
Bolivia	53.1%	National Unity Front (50%)
Sweden	43.6%	Social Democratic Party (50%) Left Party (50%) Green Party (50%) Moderate Party (2 women and 2 men to hold top 4 party positions)
Mexico	42.6%	Institutional Revolutionary Party (50%)
South Africa	42.4%	African National Congress (50%)
Namibia	46.2%	Southwest Africa People's Organization (50% Zipper/Zebra)
Nicaragua	45.7%	Sandinista Front for National Liberation (30%) Liberal and Constitutional Party (40%) Sandinista Renovation Movement (40%)
Norway	41.4%	Socialist Left Party (40%) Norwegian Labor Party (50%) Centre Party (40%) Christian People's Party (40%)
Spain	39.1%	Spanish Socialist Workers Party (40%) United Left (40%) Socialist Party of Catalonia (40%) Initiative for Catalonia (Green) (40%) Republican Left of Catalonia (40%) Nationalist Galician Block (40%) Canarian Coalition (40%)
Mozambique	39.6%	Front for the Liberation of Mozambique (40%)

Empirical evidence proves that quotas whether legislated or voluntary can generally play a major role in increasing the number of women in parliament.[25] Legislated quotas are of course preferable over voluntary quotas but only if political parties comply with the law—which they don't always do. For example, France passed the much-acclaimed Gender Parity Law in 2000, mandating that political parties have a 50–50 split between women and

---

23 "Women in National Parliaments," May 1, 2016, www.ipu.org
24 "Voluntary Political Party Quotas," IDEA Quota Database http://www.quotaproject.org

men candidates or face reduced funding from government. Unfortunately, however, the law has been weakly implemented. Even the Socialist Party, which had been a major proponent of the law, fielded only 36 percent women candidates in the 2002 elections.[26] As emphasized by Reilly and Reyes 2016, it is critical

> to ensure that the candidate list rules are enforced, for example by enforcing sanctions for those that do not comply. The sanctions may include rejecting the entire list or refusing to register the section/candidates on the list that conflict with the provisions of the law. This places pressure on the capacity of the electoral management bodies to regulate and enforce election law.

Financial sanctions are another means of trying to enforce candidate list rules, and this can include either outright penalties or the withdrawal of government subsidies to parties that violate gender parity provisions. Either way, it is essential that the sanctions have sufficient "bite" to actually enforce the rules.

Alongside legislated quotas, voluntary party quotas have shown themselves to be effective in many settings. Countries in Europe with voluntary party quotas, including Sweden, Iceland, Spain, and Norway, have relatively high women's parliamentary representation.[27] It is also important to note that, *as a rule, the bigger the party that adopts voluntary party quotas, the greater the impact.* This has been demonstrated in the experience of Norway, Mozambique, Namibia, and South Africa.

NURTURING POLITICAL PARTIES THAT ARE NOT ONLY STRONG BUT ALSO GENDER-SENSITIVE

The focus of this chapter has been on specific electoral system reform measures, emphasizing in particular the virtues of closed-list proportional representation accompanied by the zipper system. In order to optimize the capacity of such arrangements to promote gender equality, I have also highlighted the need to consider such important issues as district and party magnitude as well as electoral thresholds—and, of course, to ensure that the rules are actually enforced. The goal of gender equality can further be advanced through the imposition of other complementary types of quotas, including voluntary party quotas.

---

26 Krennerich 2009.
27 Ibid.

As noted at the outset, however, it is also essential to consider broader structural factors that are not directly captured through electoral system reform—but which can nonetheless serve to impede or facilitate the goal of giving women equal representation with men in legislatures and in other elective posts. In other words, electoral system reform should be viewed as a necessary but not sufficient condition as attention must also be given to the internal governance mechanisms of political parties. Well-conceived electoral system reform, through such time-tested measures as the introduction of CLPR systems, have a great deal of potential to nurture stronger and more coherent parties. But if electoral system reform is to succeed in the goal of balancing gender representation in the legislature, it is essential as well to ensure the nurturing of *gender sensitive and responsive political parties*. This is the double challenge faced by gender advocates, especially in countries like the Philippines where political parties are generally weak, male-dominated, and sexist. Several measures can be taken by political parties to address this problem:

1. Conduct a gender assessment of the party's structures, decision-making processes, electoral practices, and public policies.

2. Develop a gender equality policy within the party with a clear and well-defined action plan and a monitoring and enforcement mechanism.

3. Promote and invest in intensive, results-based internal training programs on gender sensitivity for party leaders and members at all levels and chapters of the party.

4. Develop and allocate funds for a capacity-building and leadership program for women members of the party to run and win elections as well as build their skills to participate meaningfully in public decision making.

5. Through the adoption of voluntary party quotas, promote gender parity in the party's list of national, regional, and local candidates with no one gender having more than 60 percent or less than 40 percent.

6. Institutionalize gender equality and women's empowerment within the party through review of internal party rules and other party documents, modifying them as required to ensure that they are in conformity with CEDAW, also known as the International Bill of Women's Rights, and the Philippines's Magna Carta of Women. The latter needs to be amended to push it from aspirational targets to implementation through enforceable mechanisms.

In the election campaign of 2016, several national and local candidates resorted to sexist methods to attract voters. In response, women's groups drafted a "Gender Sensitive Code of Conduct for Candidates and Political Parties" that they then submitted to COMELEC through its Gender and Disability Committee Chair, Commissioner Rowena Guanzon. Specifically, it asked COMELEC to adopt punitive measures ranging from reprimand to disqualification against candidates and political parties engaged in any of the following:

1. Sexist remarks, jokes, songs, that disrespect, insult, degrade women, the LGBT community, persons with disability, senior citizens, indigenous people, and other marginalized groups.

2. Kissing or touching of women supporters as well as other sexual advances, welcome or unwelcome.

3. Hiring women to perform sexually suggestive dances such as twerking in campaign rallies.

4. Campaign paraphernalia such as leaflets, posters, or tarpaulins containing any sexually suggestive content or message.

COMELEC responded favorably to requests to organize seminars to heigthen gender sensitivity and awareness among candidates and political parties at the national, regional, provincial, municipal, city, and barangay levels.

CONCLUSIONS

In the present national context of widespread discussions of possible constitutional change, it is appropriate and relevant to push for electoral system reforms that will work for women. There is a need to rectify the anomalous situation where more women vote than men but more men run and win in national, local, and barangay elections. Though the number of women in Congress has progressively increased, there has never been a time when their representation reached the critical mass of 30 percent of the total membership in either the House of Representatives or the Senate. In the wake of the 2016 elections, the House came close to that target (with 87 women out of 297 representatives, or 29 percent) while the Senate was a bit lower (with 6 women out of 24 senators, or 25 percent). But among all national and local officials (the latter at provincial, city, and municipal levels), a mere 18 percent were women. This is shown in Table 5.3, which also includes percentages of women holding posts at the barangay level: 18 percent of barangay captains and 27 percent of barangay councilors.[28]

TABLE 5.3: COMPARATIVE STATISTICS OF WOMEN AND
MEN VOTERS, CANDIDATES AND WINNERS

Elections	Actual Voters	Candidates	Winners
National and Local (2016)	Women: 50.66%	Women: 19.36%	Women: 17.9%
	Men: 46.92%	Men: 80.62%	Men: 82.5%
Barangay (2013)	Women: 50.63% Men: 48.51%	*Barangay Captains* Women: 18.74% Men: 81.26%	*Barangay Captains* Women: 18.35% Men: 81.65%
		Barangay Councilors Women: 26.96% Men: 73.04%	*Barangay Councilors* Women: 27.04% Men: 72.96%

Ladra, Esmeralda. "Election-Related Sex Disaggregated Data," 2016. The original source of the data provides no explanation as to why the gender disaggregation does not always add up to 100 percent.

The present government proposes a shift from the unitary to a federal system wherein the country would be divided into a certain number of regions each with its own executive, legislature, and possibly even judiciary. Regional legislative assemblies are to be created and the manner in which the members would be elected could be reviewed and possibly changed. This discussion of constitutional revision presents an opportunity to shift from the traditional plurality system, known to limit women's prospects of winning, to more creative systems that work for women. Amidst the national debate on constitutional change, it would be foolhardy to ignore global best practices in favor of a narrow-minded adherence to electoral systems that have prevailed across past decades in the Philippines. Done well, electoral system redesign presents enormous potential to enhance the role of Filipino women in shaping the nation's political future. This is obvious from comparative examination of the experience of the broad range of countries that have high numbers of women in their legislatures—from northern Europe (Sweden, Finland, and Norway) to Latin America (Nicaragua, Costa Rica, and Mexico) to Africa (Rwanda, Namibia, South Africa, and Mozambique).

Recent experience has revealed an openness to electoral system innovation in the Philippines. The mixed system was proposed in the Bangsamoro Basic Law

---

28 https://www.rappler.com/newsbreak/iq/140715-17th-congress-philippines-composition-numbers

introduced in the 16th Congress (2013–2016) and the 17th Congress (2016–2019) for the election of members of the Bangsamoro Parliament. Under this system, 50 percent of the members will be representatives of political parties elected through proportional representation based on the whole Bangsamoro territory, 40 percent shall be elected from single-member parliamentary districts apportioned for the areas, and 10 percent shall be sectoral representatives including two reserved seats for non-Moro indigenous communities, settler communities, and women.[29] However, to ensure that women's representation will be increased through PR the parties should adopt a closed-list zipper system with strict alternate ranking of women and men candidates. To prevent proliferation of small parties, a legal threshold of at least 5 percent can be considered. Should federalism be adopted, this system could be used for the regional assemblies. Whether or not federalism is adopted, this system could be put in place in the national-level legislature (the House of Representatives in the current system, or potentially the national parliament should there be a simultaneous shift to a parliamentary system).

In conclusion, getting the right electoral system is the critical first step in promoting women's equal representation with men in legislatures and other elective bodies. As I have argued above, the best combination of reforms is closed-list proportional representation with a zipper system, large multi-member districts, and a high electoral threshold. These can be considered not only for national-level legislative bodies but also for councils at lower levels: provinces, cities, municipalities, and even barangays. These arrangements then need to be accompanied by other types of quotas, including voluntary party quotas. Looking beyond specific electoral reform measures, another critical element of the winning formula is to nurture gender-sensitive political parties. In addition, other economic and socio-cultural barriers to women's political participation inherent in patriarchy must be addressed as well. Women cannot run and win against men on equal terms if they are economically disempowered, deprived of education and health care, assigned gender stereotype roles in the household, and threatened by sexual and gender-based violence inside and outside their homes. It is imperative, moreover, to broaden the base of political recruitment to include women across social classes, ethnicity, race, and religion. Finally, it is crucial to embrace gender diversity where each person regardless of sexual orientation and gender identity has the right not only to vote but also to be voted into public office.

---

29 Sections 4, 5 and 6, Article VII of House Bill 4994 or the Bangsamoro Basic Law.

Indonesia's shift from closed- to open-list proportional representation led to new styles of campaigning—away from a primary focus on the party's brand (e.g., through party flags) and towards a primary focus on individuals (e.g., through candidate posters). This candidate of *Partai Kebangkitan Bangsa* (National Awakening Party) is seeking election to a regional legislative assembly in West Java.

Photograph by Edward Aspinall

CHAPTER SIX
LESSONS FROM A NEIGHBOR: THE NEGATIVE CONSEQUENCES OF INDONESIA'S SHIFT TO THE OPEN LIST

EDWARD ASPINALL

INTRODUCTION

Since making the transition to electoral democracy almost two decades ago, Indonesia has moved gradually toward adopting an electoral system that emphasizes a personal rather than a party vote. This shift has been evident both in the executive, where indirect elections of the president and regional heads were replaced with direct elections, and in Indonesia's legislatures. In Indonesia's first post-Suharto national legislative election in 1999, Indonesia used closed-list proportional representation (CLPR) and, partly as a result, the election was strongly party-centered, with campaigners emphasizing party identities and programs. By the time of the 2014 legislative election, fully open-list proportional representation (OLPR) was in operation, with the result that candidates viewed their intraparty colleagues as their main competitors and concentrated on boosting their personal rather than party votes. This dramatic alteration of electoral dynamics in Indonesia thus strongly confirms a central point made in Chapter Three's overview of electoral systems: CLPR fosters party-centric politics while OLPR privileges candidates over parties.

Advocates of this system argued that it created a more direct form of democracy, in which there would be clear connections of accountability between voters and elected representatives. They were also motivated by widespread disillusionment with the corruption of the parties and the elites that ran them. Yet in many respects, Indonesia's transition to direct elections, especially to the open list, is a study in the unintended consequences of electoral system reform. The transition prompted the decline of party coherence. It also drove an increase in vote buying. Rather than improving the representativeness of Indonesia's democracy, it weakened Indonesia's political parties and undermined the possibilities of programmatic politics.

This chapter provides an account of electoral system changes in the Philippines's largest Southeast Asian neighbor. It begins with a general background of Indonesia's democratization and the electoral system, proceeding to analysis of the shift to the open-list PR and its effects on campaign patterns and patronage distribution. The penultimate section explains how other features of Indonesia's electoral system—most importantly the tough rules that govern party registration—help to counteract the decline of party solidarity and the rise of personalized campaigning. As a result, Indonesia retains a relatively robust party system when compared to the Philippines and certain other Asian countries. Different parts of Indonesia's institutional architecture thus push electoral competition in different directions: whereas electoral rules push toward fragmentation and individualized campaigning, party and candidate registration requirements enhance the role of parties. The result is that parties survive as an important component of Indonesia's electoral architecture, but they are increasingly reduced to the role of gatekeepers—levying fees (sometimes quite literally) to determine who runs, but then playing relatively little role in campaigning. The concluding section of the chapter summarizes the depth of the damage done by Indonesia's shift to an open-list system.

POST-SUHARTO DEMOCRACY

Indonesia made a rapid transition to democracy after President Suharto's 32-year authoritarian regime collapsed in May 1998. Political controls were loosened by Suharto's successor, B.J. Habibie, and a vigorous multi-party system came into being. Forty-eight parties contested the first post-Suharto legislative election in 1999, with the five biggest parties attaining over 86 percent of the vote. Many of these new parties were founded on the basis of longstanding political traditions and resilient social identities (Mietzner 2013). For example, the largest party, the PDI-P (*Partai Demokrasi Indonesia* – Perjuangan, Indonesian Democracy Party – Struggle) led by Megawati Sukarnoputri, was the inheritor of the tradition of pluralist nationalism established by the PNI (*Partai Nasional Indonesia*, Indonesian National Party) and Megawati's father, Sukarno, in the 1920s. It attained 33.7 percent of the vote. Likewise, several parties endeavored to appeal to various sectors of the Islamic community, and did so through links with very resilient and influential Islamic mass-based social organizations.

Democratic Indonesia inherited from the Suharto regime a system of proportional representation (PR). Representatives to the People's Representative Council (DPR, *Dewan Perwakilan Rakyat*), the national parliament, were elected from multi-member constituencies, which could be an entire province in less populous regions, or a part of a province in densely populated areas. Most of those in charge of Indonesia's political reform process agreed that it was best to maintain PR, believing that this system was a better guarantor of social peace: by preventing the winner-takes-all outcomes associated with single-member districts it would allow a richly multi-party system to develop—avoiding political polarization and, importantly, facilitating political representation of key minority groups. For example, in the 1999 election, about a third of the vote was captured by Islamic parties of various stripes. Many reformers agreed that it was better to have such groups represented inside Indonesia's democratic institutions rather than being left to fester outside of them, and there is indeed evidence that this inclusion has promoted moderation among the Islamic parties (Buehler 2013).

At the same time, the designers of the electoral system did not want regional or ethnic elites to be represented by way of their own parties. They thus introduced onerous national registration requirements for political parties, essentially foreclosing the possibility of locally or regionally based parties. This requirement has persisted to the present, with one exception as provided to the semi-autonomous province of Aceh in the 2005 peace accord that ended a 30-year secessionist challenge led by the Free Aceh Movement.

The specific type of PR system that Indonesia inherited was closed list. Under this system, citizens did not vote for individual representatives. Rather, on the ballot paper they punched a hole in a symbol representing the party of their choice. Seats were then allocated proportionally according to each party's relative share of the vote in the electoral district concerned. The individuals who took these seats, however, were chosen on the basis of their position on the candidate list *determined by the party prior to the election*: if a party won one seat, its top-placed candidate would win the seat; if it got two, the first two would be allocated seats; and so on. This system placed a great deal of authority in the hands of the party elites who controlled the allocation of positions on the party lists, with the result that struggles to control party branches were often fierce. It also meant that elections were very party-focused: candidates lower down the list all had a strong incentive to boost their party's vote and so increase their own chances of being elected. Candidates and their parties all had an incentive to pull in the same direction.

Another inheritance from the Suharto period was a system of indirect elections of executive government heads at the national and local levels. In the early years of post-Suharto democracy, rather than being directly elected by the people, heads of national and local government—the president at the national level, governors in the provinces, and *bupati* (regents) or mayors respectively in rural and urban districts—were elected by the legislature in the area concerned. (The president was elected by a slightly different body, the MPR or People's Consultative Assembly, which consisted of the members of the national parliament plus some appointed members.) With a few rare exceptions, Indonesia's fractured political map meant that no single party enjoyed a majority in any such legislature. As a result, these elections necessarily involved horse-trading and deal-making between parties and candidates. The most dramatic such example occurred in October 1999 when Megawati Sukarnoputri, despite being the leader of the party that gained by far the largest share of the popular vote in the parliamentary election, failed to secure election as president. The MPR instead chose Abdurrahman Wahid, whose party had secured only 12.6 percent of the popular vote.

It did not take long for dissatisfaction to begin to develop with this system, and with the political parties more generally. This dissatisfaction drove calls for electoral system change. It had several causes. One that stands out is the elections of executive government heads. It was not simply that the system of indirect elections produced many victories for candidates who were not associated with the party that had garnered the largest number of seats in the regional legislature concerned (as with Megawati at the national level). It also produced a profusion of vote buying within regional legislatures, with local parliamentarians often selling their votes to candidates willing to pay them the greatest amounts of cash, or to provide them with other benefits. In many cases, the elections of governors, *bupati,* and mayors degenerated into scandal and protest, with parties splitting asunder and many shocking revelations of corrupt deal-making reported in the press (according to one NGO, 80 percent of gubernatorial elections and 30 percent of district head elections were affected by conflicts triggered by "money politics" in local parliaments; see Hukumonline 2002). Many of the beneficiaries of this system were entrenched elites—incumbent regional government heads, former bureaucrats, wealthy businesspeople, and military officers—who had the political connections and material resources to bribe their way into office. Many Indonesians came to believe that the system of indirect elections of executive government heads was too easily corrupted, and was not producing a fully democratic system in which chief executives at every level were truly accountable to the people.

However, disappointment with these elections was just part of a much wider sense of political disillusionment that developed during Indonesia's first decade of post-Suharto democracy. Indonesia's political system rapidly became afflicted by widespread corruption and rent-seeking by many political elites, including parliamentarians. Predatory and clientelistic practices that had become entrenched during the Suharto regime hardly seemed to decline at all; in fact, they were adapted to the free-wheeling and fragmented political landscape of newly democratic and decentralized Indonesia. A voluminous literature, which we do not have space to explore here, discusses these phenomena, mostly ascribing them to the nature of Indonesia's democratic transition and the entrenched influence of an "oligarchy" that had become established during the Suharto years (see, for example, Hadiz 2010).

Many members of the public, as well as liberal intellectuals and reformers, observed such developments with distaste. Among the major casualties of the increasingly sour mood concerning official politics were Indonesia's parties and legislatures, with public trust in both institutions declining sharply. Citizens increasingly viewed parties as being unresponsive, out of touch, and corrupt. For critics of the parties, the closed-list system was part of the problem, because it meant that citizens did not play a direct role in determining their representatives; instead, it was the candidates whom party elites placed highest on their party lists who won seats. Most of the winners were themselves party leaders, while some were wealthy individuals who had simply purchased high positions on a party list by bribing party officials. In response to this strong structural position of the parties and their leaders, an anti-party mood rapidly began to develop, especially among Indonesia's reforming intellectuals. Many of them began to use terms like "party dictatorship" and "party oligarchy" to describe Indonesia's political system (Tan 2002).

The closed-list system made it hard to target individual legislators who were known to be corrupt or otherwise had poor records. Many members of the public knew little about the individual candidates on party lists, preferring to vote for parties because they identified with their image or their national leaders, or because they were connected to a social milieu or socio-religious identity they felt was represented by the party. In 2004, a coalition of NGOs ran a campaign which they called the "Don't choose rotten politicians" movement where they identified candidates who had particularly poor records for probity or human rights—and appealed to voters not to support them. Because voters did not vote for individual candidates but rather for parties, the campaign had little effect.

ELECTORAL SYSTEM REFORM

This was the context underlying the shifts in Indonesia's electoral system. The first changes, which were welcomed most enthusiastically by voters, were the transitions to direct elections of government heads. For many Indonesian reformers—including members of parliament—this change was a natural outcome of the post-Suharto reform effort and a culmination of Indonesia's democratization. The shift began in 2004 with Indonesia's first direct election for the president, and the victory in that year's second-round vote of Susilo Bambang Yudhoyono—a man who enjoyed popular support but lacked a strong party base.[1] In the following year, Indonesians began voting directly for governors, *bupati*, mayors, and their deputies. In many cases, they elected popular figures who lacked strong links to political parties and, in some cases, punished incumbents who were particularly corrupt or incompetent (Mietzner 2006).

Over the years, some of the gloss has rubbed off the system of direct elections of executive heads. It has become obvious that powerful local oligarchs and dynasts can win these elections, too, by mobilizing financial resources and political networks. Some national elites—such as former president Megawati Sukarnoputri (who lost to Yudhoyono in 2004 and 2009) and Prabowo Subianto (who lost to Joko Widodo in 2014)—have occasionally criticized direct elections as being too expensive and "un-Indonesian" (because they allegedly undermine social harmony). Even so, the system continues to enjoy popular support—as attested to in numerous opinion polls.[2] There was a public outcry when a coalition of parties associated with opposition to incoming President Joko Widodo, and headed by then opposition leader Prabowo Subianto, voted in Indonesia's national parliament in 2014 to go back to the system of election of regional heads by legislatures. Outgoing President Yudhoyono intervened to reverse the change.

Indonesia's party leaders were not directly threatened by the transition to direct elections of executive government heads, and they built safeguards into the new system that preserved some role for the parties. Most obviously, candidates for

---

1 Indonesia adopted a two-round system (TRS) in its post-Suharto electoral reforms. As explained in Chapter Three, this system requires a second election in the event that no candidate has received a majority of votes in the first round. In the Philippines, a president can assume office with a mere plurality. (This was most dramatically the case in the 1992 elections, when Fidel V. Ramos became president with less than one-quarter of all votes, but in no subsequent elections—1998, 2004, 2010, or 2016—has any winning candidate come into office with more than 42 percent of the vote.) In Indonesia, by contrast, presidents must win at least 50 percent of the votes. If no candidate receives a majority in the first election, a second election pits the top two candidates against each other. A further feature of the Indonesian electoral system is the need for winning presidential candidates to receive at least 20 percent of the votes in at least one half of the country's thirty-four provinces.

2 For example, the Lembaga Survei Indonesia (Indonesian Survey Institute) conducted a national poll in 2012 in which 86.7 percent of respondents stated they preferred direct elections of regional heads to indirect elections by local parliaments; when the institute conducted another poll in late 2014, at the height of efforts by opposition parties to do away with direct elections, it found that 84.1 percent of respondents still supported the system. See: Abba Gabrillin, "Survei LSI: Masyarakat Masih Menginginkan Pilkada Langsung" [LSI Survey: The People Still Want Direct Elections", *Kompas*, 17 December 2014. At: http://nasional.kompas.com/read/2014/12/17/12521451/Survei.LSI.Masyarakat. Masih.Menginginkan.Pilkada.Langsung

executive office could only be nominated by parties or coalitions of parties that had won a minimum proportion of the votes or seats in the relevant legislature. Although the Constitutional Court eventually decided that independent candidates should also be allowed to run, the requirements for independent candidates remain onerous so that parties retain an important gatekeeping function.

Party elites were more reluctant to embrace change in the electoral system for legislatures, despite continuing to face considerable pressure from reform-minded intellectuals, NGO activists, and others to extend the benefits of "direct" elections to the legislative field (with "direct" here suggesting less orientation to parties and greater orientation to candidates). Reform happened in 2004, but it was minimal. In that year a semi-open list was introduced: voters could vote *either* for the party of their choice *or* for one of the candidates nominated by the party in that electoral district. There was a catch, however: to be elected, the *individual candidate* had to win a proportion of the vote equivalent to or greater than the entire quota necessary *for the party as a whole* to elect one representative in that electoral district (for example, 10 percent of the entire vote in a district with ten seats).[3] If no candidate achieved such a high result, the party list determined who got elected. In the end, only two candidates at the national level passed this very high bar. In the lead up to the 2009 election the law was changed slightly again, reducing the benchmark for individual candidates from 100 percent to 30 percent of a vote quota. Indonesia's elected party representatives in parliament were slowly, but surely, giving way to reformers pushing for more candidate-centric elections.

In the end, however, it was Indonesia's Constitutional Court that initiated dramatic change. In 2009, a few months before the election, in response to a challenge to the electoral law by two candidates who were not placed high on their party lists, a majority of the court held that the requirement that candidates win a fixed share of a quota conflicted with the provision of Indonesia's Constitution that based Indonesia's democracy on "people's sovereignty." If the party list determined who would be elected, the judges determined, then the people were not truly sovereign. They ruled that, so long as a party received enough party and individual votes in an electoral district to elect at least one candidate, then it should be the candidate(s) with the highest individual vote(s) who should take the seat(s). This decision moved Indonesia to a system of fully open-list PR.

Many civil society activists, intellectuals, and reformers celebrated the decision. The new system, its supporters claimed, would initiate a new era of

---

3 In other words, it was necessary for an individual candidate *on his or her own* to receive 10 percent of the votes. This required far more popular support than simply being the highest placed candidate on the list of a party which—when the party vote as well as the votes for all of its candidates are added up—receives 10 per cent of the overall vote.

accountable government by making parliamentarians directly accountable to voters who elected them, rather than to the party elites who placed them on party lists. But what *really* happened?

THE FIRST MAJOR EFFECT OF THE OPEN LIST: FROM PARTY CAMPAIGNS TO INDIVIDUAL NETWORKS[4]

A first major impact was on the style and organization of campaigns. Early in the democratic transition, Indonesia's elections were strongly party-focused. Campaigns were organized collectively by party leaders and cadres. They emphasized promoting a party's brand, with large "color-coded" open-air election rallies, parades, and other events where the party faithful literally hoisted the party flag. Especially in the first post-Suharto election, there was a strong ethos of voluntarism associated with these campaigns, with ordinary people who strongly identified with the parties contributing their own time and effort.

This party-focused campaigning was logical under the closed-list system. Under the open-list system, however, it conflicted with the main axis of competition, which was now among candidates from the same party. Candidates now saw their own party colleagues—at least those who were running for seats in the same electoral district—as rivals, not as running mates. In 2009 the effect of this change was visible almost immediately on the streets of Indonesia after the Constitutional Court brought down its decision, as candidates erected billboards and posters that emphasized their personal qualities. By the time of the 2014 legislative election, candidates had already learned how the new system operated and they were prepared for it. There was thus typically very little coordination of campaigns by candidates running for the same party (unless they were running for seats at different levels—district, provincial, national—in the same region, in which case some cooperation was possible, though often fractious). Instead, candidates devoted their resources, time, and energy into constructing personal campaign teams that reached down, through layers of brokers, to voters in rural villages and urban communities. Greatly diminished was the spirit of voluntarism so apparent in earlier years—and the party flag was now overshadowed by candidate posters that tended to relegate party logos to the margins.

This dynamic generated a logic of electoral competition that was remarkably fractured at the grassroots, adding to existing sources of fragmentation arising from decentralization and other aspects of the political economy. In our extensive

---

4 Parts of this and the next section are modified from Aspinall 2014.

research fieldwork during Indonesia's 2014 legislative election,[5] it was easy to encounter candidates who complained about the effects of the open-list system and believed that parties were losing relevance in Indonesian politics. In stark contrast to previous elections, the centrality of the personal vote put the emphasis on the personal qualities of each individual candidate. As one *Partai Keadilan Sejahtera* (Prosperous Justice Party, PKS) candidate in South Sumatra explained, using phrasing that is echoed nationwide and across all parties, "voters now don't look at the party but at the figure [of the individual candidate]."

Deemphasizing their party brand, candidates concentrated on forging personal connections with voters, with most adopting a meet-the-people style of campaigning. Rather than emphasizing media or large open-air party rallies, most candidates instead participated in small-scale meetings in village and urban neighbourhoods every day, often until late at night. These gatherings tended to involve just a few dozen, at most a couple of hundred, participants. They typically featured a small meal or snacks, and plenty of opportunity for informal interaction between candidate and voters. Such grassroots meetings also became a means for community members to ask for or receive individual or collective gifts from their would-be representatives.

Of course, it could be very challenging, if not impossible, for legislative candidates to rely exclusively on such an approach. Especially in the large national legislative campaigns, it was not physically possible for one person to visit all communities in a constituency, or at least to do so sufficiently regularly to be able to build the personal rapport that voters value. Serious candidates therefore supplemented their individual efforts by forming teams of vote brokers who did much of the one-on-one personal contacting on their behalf.

Usually called "success teams" (*tim sukses*), these teams have a pyramidal structure that will be immediately recognizable to readers familiar with clientelistic and brokerage politics elsewhere, including in the Philippines, where vote brokers are known as *liders*.[6] Typically coordinated by a core team whose members work closely with the candidate, the structure progresses downward (depending on the size of the constituency) through layers of district, subdistrict, village, and polling booth coordinators, to individual team members (often called "volunteers" or *relawan*) embedded in local communities. The largest teams constructed by wealthy national legislative candidates could have 3,000 or more members. The base-level brokers—like the *liders* in the Philippines—are thus key. They are charged with "recruiting" anywhere between five and fifty voters each, typically from among

---

5   As part of the same "money politics" project described by Meredith Weiss in Chapter Eight.
6   The similarity with vote brokerage networks in Thailand is especially strong; see Chattharakul 2010.

household members, relatives, friends, neighbors, and other social intimates. These vote brokers are supposed to deliver information about the candidate to voters, draw up lists of individuals who are prepared to vote for the candidate, and then ensure that they actually turn out on polling day. Often, they also deliver cash or goods to seal the deal, a topic we return to below.

The motivations of success-team members vary, but in most cases they are driven by material reward. Only the wealthiest candidates pay their brokers a regular salary; more often candidates cover their expenses—money for fuel, food and drink, arranging meetings, and such like—but usually generously enough that brokers can use such payments to supplement their normal income. If their tasks include handing out cash to voters as polling day approaches, they usually get a fee for this job too. Some candidates also apply a bonus system: team members who exceed a minimum target of votes in their subdistrict, village, or polling station can expect a cash reward or a gift of some kind. Many success-team members also have longer-term goals. For instance, should the candidate be elected *and* attain a reasonable number of votes in the community where the broker was working, that broker can hope to benefit from village-level development projects and assistance packages that their new representative will be able to direct their way. This pattern of voter mobilization is now becoming so institutionalized in Indonesia that one can observe the emergence of a layer of semi-professional and highly experienced vote brokers who are able to sell their services to different parties and candidates during election season.

Critically, these teams are usually established completely outside party structures. This is because the party machine is itself usually a site of contestation given that multiple candidates from a single party are contesting in each constituency. Often, the candidate who is strongest in the local party hierarchy (typically, the chairperson of the local branch) will be able to dominate the machine and direct it toward supporting his or her personal campaign. In such cases, the party becomes, in effect, a personal success team. In other cases, the local party machinery becomes riven with division as rival candidates actively seek to gain the sympathy of different subdistrict or village branches, or of individual party leaders and activists. In yet other cases, local party activists simply act much like other vote brokers, selling their services to whatever candidate can offer the best rewards—even if, sometimes, that candidate comes from a rival party.

In seeking to win enough personal votes to defeat their intra-party rivals while avoiding expending resources unnecessarily, candidates employ various targeting strategies. In places where the party has a solid base of support, its candidates will often work only within that base community, trying to win over loyal party voters to their individual candidacy. Other candidates will target their own district, subdistrict, or village and attempt to get the lion's share of their votes—thereby exploiting hometown loyalties and promising to bring home development projects and other benefits. Candidates also target voters by working through existing social networks and recruiting their leaders as success-team members. For example, in parts of the country where clan structures are strong, candidates generally integrate their success teams into those clans. Elsewhere, candidates try to mobilize voters through networks of community-level organizations (prayer groups, martial arts clubs, youth associations, farmers' cooperatives, and so on), or they try to integrate formal and informal village leaders into their teams.

One effect of this style of campaigning is that it almost entirely closes the space for programmatic contestation. The open-list system has shifted the scale at which legislative election campaigns occur: from the general and collective to the specific and individual. Candidates try to build direct connections with voters, and emphasize their personal qualities, such as their openness, generosity, helpfulness, piety, honesty, and so on. The emphasis is on the interpersonal and the immediate, leaving little room for emphasizing grand programmatic issues such as nationwide welfare policies or governance reforms. To be sure, there is still scope for socio-cultural differences to play a role—thus, Islamic party candidates are still more likely to reach down to voters using religious networks, and to host events that are more religiously tinged. But in a world of political connections based on personal ties, even these lines become blurred. Non-religious candidates are able to use religious networks if they have the right personal connections with key leaders in those networks, and vice versa (Rubaidi 2016). By the time of the 2014 general legislative election, wider policy contestation had almost disappeared from grassroots political campaigning (although it played a larger role in the subsequent presidential election).[7] Candidates frequently complained that the voters had no real interest in party labels and programs, and acknowledged that they themselves did not emphasize such matters. Instead, they said, voters were merely interested in "concrete" benefits.

---

7 In post-Suharto Indonesia, legislative elections have thus far been held prior to presidential elections: in 2014, the legislative election was held in April and the presidential election was held in July. In that same election, only parties which won a certain minimum proportion of seats (20 percent) or votes (25 percent) in the national legislative election had the right, either singly or in coalition with other parties, to nominate presidential and vice-presidential candidates (who always run as pairs). (In practice, it is always coalitions rather than individual parties which nominate such pairs.) If no candidate pair wins 50 percent of the vote in the first round of the presidential election, a second round is held some months after the first round (in 2014, there were only two presidential candidates, and Joko Widodo won in the first round, making a second round unnecessary). In 2019, for the first time, Indonesia will run its legislative and presidential elections concurrently, on 17 April. The parties' vote shares in the 2014 legislative election will be used to assess their eligibility to nominate presidential (and vice-presidential) candidates.

THE SECOND MAJOR EFFECT OF THE OPEN LIST: FROM PROGRAMMATIC POLITICS TO PATRONAGE GOODS

A second effect of the transition to the open list was thus to greatly increase the scope and volume of patronage politics—that is, the distribution of cash, goods and other material benefits in exchange for support, especially vote buying.

It would be naïve, of course, to argue that the open list was the primary *cause* of patronage politics in Indonesian elections. Patronage has been a feature of Indonesian politics since the 1950s, though its form has changed greatly with each new regime. Even in the early post-Suharto period there was plenty of patronage amidst the enthusiasm engendered by the transition to democracy. However, given the party-focused nature of the electoral system at that time, most of the key exchanges occurred within the parties or inside the political elite—for example, in the form of payments to party leaders by candidates seeking to secure a high position on a party list, or as bribes paid to legislators to ensure their vote for one of the contenders in a gubernatorial election.

The adoption of the open list changed the locus of electoral corruption, making interactions between individual candidates and voters an important site of material exchange (in addition to the interactions among different levels and categories of politicians who had been most prominent under the closed-list system). Candidates who were trying to build their personal reputation and connections with voters faced a strong incentive to distribute patronage. Most candidates now saw their own party colleagues as their main competitors, and they could not therefore differentiate themselves from their chief rivals by way of programmatic appeals or party identity. Moreover, the large number of candidates competing individually—and working independently to construct their own teams—doubtlessly increased the overall volume of patronage distribution at election times.

By the time of the 2014 general election, the vast majority of candidates relied on patronage distribution as the central component of their campaign strategy. The key components of the campaigning style described above make most sense when placed in this context. The small-scale meetings to bring candidates together with community members (as described above) were typically occasions at which deals were discussed or transacted to provide communities with either individual or collective benefits. Voters, in turn, valued one-on-one personal connections with their representatives because they hoped they would later be able to leverage those connections if they needed help accessing government services. And the success team structure was all but ubiquitous because it provided the most effective means for candidates to provide gifts of cash and goods to voters while maximizing their return in terms of votes. Thus, success teams drew up lists of voters and repeatedly checked the voting intentions of those on the lists to ensure that the candidate would not waste his or her cash by passing it to voters who had committed themselves to a different candidate.

The variety of patronage encountered during the course of the 2014 election was mind-boggling. A first, and ubiquitous, category was collective gifts. These included donations to clubs or organizations: for example, cutlery, plates, and plastic chairs to a women's communal savings group; uniforms and equipment to a village sports club; tarpaulins, mats, a sound system, and a generator to a Koranic recitation group; fertilizer, seedlings, hand tractors, goats, cows, nets, or fuel to a farmers' or fishermen's cooperative; and so on. More sizeable collective gifts included donations in cash or kind to assist in the construction or renovation of a mosque, church, or other house of worship, or to help build a road, a drainage canal, a bridge, a sports field, a village hall, or some other community facility, or perhaps to connect the community to the electric grid, or to provide public lighting, etc. Some candidates also provided services such as ambulances, roving television shows, hearses, fire trucks, or garbage disposal for communities.

A second category was small getting-to-know-you gifts that candidates provided to individual voters in their first interactions with them, or through their success teams. These gifts were typically in the form of memorabilia (key rings, calendars, T-shirts, and the like) bearing the party logo and the candidate's image, but they are often also objects that evoke some sort of emotional or religious meaning (including head scarves, prayer mats, prayer robes, prayer books, and even Qurans and bibles). Basic foodstuffs and household items—rice, cooking oil, sugar, packets of noodles, coffee, detergent, shampoo, and so on—were also very common, though these tended to be delivered by team members, less often by candidates. "Door prizes" at public campaign events could range from small cash gifts and household items up to sizeable gifts like motorcycles or trips to the minor haj (*umroh*).

A third category, though in practice difficult to distinguish, was vote buying: the provision of individual cash gifts to voters to encourage them to go to the ballot box and cast a vote for the candidate. Cash payments were typically handed over in the final week leading up to polling day, and sometimes on the very morning of the poll (hence the name for this practice in Indonesia: the "dawn attack" or *serangan fajar*). The amounts varied, from as little as 30–50,000 rupiah, roughly US$1–3 for a "packet" of three district, province, and national legislative candidates in parts of Central Java, to up to 300,000 or 400,000 rupiah in resource-rich parts of Sumatra or Kalimantan. Not all candidates engaged in this practice, but in some places it was all but ubiquitous, and a tremendous amount of organizational activity—and finance—was expended to ensure it went smoothly.

Of course, we should not conclude that Indonesian legislative elections are now about personalized patronage politics and nothing else. National party campaigns and presidential candidates, for example, did play a role, even if most candidates viewed them as being secondary to their own efforts. Candidates also used many methods to build personal connections with voters that did not involve patronage. Even so, for a large majority of the candidates, patronage was the critical ingredient, even if they felt trapped by voters' expectations and what they saw as the imperative to distribute material benefits. Strikingly, many candidates explicitly condemned the open-list system, and decried what they saw as its harmful effects on party cohesion, programmatic politics, and relations between voters and their elected representatives. After the election, there was something of a public outcry by many candidates and commentators that money politics had seriously undermined the quality of Indonesian elections. Some candidates who had not engaged in vote buying, and lost, publically regretted their decision. Most blamed the open list for greatly increasing the volume of vote buying.

EXPLAINING THE ENDURING ROBUST QUALITIES OF THE INDONESIAN PARTY SYSTEM

A decade ago, prior even to the advent of the fully open list, the rise of patronage and personalized campaigning styles in Indonesia prompted the political scientist Andreas Ufen to write about a process of "Philippinization" of Indonesian party politics. He argued that Indonesian parties were coming to resemble the notoriously weak parties of Indonesia's Southeast Asian neighbour, which, he wrote, were "characterised by a lack of meaningful platforms, by the high frequency of party-switching, short-term coalition-building, factionalism as well as numerous dissolutions and re-emergences" (Ufen 2006, 17).

There is certainly much evidence to support Ufen's hypothesis, including the rise of personalist, "presidentialist" parties that are formed in Indonesia with the major goal of favoring the presidential ambitions of their founders. However, Marcus Mietzner (2013) has countered by pointing out that, compared to many third-wave democracies, including the Philippines, Indonesia's party system is relatively robust. He points out that the party system is not especially fragmented, nor is the level of electoral volatility unusually high. He also argues that many parties remain socially rooted, being "closely intertwined with mass organizations and movements" (Mietzner 2013, 112) and that parties "remain the single most important entry point for citizens to engage in formal politics" (Mietzner 2013, 198).

How do we reconcile the continuing relative robustness of the Indonesian party system with the trend toward personalization and patronage that has been so clearly accelerated by the shift to the open-list electoral system (and encouraged also by the rise of direct elections for executive government heads)? The answer is that four features of Indonesia's institutional design have prevented dissolution of the party system. First, according to Indonesian law, only party nominees can stand for legislative office; independent candidates cannot do so. Second, increasingly onerous registration requirements for parties seeking to contest legislative elections constitute a significant barrier to entry: parties have to show that they have functioning branches in a large proportion of the regions that make up Indonesia before they can nominate candidates. This makes it hard for cliques of local politicians to establish their own micro parties, as often happens in the Philippines. Third, Indonesia's elected legislators are also prohibited from switching parties while still holding their parliamentary seats, meaning legislators cannot desert their own party in favor of that of a newly elected president, another common pattern in the Philippines (instead, in Indonesia, the pattern is that parties will move *en masse* to support a new president, hoping to join the government and in this way gain access to patronage resources). Fourth, parliamentary threshold rules have further checked the proliferation of small parties. In 2009 parties had to attain 2.5 percent of the national vote to be represented in the national parliament, and in 2014 this threshold rose to 3.5 percent.

In other words, even if personalization and patronage have been pushing Indonesian parties in the direction of a Philippinized system, aspects of Indonesia's institutional design have slowed—but not halted—this movement. Even so, the relative robustness of Indonesia's party system in terms of formal party system institutionalization *coexists* with the largely non-party organization of election campaigns and personalized patronage politics discussed above. As a result, parties primarily play an important role as *gatekeepers* in electoral competition, largely determining who can compete for elective office. They do thus remain an important entry point for politicians seeking to participate in formal political institutions, even if in other ways their influence is declining.

CONCLUSION

Overall, Indonesia's experience with open-list PR provides a salutary lesson about the unintended consequences of reform. Driven by an understandable desire to enhance vertical accountability between voters and their elected representatives, Indonesian reformers pushed for a system in which voters rather than parties would determine which candidates on a party list would be elected to legislatures. Ultimately, it was the country's Constitutional Court which decided to fully open the list system, though the Court's decision-making was presumably influenced by the years of public campaigning and lobbying that preceded the decision in 2009.

The consequences have been largely negative for Indonesia's democratic system. By undermining the coherence of parties, the open-list system has reduced the scope for programmatic competition in Indonesian elections, though policy-based political contestation is exactly what Indonesia needs. At the same time, the system has greatly increased the scope and reach of patronage politics, especially vote buying. A growing part of the electorate has come to view elections as primarily—or at least partly—an opportunity to extract material resources from their representatives, rather than to choose between them on the basis of their programmatic and policy offerings. The increased expenditure on campaigning that results from this system has in turn greatly heightened pressures on candidates to raise finances, encouraging them to engage in corruption. Candidates speak openly about the need to recoup the "investments" they make in their campaigns, and their chief means of doing so is manipulating state budgets and extracting bribes from business interests who stand to benefit. The system has thus fuelled a vicious cycle in which electoral patronage fuels corruption which in turn erodes the faith of Indonesian voters in their parties and elected representatives, making them ever more susceptible to patronage politics. Throughout the country voters express a cynical disdain for politicians, suspecting them of self-interest and corruption and stating that elections are best viewed as a time to extract personal material benefits rather than to hope for substantive change.

From time to time, strong support has been expressed in Indonesia for a reversion to the closed-list system, though efforts to effect this change have for the time being receded (national parliamentarians are, after all, those candidates who have shown they can win under the open list, and thus have little incentive to change). Reversion to a closed-list would tilt the incentive structure back in favor of parties and programmatic competition. However, two electoral cycles under open-list PR have greatly expanded and deepened patronage politics, and one more election under the same electoral rules will take place in 2019. Patronage politics have spread so widely that it would likely take many more elections to reverse the negative consequences of Indonesia's highly problematic shift to an open-list electoral system. Sad to say, Indonesia provides a clear example of the unfortunate legacies that can result when ill-considered political reforms are put in place.

Five of the six post-Marcos presidents gather at Malacañang Palace in late July 2016. Each of the five was elected under different party or coalitional affiliations: former President Joseph Estrada was elected in 1998 affiliated with Laban ng Makabayang Masang Pilipino (LAMMP), former President Gloria Macapagal-Arroyo in 2004 with Lakas-KAMPI-CMD, President Rodrigo Duterte in 2016 with PDP-LABAN, former President Fidel V. Ramos in 1992 with Lakas-NUCD, and former President Benigno Aquino III in 2010 with the Liberal Party. The late Corazon C. Aquino did not join a political party, but was elected president in 1986 as a candidate of the United Democratic Opposition (UNIDO).

Photograph from the Presidential Communications Secretary Martin Andanar. Reprinted with his permission.

CHAPTER SEVEN
THE POLITICAL PARTY DEVELOPMENT BILL: STRENGTHENING PARTIES TOWARD THE GOAL OF STRENGTHENING PHILIPPINE DEMOCRACY *

RAMON C. CASIPLE

WEAK PARTIES, FLAWED DEMOCRACY

The traditional patronage-based Philippine political system thrives amidst the severe weakness of the country's political parties. No true democracy can exist without a working political party system that is built on valid political platforms—forward-looking policy statements that intend to foster progress and development.

Our political parties should be playing a vital role in our country's quest for economic and political development. As it stands, however, they are more of a detriment rather than a boost to the country's development. The weakness of Philippine political parties is demonstrated in their continuing dependence on personalities, political families, clans, and dynasties—rather than on issues and political platforms. One can thus observe the absence of a real and democratic political party system in the country. We live in a changing society where voters are heavily influenced by media, increasingly expressing political maturity, and actively asserting their democratic participation in electoral exercises. Amidst these changes, traditional politics, particularly of the "guns, goons, and gold" variety, has found itself not only increasingly beleaguered but also a major liability to national progress.

There is an obvious need for reforms in our political party system. We have to undertake the strengthening of the political party system to one that is based on democratic principles, strong on grassroots constituency, and able to function as the primary medium for electoral and political contests. A legal institutionalized framework for our system of political parties has to be established to provide the necessary rules and guidelines for political party strengthening and conduct. The political party reform bill, therefore, is a key initiative to build a genuine political party system. In sum, we need to strengthen Philippine political parties toward the goal of strengthening Philippine democracy.

---

* Table 7.1 found at the end of the book provides a timeline on the Political Party Development Bill from 2001 to 2018.

HISTORICAL CONTEXT

The essential weakness of Philippine democracy since the fall of Ferdinand Marcos in 1986 has been the elite capture of political power. Paul Hutchcroft once argued that the Marcos dictatorship only gave way to an "elitist" democracy supporting "booty capitalism."[1] Walden Bello went so far as to characterize the post-Marcos Philippines as a "failed democratic state" (Bello 2005).

This elite capture can be seen in the strengthening of the direct hold of traditional political families and clans over political power, from the national to local levels. The role of political parties in mediating the contest for power was decidedly marginal. It is in response to this situation that the current advocacy for political party reforms in the Philippines started, along with the restoration of democratic institutions after the end of the Marcos dictatorship.

The latter, of course, had established the *Kilusang Bagong Lipunan* (KBL) or New Society Movement as the sole political party allowed during the early years of martial law. When open opposition developed against Marcos and he was forced by international and domestic pressure to relax his rule, he made sure that the dominance of the KBL was uncontested.

The only political party that consistently defied the Marcos dictatorship was the Communist Party of the Philippines. It declared its resistance upon the declaration of martial law and rose in rebellion. It also led the massive popular movements that created the conditions for the formal ending of martial law in 1981, presidential elections in 1981, parliamentary elections in 1984, and the 1986 snap presidential elections. However, it was not prepared for the possibility of parliamentary struggle, having strategically rejected the latter in favor of armed struggle.

Marcos set aside the 1935 Constitution and, in farcical Citizen Assemblies in January 1973, had the 1973 Marcos Constitution "ratified." This was later upheld by a cowed Supreme Court, earning the derisive label of the "Marcos Supreme Court."

From 1972 to 1978, Marcos ruled without any legislature, using the Transition Provisions of his self-edited 1973 Constitution to provide legal cover for absolute rule. By 1976, when open opposition started to be felt in urban centers, this cover was already wearing thin and restlessness among the people surged.

Marcos decided to convene the *Interim Batasang Pambansa* (IBP) or the Interim National Assembly in 1978. The broad opposition decided to form the *Lakas ng Bayan* (LABAN) as a regional political party in the National Capital Region (NCR) to field a common ticket to the IBP. Amid accusations of electoral fraud, all twenty-

---

1 Paul Hutchcroft uses the term "booty capitalism" to describe the predatory behavior of the oligarchy in the Philippines, most egregious in the Marcos years. See Hutchcroft 1998.

one LABAN candidates lost, including Senator Benigno Aquino, Jr. Thereafter, the opposition boycotted the 1981 and 1984 elections called by Marcos.

LABAN later merged with the Mindanao-based *Partido Demokratiko Pilipino* (PDP) in 1984 and became the PDP-LABAN. In the 1986 snap presidential elections, it supported the coalition of the United Democratic Opposition (UNIDO) that fielded Corazon Aquino against Ferdinand Marcos.

Marcos defeated Aquino in the formal election count of the Commission on Elections. However, there was general disbelief in this outcome. When then-Defense Minister Juan Ponce Enrile and then-Chief of the Philippine Constabulary Fidel Ramos failed in their coup attempt, the people went to the streets to call for the downfall of the Marcos dictatorship. The successful EDSA People Power Revolution of February 1986 ushered in the post-Marcos democratic system.

The 1987 Aquino Constitution mandated the establishment of a multi-party system, along with a host of other political reforms, notably the introduction of a party list system with its own list of political groups. As explained in Chapters Nine and Ten, this would later lead to the proliferation of as many as 100–150 party-list groups contending for seats in the House of Representatives between 1998 and 2016 and hundreds of parties contending for posts at subnational levels across different elections.

An irony was the refusal of President Corazon Aquino to join any political party, not even the Liberal Party of her husband, Senator Benigno Aquino. Unfortunately, it set the tone for the continued decline of the importance of the Philippine political party system, which was already severely weakened under the Marcos dictatorship.

All presidential elections took the form of contests between or among coalitions of political parties; after the Party List Law was passed in 1995 and put into operation in 1998, it also included party-list groups. A review of the contenders in the five post-Marcos presidential elections graphically demonstrates a wild profusion of parties, far in excess of the two parties that dominated Philippine elite democracy in the pre-martial years (from 1946 to 1972). As demonstrated below, there was a weak degree of continuity in party structure from one election to the next. This extreme splintering of parties is exacerbated by an electoral system that elects the president and vice president separately—and not as part of a single ticket (Reilly and Casiple 2016).

In 1992, there were seven candidates (and political parties) contending in the presidential elections (Presidential Museum and Library 1992):

Fidel Ramos (Lakas-NUCD)[2]	23.58%
Miriam Defensor-Santiago (People's Reform Party, or PRP)	19.73%
Eduardo Cojuangco, Jr. (Nationalist People's Coalition, or NPC)	18.17%
Ramon Mitra (Lakas ng Demokratikong Pilipino, or LDP)	14.64%
Imelda Marcos (Kilusang Bagong Lipunan, or KBL)	10.32%
Jovito Salonga (Liberal Party, or LP)	10.16%
Salvador Laurel (Nacionalista Party, or NP)	3.40%

In a plurality system with no provision for a second round of voting, Ramos assumed the presidency with a mere 23.58 percent share of the votes. He would later form the "Rainbow Coalition" in order to increase his constituency and enhance his administration's credibility.

In 1998, the presidential elections followed the same pattern of multiple candidates and free-for-all coalitional politics, but with a clear winner by plurality (Presidential Museum and Library 1998):

Joseph Ejercito Estrada (LAMMP)[3]	39.86%
Jose de Venecia (Lakas-NUCD)	15.87%
Raul Roco (Aksyon Demokratiko)	13.83%
Emilio Osmeña (PROMDI)[4]	12.44%
Alfredo Lim (LP)	8.71%
Renato de Villa (Reporma-LM)[5]	4.86%
Miriam Defensor-Santiago (PRP)	2.96%
Juan Ponce Enrile (Independent)	1.28%

Based on the 1987 Constitution, Philippine presidents are normally limited to one six-year term of office. The 2004 presidential election was distinctive among all post-Marcos elections in that one of the contenders was an incumbent president, Gloria Macapagal-Arroyo, who had been elevated from vice president

---

2 Lakas ng Tao-National Union of Christian Democrats (Lakas-NUCD) is a coalition of Ramos's Lakas ng Tao and Raul Manglapus's National Union of Christian Democrats. Note that while President Aquino supported Ramos, he did not run under the same UNIDO coalition that had fielded her candidacy in 1986. At certain points Lakas ng Tao was also known as Lakas ng EDSA.

3 *Laban ng Makabayang Masang Pilipino* (LAMMP) or Struggle of the Patriotic Filipino Masses is the coalition of *Partido ng Masang Pilipino* (PMP) or Party of the Filipino Masses, *Laban ng Demokratikong Pilipino* (LDP) or Fight of the Democratic Filipino, Nationalist People's Coalition (NPC), and *Partido Demokratiko Pilipino-Lakas ng Bayan* (PDP-LABAN), or Philippine Democratic Party-Strength of the Nation. After Estrada won the presidency, the coalition renamed itself *Lapian ng Masang Pilipino* (LAMP), or Party of the Filipino Masses.

4 *Probinsya Muna Development Initiative*, or Province First Development Initiative.

5 *Partido para sa Demokratikong Reporma*, or Party for Democratic Reforms (Reporma). *Lapiang Manggagawa*, or Workers Party (LM).

to president amidst the "People Power II" uprising of 2001. After serving out the remaining term of Joseph Estrada, she was then eligible to seek an additional full term herself. Among five presidential contenders, the contest was basically between Arroyo and oppositionist Fernando Poe, Jr. The former garnered roughly the same percentage of votes as had Estrada in 1998, but it was a far less decisive plurality. Arroyo's victory in the controversial elections was punctuated by accusations of electoral cheating (Presidential Museum and Library 2004):

Gloria Macapagal-Arroyo (Lakas-KAMPI-CMD)[6]	39.99%
Fernando Poe, Jr. (LDP-KNP)[7]	36.51%
Panfilo Lacson (Independent)	10.88%
Raul Roco (Aksyon Demokratiko)	6.45%
Eddie Villanueva (Bangon Pilipinas, or BP)	6.16%

In the 2010 elections, new phenomena appeared, including presidential candidates teaming up with vice-presidential candidates from different parties—both in the formal construction of a presidential/vice-presidential ticket and in informal campaign efforts to support a president from one ticket and a vice-president from another ticket.[8] This resulted in even further innovations in the fractured incoherence of Philippine political parties. The presidential contest was basically contested by five candidates, again supported by coalitions, and Benigno Aquino III won by a clear margin with the largest plurality yet of any post-Marcos presidential election (Presidential Museum and Library 2010):

---

6 At the senatorial level, Lakas-Christian-Muslim Democrats (Lakas-CMD) joined with Arroyo's *Kabalikat ng Malayang Pilipino* (KAMPI) or Partnership of Free Filipinos, Liberal Party (LP), Nationalist People's Coalition (NPC), Nacionalista Party (NP), *Partido Demokratiko Sosyalista ng Pilipinas* (PDSP), and People's Reform Party (PRP) to form what was known as the K-4 coalition: *Koalisyon ng Katapatan at Karanasan sa Kinabukasan,* translated as the Coalition of Truth and Experience for Tomorrow.

7 A coalition of Angara's Laban ng Demokratikong Pilipino (LDP), Estrada's Partido ng Masang Pilipino (PMP) and Koalisyon ng Nagkakaisang Pilipino (KNP). The Aquino wing of LDP supported Lacson.

8 Estrada (PMP) had Binay (PDP-LABAN chairperson) as his vice-presidential candidate while Villar (NP) had Loren Legarda (LDP). To make things even more complicated, there was a separate concerted campaign to combine support for Aquino (the presidential candidate of the LP) with support for Binay (the vice-presidential candidate of Estrada), effectively ditching Manuel Roxas II (the vice-presidential candidate of Aquino on the LP ticket). In the end, it was the cross-over tandem of Aquino and Binay (dubbed "Noy-Bi") that prevailed in the election.

In addition, there were notable cross-overs in the composition of senatorial slates. Aquilino "Koko" Pimentel III (PDP-LABAN president), for example, ran for the Senate in Team PNoy (affiliated with Benigno Aquino III) despite his party's affiliation with the United Nationalist Alliance (UNA), a coalition between Estrada's *Partido ng Masang Pilipino* (PMP) and PDP-LABAN. In effect, a cross-party ticket of Estrada (running under PMP) and Binay (running under PDP-LABAN) was given a new name: UNA.

Benigno Aquino III (LP)[9]	42.08%
Joseph Ejercito Estrada (PMP)[10]	26.25%
Manuel Villar (NP)	15.42%
Gilbert Teodoro (Lakas-KAMPI-CMD)	11.33%
Eddie Villanueva (BP)	3.12%

In the most recent 2016 presidential elections, things took a turn for the worse with regards to the political party system. No political party conventions were held at all. Coalitions of parties, factions, party-list groups and other organizations were established, and turncoatism was rampant before, during, and after the elections. Five candidates contested the presidency, each again supported by coalitions, and Rodrigo Duterte emerged with a decisive plurality (Presidential Museum and Library 2016):

Rodrigo Duterte, Jr. (PDP-LABAN)[11]	38.6%
Manuel Roxas II (LP)	23.4%
Grace Poe (Independent)[12]	21.6%
Jejomar Binay (United Nationalist Alliance, or UNA)	12.9%
Miriam Defensor-Santiago (PRP)	3.4%

Hidden behind each party or coalition-building lies the political family or families that actually contend for the presidential power. The locus of the electoral contest is the race for the presidency and all other maneuvers revolve in relation to this. The role of political parties has been rendered secondary or subordinate to this objective.

POLITICAL PARTIES AND THE POLITICAL PARTY SYSTEM

Democracy is a form of government where sovereignty is vested solely in the people and all government authority emanates from them. Authority can be delegated to leaders through the conduct of free and fair elections. A level

---

9 LP formed a coalition behind Aquino manifested at the senatorial level and known as Team PNoy.

10 Estrada ran with a coalition behind him known as United Nationalist Alliance (UNA), composed of Estrada's *Partido ng Masang Pilipino* (PMP) and Jejomar Binay's PDP-LABAN.

11 *Partido Demokratiko Pilipino-Lakas ng Bayan* (PDP-LABAN), or Philippine Democratic Party-Strength of the Nation.

12 Grace Poe's candidacy was at first supported by the NPC, Villar's NP, National Unity Party (NUP), and Makabayan, a Left coalitional party. However, some of them transferred their support to Duterte later in the campaign.

playing field is essential to those who aspire to become servants of the people (Goodwin-Gill 1998).

Democracy is characterized by freedom and equality. It upholds the rule of the majority while respecting the rights of the minority. It is conducive to the growth of human rights because wherever there is the fullest expression of democracy, there is the fullest expression of human rights.

In a democracy, individuals with common ideologies, principles, and goals freely form associations and groups to advance their cause. A political party is a group of these individuals organized for the purpose of winning political power through elections. Often, members of a political party share an ideology, but that is not always the case. In some countries, ethnicity or caste is the basis on which political parties are organized, and in others the parties may be organized by competing groups of elites who seek to gain political power simply to increase their wealth.

Political parties are meant to aggregate societal interests, be the principal vehicles for electoral contestation, and act as a transmission belt of information to and from their constituents. They also, ideally, become the training ground of leaders and party workers, the embodiment of the aspirations of a party's multiple constituencies, and the organizational machinery for electoral campaigns and governance. Parties can further play a crucial role in steering a democracy away from personality politics and toward a focus on issues and political platforms.

In the current political system in the Philippines, political parties are mostly weak and serve only the various political families, clans, or oligarchies as conduits for their own real political agenda. However, the development of genuine political parties is a requirement for the people at the grassroots to enter electoral politics. As Gabriella Montinola explains, in reference to the Philippines, "Meaningful social change has been inhibited because political parties have failed to structure political competition to allow for the representation of interests of the poor and marginalized sectors .... Quality of choice depends on political parties, the main organizations that structure political competition" (Montinola 1999).

REFORM THROUGH THE POLITICAL PARTY DEVELOPMENT BILL

The Political Party Development Bill was conceived as a vital part of the package of political and electoral reforms that the country needs to undertake. It aims to strengthen the political party system in order to develop genuine political development and democratization in the country. The proposed act was drafted with the intention of addressing the chronic illness in Philippine politics hindering democratic growth and maturity.

The political party reform bill was first drafted in 2002, and endorsed by the major political parties in the first-ever Philippine Political Party Conference, chaired by then-Speaker and Lakas-NUCD chairman Jose de Venecia. At that time, the bill consisted of two separate bills, one on strengthening of the political party system, and the other on regulating campaign finance. A high-level party and legislative workshop in July 2002 sponsored by three political institutes[13] (one non-partisan and one each affiliated with Akbayan Citizens' Action Party and the Liberal Party) cemented agreements on its major contents. Later, a series of joint Senate-House committee drafting sessions consolidated these into a single piece of legislation called the Political Party Development Bill.

Election reform advocates, through the Consortium on Electoral Reforms (CER), participated in the drafting and endorsed the original bill, and later lobbied the government to pass it. Then House Speaker Jose De Venecia primarily authored the bill in the House of Representatives, while Senator Edgardo Angara likewise filed a Senate version of the bill. The latter headed the Laban ng Demokratikong Pilipino (LDP) while the former headed the ruling Lakas-NUCD, both of which were at the time among the major political parties.

The bill was intended to address the well-entrenched patronage system in Philippine politics; to promote transparency and accountability through institutionalization of reforms in campaign financing; and to veer away from the traditional personality-based politics. This was to be advanced by upholding party loyalty and adherence to political platforms and ideology as well as by encouraging party organizing and citizen-voter education.

However, the unanimous support of political parties for the bill started to crumble when then-president Gloria Macapagal-Arroyo announced her candidacy to run for re-election to the presidency in the 2004 elections. The crisis of her presidential legitimacy[14] also soon took center stage and prevented the bill from moving forward despite her own endorsement for it in her ten-point "legacy program" and its inclusion in the Medium-Term Development Program. Although the bill was passed on third reading[15] in the House of Representatives in the 13th Congress (2004–2007), it did not progress to the Senate amidst the controversies surrounding the Arroyo administration.

Nevertheless, in early anticipation of the 2010 national and local elections, the possibility of passing it once again opened. The urgency of ensuring free and

---

13 Institute for Popular Democracy (IPD), Institute for Political and Electoral Reform (IPER), and National Institute for Policy Studies (NIPS). IPD was closely associated with Akbayan Citizens' Party, IPER is non-partisan, and NIPS is affiliated with the Liberal Party.

14 In June 2005, the Garcillano tapes or "Hello Garci" controversy erupted and solidified public opinion against her and the credibility of her electoral victory. The tapes alleged that she and Commission on Elections commissioner Virgilio Garcillano conspired to add votes for her. See http://newsinfo.inquirer.net/606445/what-went-before-saga-of-the-hello-garci-tapes.

15 In Philippine legislative procedure, bills must go through three readings prior to being transmitted for consideration by the other house of Congress. See http://www.congress.gov.ph/legisinfo/#TRANSMIT.

fair electoral process in the elections in the light of the crisis of the Macapagal-Arroyo presidency gave impetus to a renewed effort to pass the bill. A workshop-conference in April 2008, convened by the concerned congressional committees and the CER, was well-attended by major political parties and came out with a resolution to undertake the passage of the bill.

The bill was once again filed in the 14th Congress (2007–2010) and all bills filed related to political party development were later consolidated as House Bill 3655 or the Political Party Development Act of 2008. The House of Representatives passed the bill on third reading in the 14th Congress. However, objections from party-list representatives and other members of the minority led to the bill's recall to second reading (a rather uncommon legislative maneuver).

The cynicism about traditional politics and politicians, the legitimacy crisis for Arroyo, and the valid concern of small parties and party-list groups were new elements that came up in opposition to the bill. The objection from various groups including a Catholic bishop, an election lawyer, a newspaper columnist, and minority representatives came as a surprise as the same bill had earlier passed on third reading by the same body in the 13th Congress without such negative reactions.

Those who opposed the bill raised several reasons—that it is unconstitutional, allegedly discriminating against small parties; that it did not include party-list groups; that spending public funds for political parties is wrong and increases corruption; and that Jose de Venecia (one of the authors) was the wrong messenger for political party reforms. De Venecia was an erstwhile ally of Arroyo, and during this period both were dogged by corruption allegations.

But the CER and other political reform advocates stood their ground and defended the bill. The political parties and advocates in Congress also supported the bill. However, time ran out prior to the adjournment of the 14th Congress in 2010 and the bill failed to pass.

After the election of Benigno Aquino III to the presidency in 2010, buoyed by the fact that a popular Liberal Party[16] president was in office, the advocacy intensified and legislative work on the bill resumed. A consortium called the Consortium on Political Party Reforms (CPPR) was formed by groups advocating for the bill to focus its effort not only on passing the bill but also on instituting comprehensive reforms in the Philippine political party system.

In time for the 2013 elections, the CPPR together with the Senate Committee on Constitutional Amendments, Revision of Codes and Laws; the House Committee on Suffrage and Electoral Reform; and the Commission on Elections held a three-day workshop-conference on Political Party Reform in August 2012. Major political

---

16 The Liberal Party was one of the most vociferous in supporting the bill in 2002 and has always prided itself as being the mainstream entity that is the nearest thing there is to a genuine political party in the Philippines.

parties such as the Liberal Party, Nationalist People's Coalition (NPC), Centrist Democratic Party (CDP), Partido Demokratiko Pilipino-Lakas ng Bayan (PDP-LABAN), Laban ng Demokratikong Pilipino (LDP), and Akbayan Citizens' Party participated in the workshop. Political institutes and party think tanks, as well as civil society organisations, also participated in the workshop conference. The participants all agreed and committed to work for the "urgent passage of the Political Party Development Act" in the remaining months of the 15th Congress (2010–2013).[17]

In the 15th Congress, efforts to strengthen the political party system were enshrined in House and Senate bills entitled "The Political Party Development Act of 2010." Senators Edgardo Angara and Jinggoy Estrada filed senate Bills 51 and 607, respectively. House Bills 49, 403, and 159 were also filed with the same topics by Representatives Rufus Rodriguez, Maximo Rodriguez Jr., Juan Edgardo Angara, and Arthur Yap, respectively, and Rep. Raymond Democrito Mendoza also co-authored the consolidated bill. The bills filed at the Senate were consolidated and adopted as a committee report with eighteen senators as signatories, while the House of Representatives again (as in the 13th Congress) approved its version of the bill on third reading and transmitted the bill onward to the Senate. However, it never reached the stage of bill sponsorship on second reading in the Senate and the 15th Congress ended without any action from the upper house.

In interviews with key legislators, it turned out that the ruling Liberal Party and President Aquino himself prevented its passage as this would interfere with the LP plans and strategies for the 2013 and 2016 elections. This may be a plausible explanation given that the bill would have curtailed a certain electoral practice enjoyed by the Liberal Party. This was the so-called "equity of the incumbent," a longstanding convention whereby national parties favor incumbents over other co-partisans who are seeking to win election to a post.[18]

This development led to half-hearted efforts to pass the bill in the 16th Congress (2013–2016). In the wake of the pork-barrel scandal that emerged in 2013, with allegations of misconduct against legislators in the 14th Congress, there were suggestions to use the anti-pork barrel public opinion to encourage the ruling Liberal Party to change its negative position on the bill. However, this came to naught when not enough momentum was generated and traditional politics entrenched itself in the party.

---

17 As agreed upon in the Declaration of the 2012 Workshop-Conference on Political Party Reforms. Manila, Philippines.

18 As Manuel Quezon III explained in a 2007 blog, during the Arroyo administration, "The 'equity of the incumbent' is a term dating back to prewar days, which simply means that in any race, the incumbent should be given preference in getting officially anointed (and funded). An administration—any administration—finds its election-related problem to be simply, too many candidates, too few positions, too many people might get mad if you play favorites without knowing who will surely win." See http://www.quezon.ph/2007/02/06/equity-of-the-incumbent/.

THE PROVISIONS OF THE POLITICAL PARTY DEVELOPMENT BILL

The bill as narrated in its historical evolution began as an overall package to reform the system governing political parties in the Philippines. It was part of the goal to strengthen democratic institutions and weaken individuals, clans, and dynasties that have long defined Philippine politics. The bill, if eventually passed, is envisioned to veer away from the personality-based politics that have incessantly undermined Philippine democracy in the post-martial law era.

Through the years, the legislative bills filed from the 12th Congress in 2002 to the current version in the 17th Congress in 2016 were all aimed at strengthening the system of political parties by: (1) upholding party loyalty and adherence to ideological principles, platforms, and programs by penalizing turncoatism; (2) reducing cases of graft and corruption by regulating campaign financing through transparent mechanisms to level the playing field; and (3) professionalizing of political parties through state subsidy by supporting them to become effective agents of democracy.

The proposed bill highlights two major categories to strengthen the political party system in the Philippines: political party development and campaign finance reforms. This section examines the contents of the proposed measure, highlighting the major provisions that have remained in the bill from the time it was first drafted in 2002 until now. This also presents other recommendations based on both the ongoing advocacy efforts and a recent gathering of major political parties, government agencies, and civil society organizations.

I. POLITICAL PARTY DEVELOPMENT

TURNCOATISM

In the Philippines, jumping from one political party to another political party has become too common, and constitutes a scandalous political practice. The largely personality-based politics in the country further encourages this practice. Political turncoatism, as defined in most versions of the proposed measure, is the act of changing party affiliation by a candidate.

In the Senate version of the bill (filed as consolidated bill SB 3214 in the 15th Congress), political turncoatism is defined as the *change of political party affiliation by any candidate within eight (8) months prior to the election.* Meanwhile, the House final version in the consolidated bill HB 6551 as approved in third reading defines political turncoatism as the *change of a political party affiliation by an elected official during one's term, except during six (6) months before the end of the term.*[19]

The proposed measure intends to suggest at least nominal discouragement of the phenomenon of political turncoatism. It promotes party loyalty and adherence to it before an election—or, if elected, after the convening of Congress—by penalizing any member of a political party from changing party affiliation for convenience's sake. A glaring omission, however, is the period immediately after the presidential election and prior to the convening of the new Congress—which is, in fact, when one can observe the strongest stampede of legislators to the party or coalition of the newly elected president. This is because, in most cases, realignments occur after candidates have identified the winnable or ruling party. It means that the shifting of party affiliation is mainly rooted in political advantages rather than in conviction. In sum, the anti-turncoatism measure provides a large loophole and reflects the reluctance of most politicians to reform current practices.

All versions of the bill, in both Houses, recommend the following penalties:

a. Removal from office if an elected party candidate changes parties;

b. Disqualification from running for any elective position in the next election immediately following the act of changing political party affiliation;

c. Prohibition from being appointed or from holding any position in any public or government office for three years after the expiration of the current term/office;

d. Prohibition from assuming any executive or administrative position in the new political party; and

e. Refunding of any and all amounts received from one's former political party, plus 25 percent surcharge thereon.

These penalties on turncoatism have proven to be among the most contentious provisions, and have hindered the passage of the bill in both the Senate and the House. This led to consideration of arriving at an agreeable

---

19 These are the most advanced formulations reached in both chambers of Congress and reflect the various negotiations among the legislators.

consensus, but in the end such a conciliatory approach was rejected. In a 2012 workshop-conference (the most recent major gathering among political parties, government agencies, and civil society organizations), it was agreed that the provisions on turncoatism need to be treated as a non-negotiable element of the bill. The anti-turncoatism provisions are deemed to be among the fundamental features of the bill, and watering them down would defeat the purpose of reforming the system governing political parties in the Philippines. The penalties in the current versions of the bill are already a result of continuing negotiations with political party representatives.

II. CAMPAIGN FINANCE

The excessive use of money during elections has characterized Philippine elections. Although there are existing government regulations in campaign financing, both in contributions and expenditures, they have always been a thorny issue in Philippine elections. Despite existing constitutional and legal provisions that aim to level the playing field for those who wish to run for office, political parties and candidates still blatantly go beyond these restrictions based on the belief that money alone can buy any political office. Transparent and effective mechanisms are indispensable to level the playing field among candidates and political parties during elections. In an election, the people express their will and delegate their power to elected officials. They entrust elected leaders to govern the state through policies that would reflect their will. As such, choosing leaders should be based on a process that is free from intimidation or influence of money.

The proposed bill intends to strictly regulate both campaign contributions and campaign expenditures, and hopes to enable both the candidates and citizen-voters to view elections as a democratic exercise and not as a form of business to amass wealth. It will institute stiffer penalties for violators and it proposes to strengthen the role of COMELEC by creating a department within the commission that is tasked with supervising and regulating campaign financing.

During the many years of discussing the bill, it has been proposed that the Commission on Elections (COMELEC) establish an office that will strictly monitor the Statement of Contributions and Expenditures (SOCE) of both political parties and candidates. A step in this direction was done by the COMELEC itself by establishing a preparatory Task Force on Campaign Finance. It has already developed the institution's capacity to fully implement the provisions stipulated in this bill.

Regulating campaign finances presents an enormous challenge in a cash-based society where unreceipted expenditures prevail and where big campaign donors are often hidden from the public. Though there are various rules on campaign contributions and campaign expenditures, these leave big gaps that often prevent the meaningful monitoring, prosecution, and conviction of violators. An example is the SOCE which does not carry the requirement for an independent audit of a candidate's or a political party's campaign funds and expenses. On the other hand, an exception is the successful regulation of the "air war" or mass media expenditures, which is facilitated by the ability of regulators to examine records of the television, radio, and print media outfits.

A. CAMPAIGN CONTRIBUTIONS

Existing laws put more focus on regulating campaign expenditures; regulations regarding contributions are limited to including the names of contributors and the respective amount given to a political party or candidates. To the extent that campaign contributions are received in cash and "under the table," the formal regulations are open to ready evasion. Surplus contributions, which can often be quite substantial, also remain effectively unregulated.

The proposed Political Party Development Act has outlined the limits for voluntary contributions to a national political party. In the 16th Congress, both the House and Senate versions of the bills have limited voluntary contributions from a natural person to not more than 1,000,000 pesos (roughly USD20,000) while a juridical person has up to a limit of 10,000,000 pesos (roughly USD200,000). This would bring the limits to a more realistic level consistent with actual expenditures. Furthermore, the bill requires disclosure of contributions to political parties, including opening an account with any reputable bank accredited by COMELEC. All contributions received in the bank account of the political party shall be published and audited. In turn, the audit can discover any big discrepancy between the reported contributions and the actual expenditures on the ground.

The bill intends to promote transparency and prevent candidates being beholden to campaign contributors. In addition, members are encouraged to pay their dues to be considered stakeholders of their respective parties. Placing limits on contributions is also an attempt to do away with the well-entrenched patronage system in Philippine politics. It emphasizes that sovereignty derives from the people and not from individuals financing electoral campaigns.

B. STATE SUBSIDY

Another component added in the measure is the provision on "state subsidy." Advocates of a comprehensive reform of the political party system believe that the role of political parties is essential to the maturation of democracy. The bill's proponents have argued that as much as the state could invest in economic institutions, the state also has the responsibility to develop political institutions.

The proposed act provides for a state subsidy to accredited and qualified political parties in order to promote professionalism and accountability among its members. Although this is one of the provisions that has caused conflict and controversy in the passage of the bill, its proponents argue that it is meant to be used to augment the operating funds of the accredited political parties,[20] therefore encouraging political parties to be true to their roles. In addition, the fund shall only be used directly and exclusively for (a) party development and (b) campaign expenditures.

The bill specified which entities are entitled to and qualified for the state subsidy. The proposed measure has set the following criteria for eligibility of political parties to receive funds from the State Subsidy Fund:

1. Current levels of political representation across the posts of incumbent president, members of congress, governors, vice-governors, and city and municipal mayors and vice-mayors;

2. Organizational strength and mobilization capability;

3. Performance and track record of the party.

The state subsidy, as practiced in many other advanced democracies, provides the minimum requirements for political parties and individual candidates to function. It is a means of trying to steer political parties away from being beholden to personalities and toward the upholding of party programs. Moreover, the creation of a state subsidy fund intends to deter political corruption by encouraging political groups to refuse funds offered by unlawful elements engaged in illegal businesses (e.g., drug and gambling lords) that would later require favors from those they have supported financially during the campaign.

---

20 There is to be a separate accreditation process for the state subsidy, limited to qualified political parties that have earlier passed accreditation as national political parties.

ISSUES SURROUNDING THE STATE SUBSIDY PROVISION

Critics of the bill have always faulted the inclusion of provisions for state subsidy, arguing that it can be a source of graft and corruption. Some even say that it makes the bill "unpalatable." But in one of the discussions among stakeholders in 2013, around the time that the pork barrel scandal took center stage in Philippine politics, it was explained that state subsidy would be given to political parties and not to individuals. It is to be under the control of parties and not individuals, and using the funds in any way counter to its purpose could be detrimental to the party. If the funds are not used properly, there would be a strong chance that the political party may lose political support in future elections. State subsidy is meant not only to provide the minimum resources for party building but also to leverage more effective auditing, transparency, and accountability in the sourcing and expenditures of party and campaign funds. In addition, because the party would control the funds, it can be expected to enhance the authority and influence that parties have over their candidates and members.

The state subsidy fund would urge political parties to develop internally to become more spirited and aggressive in pushing for their agenda. It is envisioned that this measure would lead to the political maturation of political parties as they themselves would be bound to work within a democratic framework. The expectation is that a self-checking mechanism would be put in place: political parties themselves would instill discipline among their members in order to qualify for state subsidy.

In order to have access to the state subsidy fund, a political party should pass the accreditation requirements or the criteria for eligibility—political representation, organizational strength and mobilization capability, and performance and track record of the party. These accreditation requirements encourage political parties to develop valid political platforms. In essence, they attempt to screen genuine political parties for a meaningful electoral exercise.

During the last conference-workshop held in 2012, stakeholders also recommended setting a minimum base amount from the total state subsidy, available to all national political parties and equitably shared. Beyond this minimum subsidy, it was recommended that additional funds be distributed based on the acceptable proposed criteria. Lastly, it was recommended that the largest portion of funds be allocated to party development.

C. ALLOWABLE POLITICAL PARTY EXPENDITURES

The proposed Political Party Development Act also details the allowable expenditures that can be funded out of the state subsidy fund. This is to ensure that funds coming from taxpayer's money are used only for its intended purpose. These expenditures are subject to audit by the Commission on Audit (COA) since part of the monies will come from the state subsidy fund. The latter can only be used for *party development* and *campaign expenditures*. For party development, the subsidy can only be used for those activities that foster or promote membership recruitment and education, professionalism, and accountability among its members. Similarly, only allowable campaign activities can be funded from the state subsidy.

Meanwhile, the current governing law on campaign expenditures—Synchronization of National and Local Elections Act (RA 7166) of 1991—limits expenditure of both political parties and candidates to PHP 5.00 (or roughly USD10 cents) per registered voter. The pending bill in the Senate and House increased the limit to PHP 20.00 and PHP 11.00, respectively, per registered voters due to inflation. Both versions of the bill authorize COMELEC to adjust the amount based on the Consumer Price Index every three years following the effectivity of the proposed Act.

Putting in place a cap on expenditures is seen as a regulating provision that would help provide a level playing field among political parties contesting for elective positions in government.

D. AUDIT

Lastly, the bill proposes to put in place a monitoring mechanism for funds that would be allocated once it becomes a law. The COA and COMELEC would be tasked to design and implement a monitoring and reporting system. It shall be conducted through consultation with political parties, accredited citizens' arms, the private sector, non-government organizations, and government agencies.

Given that transparency and accountability are necessary ingredients of a truly democratic country, the proposed measure requires all political parties to make full disclosure of all contributions and expenditures incurred in the use of the state subsidy fund. Furthermore, it requires political parties to submit a sworn statement of their assets and liabilities to the COA. The amount of contributions given to a party shall also be disclosed, including information on the entity that provided the contribution. All these reports would be audited by the COA, and failure to comply would result in disqualification of political parties from receiving their share in the state subsidy.

It should be noted that similar measures have been enacted in the past, but their implementation remains weak due to the lack of a monitoring and reporting system. Candidates and political parties continue to evade sanctions from overspending during election campaigns or from receiving contributions from unlawful donors. In the 2012 workshop-conference among stakeholders, additional recommendations were put forward to give more substance in the "disclosure and performance monitoring" section of the bill. Stakeholders proposed that COMELEC's campaign finance department must be empowered to be able to discharge its mandate and functions and that it should allow COMELEC to cause the investigation of pertinent violations. Lastly, it added that harsher penalties must be imposed on the misuse of state subsidy.

LESSONS FOR FUTURE ADVOCACY

The advocacy for political party reforms, and particularly for the passage of the Political Party Development Bill, is a tortuous road, littered with broken promises, half-hearted support from its direct beneficiaries, and misplaced opposition from opinion makers and the general public.

Ironically, the major obstacle to the passage of the bill comes from political parties themselves, or rather, from some key political leaders who benefit from the present personalistic politics and have opted to maintain the political party system in its present weak state to ensure their own dominance. Most often, these leaders fail to rise above their personal and partisan interests.[21] This situation calls for more creative methods and going beyond the politicians in order to undertake the strengthening of the political party system and the passage of the bill itself.

The follow-up conference to the 2015 Electoral Reform Summit agreed that the major resolutions in the campaign for political reforms revolve around the following initiatives:

---

21 There are at least two notable exceptions among political party leaders, both noted above: Jose De Venecia of the LAKAS-NUCD and Edgardo Angara of Laban ng Demokratikong Pilipino (LDP). They saw the destructive impact of unrestrained campaign fundraising and expenditures and opted to change the rules of the game. They and some others are a small few among many others who have resisted change.

- Review the Political Party Development bill and its advocacy to draw the necessary lessons in preparation for ongoing advocacy in the 17th Congress.

- Consider the key provisions to be advocated piecemeal as separate bills, e.g. turncoatism, strengthening political parties, and campaign finance.

- Strengthen the political party system and support the development of political institutes.

- Undertake constituency building and advocacy for a Political Party Development Act.

- Reiterate the focus on voter education for the political party and campaign finance (Follow-up Conference 2015).

While summit participants would likely have had a positive disposition to electoral system redesign, specific proposals were not a major focus of the gathering.

The Duterte administration offers a new opportunity to pass the Political Party Development Act in the 17th Congress. The bill did not progress well due to the antagonistic relations between the Duterte administration and its political opposition, the other priorities of Congress, and the weakened advocacy for the bill within and outside Congress. However, it is still considered a major reform issue.

In the meantime, another avenue has opened. President Duterte made changing to a federal system from the present unitary system a prominent theme in his quest for the presidency. To be sure, this can only be done through a revision of the Constitution. In early 2018, he convened a presidential body, the Consultative Committee to Review the 1987 Constitution, to craft a new federal constitution. In doing so, Duterte has signaled that the political system needs, at a minimum, further refinements, and, at the most, restructuring.

The first draft of the Consultative Committee contained an article covering political party development and most provisions in the Political Party Development Bill are incorporated in it. This is in addition to gradually replacing the existing party list system with a more standard proportional representation system and a self-executing provision on restricting political dynasties. The Commission on Elections has also been given a greater role in supervising the political party system.

The proposed constitution provides the framework for political party reforms and for the reforms in the electoral system design itself. In order to promote program-based and disciplined parties, anti-party switching rules and public financing of parties should be provided in the constitution. Another innovative proposal is the recognition of political parties as public institutions instead of semi-private organizations. Strict requirements (i.e. membership, chapter organizations, party programs, etc.) for registration of regular parties should be implemented. Another possible requirement is to accredit national political parties only. This is critical to ensuring that the political system is oriented to national public goods over local particularistic interests.

The strengthening of the Philippine political party system is a necessary requirement for a successful transition to a federal-parliamentary system.[22] It also stands in itself as a necessary ingredient of a strengthened Philippine democracy. If parties are already critical to the proper functioning of the current presidential system, all the more important is their role in a parliamentary system. Whereas presidents are elected directly by the people, the prime minister is elected by the parliament—in other words, executive authority arises out of the legislature. Without an effective party system, there will be no well-institutionalized basis for the creation of parliamentary coalitions—and one can anticipate a high degree of instability as executive authority frequently shifts from one prime minister to another.

The wind of change is here now. May it bring the flowering of genuine political parties and people's participation in governance.

---

22 At present, the Consultative Committee decided on a federal-presidential system in its draft. This is still to be approved by Congress and the president.

Ahead of the 2013 general election, party flags are hoisted on a bridge in peninsular Malaysia. In stark contrast to the Philippines, Malaysia's national political parties have long been well-established and deeply rooted.

Photograph by Paul D. Hutchcroft

CHAPTER EIGHT
PATRONAGE POLITICS AND PARTIES IN THE PHILIPPINES: INSIGHTS FROM THE 2016 ELECTIONS

MEREDITH L. WEISS

The 2016 Philippine election will probably be best remembered for the bold campaign and dramatic win of presidential candidate Rodrigo Roa Duterte, including the innovative social media strategies he adopted (Ressa 2016). In many other ways, however, the elections were altogether "normal": weak national-level parties, deeply patronage-based local machines, endemic cash payouts, and underlying fears of malfeasance and/or violence continue to characterize electoral politics across the Philippine archipelago. Drawing on in-depth collaborative field research during the electoral campaign, as well as cognate efforts in Malaysia in 2013 and Indonesia in 2014, this chapter explores dynamics of the recent campaign, and how "money politics" in the Philippines compares with that of the two neighboring states. Overall, our research concludes that—at least at the local level—money matters in Philippine elections as much as if not more than ever. This salience manifests in the "retail politics" form of payments for votes (to some extent signaling a patron's sincerity, wherewithal, and generosity, and to some extent simply buying favor); in the form of project-based contracts and concessions to be awarded post-polls, at least partly contingent on votes (with project proceeds funding subsequent contests); and in the form of national programs, association with which intensifies incumbent advantage and continues to lure legislators to the president's fold. Despite occasional efforts especially by the Liberal Party to develop a clearer identity and party loyalty, mainstream parties continue to be less clearly differentiated, reified, and meaningful in the Philippines than in Indonesia or Malaysia; where they matter is far more in the form of mayor-centered local machines (sometimes registered as parties) than as compelling nationwide entities. Mesoparticularistic inducements, or collective "club goods,"[1] designed to woo part of a known base, feature less in the Philippines than in its neighbors. The same is true of election-period development grants and projects. Meanwhile, personal (especially family) ties may either temper or amplify the effects of cash disbursements.

PATRONAGE POLITICS IN THE 2016 GENERAL ELECTIONS[2]

In the interests of space, this analysis will focus narrowly on patronage politics in the Philippine elections, at the level of both individual politicians and political parties. While there is much more to be said about the organization of, conduct of, and voter decision making in the elections, I leave that discussion to others. Even so, given the centrality of "money politics" to contemporary Philippine political campaigns, this limited investigation still illuminates key patterns. Most obvious among these practices is vote buying itself: a short-term exchange that may as often be expressed in terms of affective ties (demonstrating gratitude for support provided) as in market terms (purchasing a vote). At the same time, the enduring phenomenon of longer-term or more episodic provision of services and resources—essentially a patron-client model centered around local political machines—persists, as well.

Vote buying, largely in the form of cash payments to voters, is endemic in all but a few areas, particularly in connection with local rather than national contests.[3] Labeled as "allowances" in Pampanga, *uwan-uwan* (rain showers) in Bohol, "banquet" or *salu-salo* in parts of Laguna, or by other euphemisms, the practice extends nationwide. In actuality, as detailed below, we can differentiate between culturally somewhat acceptable, reputation-building distributions of cash, food, and other small gifts, and more targeted, often larger and/or later inducements to shift one's vote. While not new, vote buying appears to have increased in scale and scope over recent elections. One explanation looks to devolution under the Local Government Code of 1991, which has raised the stakes—and, arguably, the expense and violence—of elections, as local officials gained access to more

---

1 This form of patronage appeals not just to individuals and households, one on one (that is, microparticularism), but to targeted blocs of voters, pursued on an impersonal basis—for instance, upgrades to a church building or a new playing field for a village, to woo electoral support from that community. See Hutchcroft 2014b.

2 This section in particular draws upon the findings of members of our research team for the Philippines portion of the project, *Money Politics: Patronage, Political Networks, and Electoral Dynamics in Southeast Asia*. (Primary funding for the project is from the Australian Research Council, DP140103114.) Unless otherwise stated, the details included here are from that collective data-gathering effort. See Hicken et al., forthcoming.

3 See Hicken et al. forthcoming, or for an abbreviated overview, see Aspinall, Davidson, Hicken, and Weiss 2016. Other forms of election malpractice, too, are generally also tied more to local than national contests (Carter Center 2016).

substantial financial and other resources (as well as more steady employment for themselves and favored relatives or allies). These assets are all the more valuable where income and opportunities are otherwise scarce, as is particularly the case in the least economically advantaged regions of the Philippines. The introduction of and security improvements to electronic voting since 2010 offers another explanation, and one which goes farther to explain the uptick in individual-level vote buying in subsequent elections: lacking the opportunity for aggregated strategies through ballot-box manipulation, candidates resort instead to retail strategies.

Vote buying follows a similar dominant pattern nation-wide (and a pattern not unlike that found across Indonesia). A pyramidal campaign structure is near-universal, generally from the mayor (or sometimes governor) down to the rural sub-barangay (*purok*), urban city block, and even household level. Members of the team generally receive only a small honorarium, meals, and allowance for expenses, supplemented with the lure of post-election jobs or access to services. (Meals and transportation expenses for campaign staff and meetings constituted among the largest campaign costs, across units of electoral contestation: congressional districts, provinces, cities, and towns.) The timing for distribution of funds to cover team allowances and other expenses varies, but may begin a full year out among barangay leaders (though lower levels of the organization may be funded closer to the election time). These expenses are generally high, even apart from payments to voters, prompting calls for more realistic legal campaign spending limits.

Although officially nonpartisan, the barangay captain—or if not supportive, then a barangay council member or neighborhood or local-association leader allied to the candidate in question—is the central node in this network, coordinating campaign efforts for a given area. The opportunity for reciprocity, when barangay-level elections will lead the barangay captain to rely upon the higher-level candidate (or now elected official) he or she has just supported, helps solidify this clientelist connection. Assurance of priority in poll-watcher assignments as well as for post-election jobs helps to keep rank-and-file campaign team members committed. Given the size of the teams assembled, joining a candidate's campaign apparatus is a fairly common way to earn a bit of extra income, though being found to be disloyal will end that "career."

Some campaign organizers say they just know when a local team member, termed a *lider*, has been disloyal, but others described strategies for cross-checking or monitoring (or fielding complaints from voters who did not receive anything) to ensure *liders* distribute payments as directed. Some candidates (or their close associates) personally presented payments to voters (even if doing so problematically signaled their lack of trust in their teams), gathered supporters together for mass distributions, or tried in different ways to assess team members' loyalty and at least to sideline those they doubted. That said, teams tend to be fairly enduring, for all but brand-new candidates who were not seeking positions in the wake of other members of the family. Disloyalty was less a concern for incumbents, as well as for those candidates with prior familial campaign experience, as they tended to rely less upon short-term and opportunistic or mercenary teams.

Campaign teams typically check the ground during the campaign period, starting with an initial mapping as well as surveys to gauge potential candidates' "winnability," then conducting "straw voting" (as it is sometimes termed) or surveys to gauge voter support and "troubleshooting" worrisome areas, often starting well in advance and proceeding through several stages. Those at the lowest rung are *taga-lista* (as termed in Bulacan) "tasked with compiling": compiling lists of voters who promise to support that candidate or slate, and who will receive payments for attending events or for their votes. In Bohol, for instance, campaigns divide voters among "ours" (loyal supporters); swing voters who will accept cash from both sides but not reveal their preference; *palitunon*, or undecided, whose votes may be bought; and those clearly inclined toward an opponent, but who can be "shot" with money in hopes of changing their mind. New technologies for surveys, compiling results, and checking voters' registration status have refined procedures previously done through traditional clan or other networks, and have also fed an apparent trend toward professionalization of at least lead campaign staff.

In most cases, funds are distributed via specially trained barangay-level brokers, sometimes called *listadores*, either in one payment—via "special operations" the night before polling day, or during the *oras de peligro* (delicate or dangerous time) or "end-game" of the final two days of the campaign—or in several tranches, starting a couple weeks out. Some regions present variations. In Lanao del Sur, for instance, in what is termed "vote squatting," voters receive an initial deposit from a candidate they promise to support; if they then accept a larger deposit from a challenger, they are expected to return the first candidate's deposit. Teams worried about their vote margins as the campaign proceeds will pay a higher price for these "squat votes" than for the votes of their solid supporters. The terms used are themselves evocative: for instance, the *gapang* (crawl) of discreet, final-days vote buying, while opponents stalk the other side in hopes of catching them in the act.

Campaign strategists think carefully about how much to distribute, weighing what their opponents will likely give—since what stops any one side from abstaining is that their opponents will not. They also assess how confident they are of that voter's support, how heated the contest is, how extensive they expect their defections ("mortality rate") to be, and how much they have on hand to give. Most aim to wait until the first team has released its payments, then adjust as needed. Payments may come in phases, to counteract attempted raids on a candidate's base by deep-pocketed opponents; loyalty and general preference may be enough to outweigh a difference of a couple hundred pesos, but once the other side ups the ante further, even voters inclined toward a candidate may shift their vote. But in areas like Bukidnon, where welfare services are undersupplied, a candidate who previously provided medical or other assistance is likely to lock in that voter's support, regardless of others' payments (more on that aspect below). Nationwide, cash distributions to voters ran the gamut, from token 20 peso payments from municipal council candidates to 1,000, 1,500, or (more rarely) several thousand pesos from a would-be mayor, often inclusive of that candidate's council slate.

Currency notes are typically stapled or clipped to sample ballots or candidate handbills or cards, often in an addressed envelope, to ensure that only voters listed as likely supporters will receive payments. Some campaigns, though, were more creative in how they distributed payments. For instance, in Leyte, one candidate distributed pseudo-bank cards, to be handed over to a campaign *lider* after voting in exchange for cash.

Teams generally targeted their own supporters first. If funds permitted, though, they extended their reach to swing voters or less promising efforts among their opponents' supporters. Illustrative of the opportunistic alliances common across the Philippines—and the weakness of party loyalty—sample ballots frequently diverged from the party line. For instance, virtually all slates touted in the vicinity of Davao City had hometown hero Duterte in the presidential slot, regardless of party affiliation. Nor would most candidates there campaign for their party's actual presidential candidate, lest they hurt their own chances.

Campaigns face the challenge of being discreet, but also personal in their distributions. For instance, one team in Bulacan reportedly brought voters to a resort where they distributed funds, as going for a swim would not seem unusual. In one district in Camarines Sur, campaigns employed the majority of voters in a precinct as poll-watchers, to disguise payments made to them. Moreover, campaigns have to worry about security: an opponent may attack (or tip off the police or New People's Army guerrillas to intercept) campaign staff carrying large sums of cash for distribution, or may themselves stop rival campaign workers from distributing payments within their own bailiwick. Campaign strategists developed creative plans to deal with brute security. In some locations, these efforts involved contracting/colluding with the police or guerrillas; elsewhere, as in Lanao del Sur, having strongmen and guns (extending to stockpiled firearms, essentially a private army) is critical.

Campaign resources come primarily from the upper/middle-range candidates on the ticket, commonly those running for mayor, governor, and/or Congressional representative. Those candidates, in turn, derive their funds from proceeds from government contracts, personal wealth, family members, and wealthy or supportive friends (specifically including, in some areas, overseas Filipino workers). Businesses may donate in kind, but less often in cash, at the local level; some business leaders donate to higher-level candidates, however, and allegations of vested interests or businesses contributing to campaigns arose in some areas, such as Cebu City. Particularly where provision of infrastructure is key to building support, contractors may finance campaigns; they then quite likely expect to receive project contracts, in turn. Incumbents benefit, too, from being able to draw on local government staff as campaign workers—even though other networks may be more useful or central to their team.

Some poorer voters (Classes D and E) allegedly sold their votes more proactively. In one pattern noted in Antique Province, intermediate brokers committed a number of votes in a bundle to the highest bidder; in another pattern there, voters approached a mayoral candidate's headquarters with an offer to sell their vote to that candidate (or if they were not buying, then to an opponent). We heard discussions, too, of turnout buying—of campaigns paying voters, including entire families, not to vote, then sequestering them on polling day or marking their fingers with indelible ink to prevent their reneging—though these descriptions seemed more often discussed than actually pursued. Some campaigns purportedly also pay off voting machine programmers, as a cheaper alternative to standard vote buying, although we encountered more allegations of than evidence for efforts to tamper with voting machines.

On polling day in the Philippines, party monitors are more readily able to assess voter compliance than, for instance, in Indonesia (where vote buying is similarly rampant). It is in large part the right to appoint these poll-watchers that makes registering as or with a party appealing; the national party generally covers the cost of poll-watchers for national-level candidates and sometimes subsidizes their allies at lower levels as well. In at least some polling stations, voters sit within view of the party witnesses as they fill out their ballots (at school desks rather than in polling booths). Not all voters used the cardboard folder supplied to veil their ballot as they brought it to the vote counting machine (some of which broke down, leaving voters queued with their ballots), and the witnesses were in some cases close enough to scrutinize the ballot as the voter fed it into the machine (Carter Center 2016, 7; and our own observations). Even so, verification of vote buying seems to be far more difficult with the new automated voting system than under the previous manual-counting system, especially if voters understand that they are not to retain the receipt the machine emits (Carter Center 2016, 14). (Some campaigns allegedly counted on voters' ignorance of the rules regarding receipts, and asked voters to save and produce that record as proof of compliance.) Campaigns do not rely solely on polling-station checks, however. Some respondents noted that canvassers asked them to sign a contract promising not to vote, but that they also felt a moral obligation to follow through once they had accepted funds. In some constituencies, campaigns offered bloc payments to barangays if they "voted straight"—that is, if the full slate won the barangay.

Apart from money, candidates also distributed various goods: t-shirts, food, fans, alcohol, cigarettes, coffins, uniforms, and more, either in the course of canvassing and campaigning or upon voters' request. Provision of these items requires advance preparation and coordination, including selection of targeted beneficiaries (particularly for larger, costlier items). In some cases, distribution is at high-profile rallies, including as coveted prizes; these are not illicit hand-offs, but public displays, intended to excite the crowd. Candidates may also provide direct services during the campaign; in Laguna, for instance, both sides offered such assistance as medical aid and meals, as well as *tulong* (financial help) from their headquarters.

More broadly, beyond direct payments, however essential, other forms of patronage also play a role—in some areas, arguably a more pivotal role than campaign-time cash payments in spurring turnout and loyalty. In Bohol, such practices are termed "sowing the seeds": preparing the ground for elections via prior sponsorship, gifts, and other patronage to build reputation and accumulate *utang na loob*, or debts of gratitude. In Muntinlupa, one incumbent quite literally provided seedlings and gardening implements, to allow constituents to grow their own food and market the excess. Many Cordilleran voters in particular seemed to favor clan voting, obviating most vote buying, given expectations that elected officials would then support the familial unit; in other regions, too, volunteers eschew payment lest they then be unable to request assistance in the future.

In this vein, scholarship programs are especially prevalent. Assurances of a greater number of, and higher value to, college scholarships helped to woo young voters in Antique Province, for instance. Scholarship recipients elsewhere were likewise expected to campaign for the candidate responsible, and form an exceptionally reliable pool of volunteers. Promise of employment, particularly in poor, rural areas, performed a similar function. In such regions, incumbents in particular were also expected to have invested in poverty alleviation, health, and livelihood programs—for instance, helping with hospitalization and doctors' fees, burial assistance, or water connection costs.

Whereas incumbents could point to, and promise to continue, the projects they had brought thus far to a constituency, challengers were motivated to fund similar projects themselves prior to the campaign, to develop a record to which to refer. These projects are essential to building up the persona of, and voters' personal connection with, the candidate; pre-election walkabouts and informational leaflets alone cannot cement that relationship. The need to build name recognition leads some challenger candidates in particular to start what amounts to campaigning well before the forty-five-day official campaign period begins. In Baguio City, meanwhile, ongoing contributions include ceremonial items like gongs, chickens, and black pigs for upland rituals, alongside more common services such as scholarships, transportation assistance, medical aid, casual jobs, and disaster relief.

In addition, candidates may direct funds not at voters (and campaign staff), but at fellow candidates. Paying off rival candidates *not* to run may be an especially efficient strategy. Our team encountered reports of "splitter" candidates (the term used in Antique Province), for instance, paid by one side to split the opposition vote.[4] Lastly, the New People's Army also collects payments from candidates in the form of permit-to-campaign fees, with the amount increasing from around 40,000 pesos (or less; one city council candidate in the Compostela Valley noted that their council slate negotiated a lower group rate) to 150,000 pesos (using estimates from Camarines Sur province) with the stature of the office sought. However, these payments grant only access to voters, not assured support.

POLITICAL PARTIES AND ORGANIZATIONAL ALTERNATIVES

We know by now that political parties in the Philippines are comparatively weak, oriented around leading figures (generally the presidential and vice-presidential candidates, at election time), and typically with a minimal mass base or clear, national public image and program. This pattern is in stark contrast to Malaysia, where national political parties have long been well-established and deeply rooted; state-based or regional parties are dwarfed in significance (with the partial exception of the states of Sarawak and, to a lesser extent, Sabah; even in these exceptions, however, leading state parties commonly work in coalition with national counterparts). Indonesian political parties also remain far more cohesive than those in the Philippines, thanks to a number of regulatory features as described in Chapter Six—including requirements that all parties (with the exception of those in Aceh) demonstrate national scope and that winning presidential candidates obtain a minimal level support in one-half of the country's provinces. In the Philippines, the connection between the national and subnational levels of politics is generally far more tenuous. The local machine— often branded with its own team name and logo—is likely to be centered around a locally powerful family, allied strategically for elections with a national party, but otherwise weakly articulated with that national affiliation.[5] The latter generally

---

4 The Carter Center's observation report suggested that the high share (15 percent) of uncontested single seats may in part reflect increasing deals among powerful local families (2016, 5).

5 Where the presidential candidate is connected directly with a local machine, party still may fade to the background: incumbent vice-president Jejomar Binay's Team Binay ran as a "family brand" to secure their longtime stronghold in Makati, rather than emphasize the larger party (United National Alliance, UNA), even as patriarch Jejomar headed up the ticket to contest the presidency.

provides nothing other than a brand, endorsement, and coordination; the party itself focuses more on the national campaign, as well as on structural resources such as poll-watchers, and only sometimes feeds other resources downward. (Congressional candidates are packaged as part of the broader party ticket, though they generally also have strong local ties.) The would-be mayor typically selects a slate for city council, then the team's machinery urges voters to "vote straight," or support the full slate (a win for the slate is termed *ubos-kun-ubos* in Naga City, for instance). Canvassers may also encourage support for the upper echelons of the ticket, but less consistently or forcefully. Candidates for city or provincial councils may have supplemental teams of their own, in addition to the full-slate team. Team-based appeals aside, candidates still effectively compete with members of their own party in multi-member council districts, so individual name recognition matters.

Voting in a full slate facilitates enactment of a legislative platform, including provision of the sorts of programs and jobs essential to extending and sustaining support. Furthermore, a distinct feature of Philippine local politics is its emphasis on participatory budgeting and inclusion of non-governmental and people's organizations in governance. That structure not only opens communication channels between citizens and policymakers, but also grants access to a vote-bank and a campaign apparatus that draws on the leaders (reputable, clued in to local concerns, loyal, and already effectively compensated) of participating organizations (Borromeo-Bulao, in Hicken et al. forthcoming).

Whatever their weaknesses, parties (particularly the Liberal Party, LP, at least in this election) may supplement local campaign machinery and funding, as well as provide campaign headquarters apart from the candidate's home (a common option otherwise)—but such support is inconsistent across regions and contests. Parties claim specific strongholds, whether fairly enduringly or, for instance, in the home town or province of their "presidentiable." Machinery is key, given the prevalence of house-to-house campaigning (or "handshaking") as a supplement to wider-scale start-of-campaign proclamation rallies, end-of-campaign *mitings de avance* (which may draw crowds into the tens of thousands), caucuses (where platforms are presented and discussed, alongside entertainment and refreshments), motorcades, and smaller gatherings.

The LP claimed a strong machine in a number of areas nationwide (Holmes, in Hicken et al. forthcoming)—though that pattern has since shifted now that the president comes from a rival party (Partido Demokratiko Pilipino-Lakas ng Bayan, or PDP-LABAN). In the 2016 elections, though, LP "foot soldiers" worked the ground in various areas, and national and provincial party headquarters provided at least some funds to support them. (Elsewhere, party support, even from LP, was fairly minimal.) Dynastic politics are not necessarily at odds with party bailiwicks,

142

either: in Siquijor or Pangasinan, for instance, key families form the core of a well-oiled local LP machine. Moreover, the LP had tried under Aquino to broaden its support by channeling "pork" not only to its own people but also to those in rival camps. By *not* requiring that one be a party member to access state services and funds—in essence, to go by the actual rules and bring about the programmatic delivery of what are in any case supposed to be non-contingent programs—the LP aimed to encourage politicians to join or support the party (Vitug 2016).[6]

Whether this actually succeeded, however, is another question. Respondents who had earlier committed to strengthening the party-based appeal and reach of the LP admitted to us that they would likely shift their machinery over to the new presidential power-holder. Doing so brings PDP-LABAN the benefit of local patronage resources, while encouraging the ruling party to channel state largesse (contracts, infrastructure projects, jobs, etc.) to that locality. Newly inaugurated president Rodrigo Duterte himself had longstanding but not deep ties to PDP-LABAN, having previously served as the party's sole member of Congress, and the party provided a useful vehicle in his teasingly indecisive (and headline-grabbing) initial entry into the presidential race: six weeks after the deadline for filing for candidacy, he replaced the party's Michael Diño on the ticket. In the words of one analysis, "Duterte was purely a local/provincial personality, not a celebrity; did not have the support of traditional money politics or a pre-existing network of local political bosses supporting him; was not the candidate of a major party; and is not the scion of a generations-old, national-level political dynasty" (Cook and Salazar 2016, 3). Cook and Salazar attribute Duterte's win to a combination of regional (including familial) loyalties, his anti-crime and urban-order-restoring message, a promise of federalism, his openness to negotiation with (and access to) both communist and Moro/Muslim insurgents, the endorsement of the Iglesia ni Cristo (or INC, which purportedly could offer a bloc of up to two million votes), as well as his outsider status, use of social media to connect with both domestic and overseas voters—and the simple fact of weak parties and "fluid" loyalties (2016, 4–7, 10). Some of these attributes apply more widely as ways of building support; others suggest the innovations of Duterte's populist campaign.

Parties may lose even more of their raison d'être in an era of social media: the Duterte campaign effectively let social media—among a populace with the world's highest daily rate of social media usage (Kemp 2017)—take the place of machinery, as it reported the lowest spending among the four main candidates. His tech-savvy team still strategized carefully for how to harness these media, but online amplification reduced the investment needed (Cook and Salazar 2016, 8–11). Elsewhere—including outside highly urban areas—campaign teams used

---

6 We heard this sentiment in interviews also.

social media both proactively, to promote candidates, especially among younger voters or those overseas, and also to respond to or engage in "black propaganda." Still, at the local level, our findings suggest social media platforms hardly featured in political campaigning in some regions. Meanwhile, mainstream media took on partisan roles in several constituencies, such as Cebu.

Other networks besides parties are also important for canvassing and may deliver blocs of votes. The Iglesia ni Cristo is the best known of such groups—purportedly able to deliver 80 percent of its members' votes as promised, for local as well as national offices—and appears among the key networks activated across our sample constituencies. Other networks that perform similar roles include transport ones (for instance, Tricycle Operators and Drivers Associations; these groups are especially valuable allies since their members interact with, and can eavesdrop on and influence, so many voters as passengers, and can post stickers on or play jingles from their vehicles) as well as organizations or groups centered around fisherfolk, students and youth, women, farmers, or LGBTs. However, those organizations seem less reliable than INC at delivering blocks of votes. Perhaps for this reason, we saw relatively little prevalence of mesoparticularistic (or club-good) distributions, in terms of grants or donations to organizations or targeted communities. When members were offered items (for instance, groceries for members of a pedicab drivers' association), it tended to be in line with a strategy of campaigns targeting individual voters, albeit via an organization. Still, certain areas saw donations for things like basketball court repairs, village signage, and so forth, and candidates wooed some local *liders*, for instance, offering "a little extra" for *merienda* ("snacks") for the *lider* and their community in Laguna. While in some areas distribution of resources may have mattered for endorsement by religious or other groups (including INC), we saw far fewer election-time grants or promises to congregations, schools, or comparable entities than in Indonesia or Malaysia. That said, at least one candidate in Camarines Norte characterized middle class voters as swayed by "collective benefits" rather than individual favors.

COMPARISON WITH MONEY POLITICS IN MALAYSIA AND INDONESIA

The most definitive comparison we might draw is also the most banal: money politics is complex in its manifestations, its cultural resonances, and its implications, within and across states. Practices that clearly fit a definition of "vote buying" may be differently understood and carry little expectation of "buying" a vote—or they may clearly intend to purchase support. Indeed, use of the term "vote buying" may be anachronistic and obfuscatory: when these payments serve as means of consolidating and confirming support, rather than of purchasing votes per se, we should rightly develop a more appropriate term.

Also, while candidates across countries build elaborate teams of campaign workers, the specific character of those machines, and their alignment with or dissociation from political parties and other networks, varies both among and within political systems. Important, too, for efforts at reform: in the Philippines as in Indonesia or Malaysia, candidates may brand themselves as anti-corruption and opposed to money politics and patronage—a major theme in some localities—yet voters still expect to receive gifts, whether t-shirts or cash, from them. Candidates oblige since they see doing so as necessary and unavoidable.

In all three states, some distributions function as a sort of culturally acceptable stipend, read as signs of kindness, generosity, approachability, and concern, rather than as "vote buying" per se. *Not* to provide a bit of "pocket change" to someone who needs it reflects poorly on a candidate. In Malaysia, the comparable concept would be provision of transport or missed-salary subsidies to lighten voters' burden, or of (Muslim, Christian) charity for those in need; in Indonesia, those same readings of facilitating civic duty and offering the charitable beneficence expected of a wealthy and/or righteous person likewise offer alternate interpretations to vote buying. While payments stapled to a sample ballot in the Philippines are widely declaimed as vote buying, however clearly token the amount, even there voters may not see these distributions as payment so much as a show of reliability or generosity. Regardless, in especially poor areas across the Philippines, elections may be seen as a chance to redistribute wealth and share local officials' "loot."

Overall, campaign-period patronage in the 2016 Philippine elections was more heavily in the form of "retail" payments to individual voters than elsewhere in the region. While such payments were also endemic in Indonesia (albeit more frequently delivered to families, rather than individuals, than seemed the case in the Philippines), block grants to mosques, community organizations, and other intermediary associations loomed larger among candidates' expenditures in Indonesia as compared to the Philippines. At the same time, the fact that candidates throughout the Philippines are expected to provide pre- and post-election development projects, job opportunities, and more—and that their persona (and usually family) matters— suggests that a patron–client model still survives to some extent at the local level in many parts of the country.[7] Iterative, personal, mutual exchange (all of which

---

7 Chapters within Hicken et al. 2016 illustrate these patterns. See, especially, Hicken et al., "Introduction: The Local Dynamics of the National Elections in the Philippines," which emphasizes how much has changed in Philippine politics since the patron-client framework developed more than half a century ago. Alongside multipurpose, affective, long-term clientelistic ties are relationships that tend to be single-purpose, instrumentalist, and short-term in character (for example, brokers willing to sell their services to the highest bidder).

generate a sense of *utang na loob*) characterize this model, rather than a simple cash-for-votes transaction. On the plus side, in policy terms, this enduring connection does at least signal space for prospective voting, rather than just a retrospective assessment of what has already been provided or accomplished. It further suggests a longer time-horizon that goes well beyond a mere momentary exchange, as one would expect given the intended longevity of specific leaders and their teams. Still, campaign promises verge toward the unachievable, as for traffic miracles and free services of all sorts,[8] so the retrospective angle of weighing a candidate's patronage record thus far likely still dominates among reasonably savvy voters.

However important patronage may be, in the Philippines as in Malaysia and Indonesia, the specific person—charisma, reputation, familiarity—also matters. In Malaysia, nearly all politicians refer to the "personal touch"; in Indonesia, the term *figur* (figure, personage) is common. The same pattern applies in the Philippines, although dynastic politics—nurtured by political culture/habit as well as the rotational impetus of term limits—offers something of a shortcut to recognition for some candidates. Across all three countries, campaigning typically requires preparatory activities meant to establish one's name and reputation. In Malaysia, would-be candidates set up service centers and start making the rounds of weddings and funerals. In Indonesia, aspirants build roads and offer tutoring and other classes, starting months or years in advance. In the Philippines, even candidates with a known family name will often start laying the groundwork well before the official campaign period: attending wakes, birthday parties, and other local events, or serving as *kumpare/kumare* (godparents) to build up recognition and rapport. In some areas, a candidate's barangay-level *liders* effectively stand in for the patron—not just in vote-related transactions, but as the normal go-to person when one seeks political intercession or support. The underlying fiction is that the barangay leader is not working for herself but is rather representing the mayor (or other political official), who will then expect and deserve the vote of the citizen supplicant.

Across the Philippines, it is critical that candidates cultivate a reputation for being helpful and not stand-offish, ideally supplemented by a prominent family name as well. Poorer voters in particular may have sought and appreciated a politician's material assistance in the past—although one cannot disentangle gratitude for concrete aid from appreciation for a benevolent mien. The emphasis on what a candidate has done for the local community favors incumbents in the Philippines, as it does in Malaysia and Indonesia. Some of what incumbents tout are their own charitable or other contributions, yet being able to claim credit for securing or facilitating state economic development or

---

8   For example, in Muntinlupa, four candidates were dubbed "Mr. Educator," "Mr. Free Water," "Mr. Free Notary Public," and "Mr. Health," respectively, signaling the electoral allure of (free) services.

infrastructure projects falls within the same frame. In all three political systems, a good politician also helps to smooth voters' access to state services and welfare support (whether or not their intercession is really required): use of local health offices, educational support, and the like. Non-incumbent challengers turn to cognate strategies of developing clientelistic networks and distributing patronage—but, unlike their opponents, cannot draw on resources attached to or available via an office they hold.

IMPLICATIONS AND ASSESSMENT

Not just the complexity of "money politics," but also these practices' embeddedness in political culture, makes reform difficult. On the one hand, Duterte's win suggests that reliance on identifiable campaign themes persists—but his win is at the presidential level; local-level dynamics continue to center around patronage-based machines, the doling out of large quantities of cash, and underlying fears of malfeasance and/or coercion. If deeply entrenched patterns of patronage politics are to diminish in scope and salience, something else needs to take their place.

At the most basic, "band-aid" level, our research suggests the need for targeted strengthening of the Commission on Elections (COMELEC), both in terms of increased staffing (including for voter education on responsible voting) and perhaps of the ability to investigate without waiting for someone to file a complaint. The problem is more complex than candidates simply under-reporting standard campaign expenses and COMELEC being ill-equipped to investigate.[9] Distributions of money and gifts to voters would be unlikely to feature in those reports, regardless, requiring a smarter regulatory approach than simply raising unrealistically low campaign spending limits, monitoring licit spending, and scrutinizing campaign finance reports (Statements of Contributions and Expenditures) more carefully. For instance, COMELEC might consider best practices from elsewhere to determine new methods for tracking both financial inflows and outflows, or enact stiffer penalties to discourage offering payments for votes.

Looking beyond superficial remedies, we might ask what sort of parties the Philippines most needs if the goal is to shift away from personalistic,

---

9 Meanwhile, campaign overspending allegations and convictions are themselves part of the political game: in Laguna, one candidate, for instance, entered his son provisionally in his place in the gubernatorial race while he waited for COMELEC to exonerate him of charges his rival pressed, related to the 2013 election; he was belatedly cleared to contest. However, both his and his son's name remained on the ballot, splitting their votes.

patronage-laced appeals and toward more programmatic emphases. Closed-list proportional representation (CLPR) might be an option, given its capacity to create more party-centric incentives. This option is not without risks: Indonesia's experience, of within-party money politics and machinations, would likely be even more problematic in the clan-riddled Philippines. But arguably the greatest risk of all is the maintenance of the existing electoral system, the many elements of which (as noted in Chapter One) combine so effectively to undermine the strength and coherence of Philippine political parties. At present, ideology is essentially absent from the mainstream political landscape, offering little grounds to distinguish among parties beyond their respective rosters of candidates, proximity to national and provincial executives, and resources available. A core goal of electoral system redesign, based on careful study of comparative experience, would be to induce parties to develop differentiated and coherent platforms, to provide incentives for candidates to articulate these platforms, and thus eventually to shift the basis for voters' assessments. As we know from experience, good intentions and sincere pronouncements are not sufficient: segments within the LP claim to have begun this process prior to the 2016 election, in order to strengthen the party—apparently without substantial success, given how quickly the party declined in the wake of Duterte's victory. Well-designed electoral system reform is thus a necessary first step to creating effective incentives for the emergence of stronger parties.

One externality worth considering, though, if the Philippines moves toward parties, and not families, as the nodes of political allegiance: the dynastic system, for all its flaws, has propelled a significant number of women into office who might otherwise not have had that chance, given their lack of independent access to the sort of patronage resources and clientelist connections otherwise essential.[10] Empirically, too, even if sometimes structurally positioned merely as placeholders for term-limited male relatives (Carter Center 2016, 16), once in office, women need not, and frequently do not, act as such. As Socorro Reyes discusses in Chapter Five, the Philippines might consider some sort of quota system, "zipper" rule (requirement of alternating male and female candidates in a party list, with proportional representation rather than plurality/majoritarian voting), or other mechanism to encourage or oblige parties to include women not only among candidates, but among the ranks of party decision makers. The adoption of closed-list PR entails its own risks, as noted above, but at the same time provides opportunities not only to build stronger parties but also to promote greater degrees of women's political participation.

---

10 For a relevant exploration of these dynamics in Thailand, see Bjarnegård 2009.

While the risks of undue optimism are clear, the increasing salience of new media and social media in this election suggests the availability of new ways *both* to monitor corruption—since what fuels many of these election-time distributions are effectively side-payments from contracts in the intervening years—*and* to offer citizens new evidence and criteria with which to evaluate candidates. Incumbents might find themselves disadvantaged by the emergence of new techniques for others to smoke out corrupt deals, but very much advantaged by new opportunities to publicize their own achievements in policy making and in the delivery of patronage to their districts. And perhaps most problematically, reliance on these media requires that they be of reasonably high quality (as in the strong Philippine tradition of investigative journalism). Where media are of low quality, as was amply demonstrated in the concerted manipulation of social media in the 2016 elections, corruption monitoring is likely to be more distorting than revealing.

At the same time, there is no reason to expect that voters who based their decisions on the size of payments received were oblivious to or ignorant of the various candidates' qualities. Unless and until most citizens have, and know they have, equal access to state services, it may not be rational for many to prioritize a long-term, but abstract, policy record over an immediate, and likely one-time, payment. A core goal of electoral system reform, as explained in Chapter Two, is to move a polity from a candidate-centered system, marked by particularistic inducements, to a more party-centered political system oriented to the provision of national public goods that are critical to sustained developmental success. Concomitant to such a re-orientation, however, is the need for significant, meaningful improvement of public administration and the delivery of programmatic welfare services. One can hope, in other words, that successful electoral reform might put the spotlight as well on the longer-term but also critical task of building an effective bureaucracy able to deliver services more fairly and effectively to the Philippine citizenry. If so, the strengthening of two critical political institutions—political parties and the bureaucracy—could happily prove to be mutually reinforcing processes.

Between 1998 and 2016, an average of 104 party-list organizations participated in party-list elections. This 2016 ballot lists the more than 100 parties that vied for the 59 available seats in the Philippine House of Representatives; after the results had been tabulated, a record number of 46 party-list organizations received at least one seat.

Photograph from the Commission of Elections.

CHAPTER NINE
UNTANGLING THE PARTY LIST SYSTEM

JULIO C. TEEHANKEE

The 1987 Constitution introduced a novel pathway for marginalized sectors to be represented in the corridors of power, as one-fifth of the members of the House of Representatives came to be elected via a party list system (PLS) elected from one nationwide district. The remainder of the House has continued to be elected on the basis of the system retained from the 1935 Constitution, namely "first past the post" (FPTP) or single-member district plurality: one member from each district, with the winner needing to win the largest number of votes (i.e., a plurality). The Philippines was thus adopting a mixed electoral system, as had a number of other countries around the world (including Japan, New Zealand, Italy, and Russia) (Dunleavy and Margetts 1995; Scheiner 2008). Aside from this surface similarity, however, the Philippine PLS has core features—as discussed below—that make it unique among the world's electoral systems.

Reform constituencies initially acknowledged the promise of the PLS but were later frustrated by its sloppy implementation (Rodriguez and Velasco 1998; Garcia 1998; Santos, 1998; Rodriguez 2002; Pangalangan 2011). Since its inception, the Philippine PLS has been saddled by problems of definition, implementation, and interpretation. Most fundamentally, the system is highly disproportional and thus distorts the democratic will by allocating seats in a manner quite at odds with the preferences of the electorate. Despite its original intentions, moreover, the PLS has failed in its objective of fostering greater political participation by those sectors of Philippine society that are marginalized and underrepresented. As it generates dozens of tiny parties, finally, the PLS contributes to the weakness and incoherence of the Philippine party system. Whereas political parties are meant to *aggregate* societal interests, the PLS *splinters* them instead.

Not a few sectors have declared it a failure and some even call for its abolition (Wurfel 1997; Tuazon 2007, 2011; Tucay 2016). *This chapter argues that the solution is not to abolish the PLS but rather to reform and strengthen it by instituting the features of a closed-list proportional representation (CLPR) system as generally practiced in other parts of the world.* The current mixed electoral system should stay in place, in order to retain the essential grounding of geographic representation, but it is time to reform the party-list component with three major objectives: 1) make it truly proportional, and thus more reflective of the democratic will; 2) use the capacity of CLPR to promote very systematically the political participation of marginalized and underrepresented groups (including women, minorities, and the poor); and 3) tap the enormous potential of CLPR to strengthen not only parties but the party system as a whole.

ELECTORAL SYSTEM DESIGN AND POLITICAL PARTIES

Political institutions provide the "rules of the game" that govern the practice of democracy. The electoral system is generally viewed as the most malleable among political institutions, and the choice of electoral system not only determines how votes are translated into legislative seats but also shapes the type of party system that develops. As explained by Reynolds et al., the "number and relative sizes of political parties in the legislature...is heavily influenced by the electoral system" (2008, 6). Electoral systems also play an important role in influencing voter behavior as well as in shaping the processes through which political power is transferred and policies are made. Indeed, as Allen Hicken explains in Chapter Two, the way in which electoral systems "shape the capacities and incentives of key actors and decision makers" helps to influence a country's "level and pattern of development." From the standpoint of democracy, an electoral system provides two major functions: to represent the multifaceted interests in society (*representation*) and to transform votes into seats or mandates (*integration*) (Gallagher and Mitchell 2005; Reilly 2006; Reynolds et al. 2008).

Principles of electoral systems can be defined according to two criteria: the formula of decision and the objective of representation (Nohlen 1984).

- *Formula of decision refers to the formula by which electoral winners or losers are determined.* Plurality and majoritarian systems involve the election of individual candidates or personalities, and the winning candidate must obtain a plurality or majority of votes. Because the losing candidates get nothing, these are sometimes referred to as "winner-takes-all" systems. On the other hand, proportional representation systems usually involve election of party lists: it is the share of votes that determines the (multiple) winners, with the proportion of seats won based as closely as possible on the number of votes received.

- *Objective of representation addresses the functions that representation should fulfill in legislative assemblies.* For plurality and majoritarian systems, the key objective is the formation of a legislative majority, while in proportional representation the primary goal is to reflect the structure of the electorate.

TABLE 9.1: MAJORITARIAN AND PROPORTIONAL
REPRESENTATION ELECTORAL SYSTEMS

Basic Types of Electoral Systems	Formula of Decision	Objective of Representation
Plurality and majoritarian systems	The plurality (or majority) wins	Formation of a legislative majority
Proportional representation system	The share of votes decides	Reflection of the structure of the electorate

Adapted from Nohlen 1984

Moreover, the choice of electoral system also influences the type of political party system that will develop: two-party or multiparty system. A political party system cannot be legislated; rather, it emerges to a significant degree from the choice of electoral system. French political scientist Maurice Duverger observed that a two-party system usually emerges from plurality and majoritarian electoral systems, while a multiparty system usually emerges from a proportional electoral system. This is due to two underlying reasons. First is the *mechanical effect* under plurality or majoritarian ("winner-takes-all") electoral systems, which make it difficult for small parties to win seats. Second is the *psychological effect* in which voters are less inclined to vote for smaller parties where their votes can be wasted (Benoit 2001; Farrel 1997; Grofman and Lijphart 2003; Gerring 2005).

In recent years, a number of countries have shifted from either a pure majoritarian or pure proportional representative electoral system to a mixed electoral system (MES). Massicotte and Blais (1999, 345) define MES as "the combination of different electoral formulas (plurality or PR; majority or PR) for an election to a single body." Typically, voters will cast one vote in a plurality/majority contest and one vote in a proportional representation contest (not unlike the current Philippine system, where voters cast one vote for their district representative via FPTP and one vote in the PLS).

Essentially, the MES combines the direct election of legislators in geographically defined districts with some form of a list proportional representation system (List PR).[1] As shown in Table 9.2, there are two broad subtypes of the MES, one "compensatory" and the other "non-compensatory".

- *Compensatory, or mixed-member proportional (MMP) system.* This is a "mixed system in which the choices expressed by the voters are used to elect representatives through two different systems—one List PR system and (usually) one plurality or majority system—where the List PR system compensates for the disproportionality in the results from the plurality/majority system" (Reynolds et al. 2008, 95). The MMP, as practised in Germany, links two tiers and compensates for any disproportionality produced by the district seat results. For example, a party that wins 10 percent of the national vote but doesn't win any district seats can be compensated in the PR List to receive as many as 10 percent of the legislative seats.

- *Non-compensatory, or parallel system.* This is a "mixed system in which the choices expressed by the voters are used to elect representatives through two different systems—one List PR system and (usually) one plurality/majority system—but where no account is taken of the seats allocated under the first system in calculating the results in the second system" (Reynolds et al. 2008, 104). Unlike in MMP, therefore, the parallel system does not link the tiers and does not compensate seats. Even so, minority parties nonetheless still have ample opportunities to win seats in the proportional representative portion of the election.

At least in theory, the non-compensatory parallel system should lead to less party system fragmentation as compared to the compensatory MMP (Reynolds et al. 2008, 91).

TABLE 9.2: TYPES OF MIXED ELECTORAL SYSTEMS

Mixed Electoral System	Linkage	Allocation of Seats
Mixed-member proportional	Yes	Compensatory
Parallel system	No	Non-compensatory

Adapted from Shugart and Wattenberg 2001

---

1 As explained in Chapter Three, there are two major types of list proportional representation: closed-list PR (CLPR) and open-list PR (OLPR). For reasons discussed below, I advocate CLPR for its capacity to strengthen party institutions relative to the personalistic, candidate-centered orientation that currently prevails in Philippine politics.

HOW DOES THE PHILIPPINE PARTY LIST SYSTEM COMPARE WITH STANDARD PR SYSTEMS?

As noted at the outset, the party list system in its current form in the Philippines is unique among the electoral systems of the world. As a foundation for the proposals that I will present in this chapter, it is important to understand the key differences between PLS and a standard PR system.

As explained by Australian political scientist Ben Reilly, there are three characteristics of standard PR worthy of particular emphasis:

> *First*, there is no upper limit on the number of seats that a party can receive. For example, a party that wins two-thirds (or more) of the vote should win two-thirds (or more) of the seats.

> *Second*, in order to rule out parties with very low support levels, a minimum vote threshold of between 3–5 percent is commonly applied. This deters small fringe groups from entering the legislature.

> *Third*, all parties are allowed to compete (i.e., the system is not reserved for specific types of parties representing specific constituencies) (Reilly 2016, emphasis added).

The Philippine party list system operates in very different ways. As Reilly further explains, "any party, group or coalition receiving at least 2% of the votes wins a seat, up to a maximum of three seats in total."[2] There are three key features that distinguish it, quite dramatically, from a standard PR system:

> *First*, the three-seat ceiling goes against the principle of proportionality. *If a party were to obtain 20% of the vote, it would still be given only three seats.* In a truly proportional system, a party obtaining 20% of vote would get 20% of the available 59 seats, or at least 11 seats.

---

2 The 1995 PLS law mandates that a house seat is allocated to a party-list organization "if it gets at least 2 percent of the total number of votes cast for the party list system (Sec. 11). It also provides parties garnering more than 2 percent of the votes additional seats in proportion to their total number of votes . . . .However, Sec. 11(5) established a 'cap' on the number of seats that political parties in the list system can win" (Manacsa and Tan 2005, 758).

At the other end of spectrum, parties with very low popularity can also end up winning some of the remaining seats once the more popular parties have reached their limit. *In other words, the percentage of seats that they obtain can be significantly greater than their percentage of the vote.*

Second, there is no [clear-cut] minimum vote threshold in the Philippine party-list system. This reinforces the opportunity for a party of very low popularity to gain a seat in Congress.

Third, the system was originally limited to "marginalized groups" such as youth, labour, the urban poor, farmers, fisherfolk, and women. With major parties still unable to compete directly (as long as they are also contesting seats in the district elections), the goal is for party-list representatives to bring more diversity to Congress and to inject some new voices into government processes. In practice, however, some traditional politicians learned to use the party-list system to enhance their own voices in Congress— albeit in the name of marginalized sectors. It remains common for politicians to use the party list to enter Congress when their relatives have already filled up the district seats (Reilly 2016, emphasis added).

ISSUES WITH THE CURRENT PARTY LIST SYSTEM

The Philippine PLS is beset with problems. These can broadly be found across two categories that correspond to the two major democratic functions of an electoral system as explained above: integration and representation.

- *Issues of integration* relate to the translation of votes into seats and mandates.
  - o The three-seat cap on the number of seats not only distorts proportionality but also fragments the vote across a large number of very small parties. This, quite obviously, undermines the fundamental role of political parties in aggregating (rather than splintering) societal interests.
  - o The absence of a clear minimum-vote threshold results in a proliferation of parties—some of which, as noted above, may enjoy very minimal levels of popular support.

- *Issues of representation* refers to the goal of ensuring that a broad spectrum of societal interests are represented in the legislature. The PLS was originally intended to represent marginalized sectors, but has been captured to a significant extent by elite and other interests. There has also been considerable confusion in the interpretation of sectoral and proportional representation, not to mention the impossibility of listing down all the sectors in society to be represented in the legislature.

INTEGRATION: THE TRANSLATION OF VOTES INTO SEATS

If an electoral system is unable to translate votes into seats or mandates that will form legislative or governing majorities, it is failing to perform one of its core functions. The Philippine PLS, through its generation of a large number of political parties, does little to contribute to this goal. As demonstrated in Table 9.3, the numbers are quite extraordinary: between 1998 (when the party list system was put into operation) and 2016, an average of 104 party-list organizations participated in the party-list elections and the average number of winning parties exceeded 25! This underperformance can be directly traced to basic deficiencies in the PLS brought about by the three-seat limit and the unclear minimum electoral threshold (Muga 2007; Rivera 2007). In addition, as discussed further below, conflicting interpretations of the law have also contributed to the underutilization of the party-list seats: an average of only 34 seats out of the 50-plus seats have been filled up during these seven electoral cycles.

TABLE 9.3: PHILIPPINE PARTY-LIST ELECTIONS: 1998–2016

Party-List Election	Total Number of Available Seats	Actual Number of Seats Allocated	Number of Winning Parties	Number of Participating Parties
1998	52	14	13	122
2001	52	20	12	46
2004	53	24	16	66
2007	55	23	17	92
2010	57	41	31	150
2013	59	59	43	136
2016	59	59	46	116
Averages	55.3	34.3	25.4	104

Adapted from Muga 2011

The extreme proliferation and fragmentation of party list organizations have hindered the maturation of the party list system. As a formula for electoral decision, the Philippine party list system has directly gone against the very notion of *proportional* representation. According to mathematician Felix P. Muga II (2007a, 107), "the principle of proportional representation is negated by the seat allocation method specified in the [1995] Party-List System Act...which contradicts its statement that it is the policy of the State to promote proportional representation in the election of representatives to the House of Representatives."

Another source of major confusion for the PLS is the interpretation of the seat allocation formula of the Party List Law (as summarized in Table 9.4). Given the lack of a clear proportional formula in the law, COMELEC has had to struggle with various interpretations in allocating seats for the PLS. Initially, COMELEC only allocated seats to those parties that obtained 2 percent of the total votes cast for the party list election, and did not allocate any additional seats to fill up the (then 52) reserved party list seats. This changed with the interpretation handed down by the Supreme Court in a 2000 decision, *Veterans Federation Party, et al. v. COMELEC*. This interpretation, popularly called the Panganiban formula, allocates seats on the basis of the number of votes obtained by the top-performing party. As Felix Muga explains, it uses "the first party's additional seats and its votes to compute the additional number of seats for those parties that qualified to obtain a seat" by meeting the 2 percent threshold (Muga, 2007a, 107). Nine years later, in the 2009 decision on *BANAT, et al. v. COMELEC*, the Supreme Court applied the so-called Carpio formula and declared the 2 percent threshold unconstitutional as regards additional seats. In doing so, the Supreme Court managed to move the PLS even further away from the principle of proportionality: not only (as provided in the 1995 law) are parties that obtain *high numbers of votes* limited to a mere three seats, but now (with the 2009 decision) parties that obtain *less than 2 percent* of the vote are nonetheless able to seat candidates in the House of Representatives. Thus the basic precept of proportionality is violated in a new way, as parties with minimal popularity receive a percentage of seats in excess of the percentage of votes they have received from the electorate.

TABLE 9.4: SEAT ALLOCATIONS UNDER THE PHILIPPINE PARTY LIST SYSTEM

Method	Mechanics	Legal Basis
COMELEC formula	One seat awarded for every 2 percent of votes received for the party-list election with a 3-seat cap.[3] As shown in Table 9.3, only 14 of 52 available seats were allocated in the 1998 election, the only instance in which this formula was in place.	The Party-List System Act of 1995 (Republic Act 7941)
Panganiban formula	The number of seats to be obtained by those parties exceeding the 2 percent threshold is dependent on the number of votes received by the top-performing party. Only the top-performing party is entitled to the maximum of 3 seats, while its "excess" votes are allocated to other parties (thus enhancing their prospects for gaining additional seats).	Supreme Court G.R. No. 136781 (Veterans Federation Party et al. v. COMELEC), 2000
Carpio formula	Two percent threshold applies only to the first seat of winning party list organizations. If the number of seats allocated has not been filled up, additional seats shall be awarded to less-popular qualifying parties even if they have not reached the 2 percent threshold.	Supreme Court G.R. No. 179271 (BANAT et al. v. COMELEC), 2009

Collated by author from Supreme Court decisions

Under the current system, based on the Carpio formula, those parties that garner more than 2 percent of total votes are sure to receive one seat each. Additional seats are then proportionally distributed to succeeding parties that did not breach the 2 percent threshold (starting with those closest to receiving 2

---

3 This was based on the Neimeyer formula, which was originally envisioned as the proper seat allocation formula for the PLS in the original 1995 enabling law but rejected in 2000 by the majority decision in the Veterans Federation Party case. Under the Neimeyer formula—borrowed very roughly from Germany's system of standard PR, which of course has no ceiling on the number of seats that a party may obtain—seat allocation per party is computed by multiplying the total number of available seats by the total votes of the party list organization, and then dividing that sum by the total number of votes of parties which reached 2 percent.

percent of the votes) until all the remaining seats are allocated.[4] The application of the Carpio formula in 2009 has thus increased the utilization of the available party-list seats—from less than half in the first four elections (1998–2007) to roughly 70 percent of seats in the 2010 election to 100 percent of available seats in 2013 and 2016.

Across the past two decades, there has been an enormous degree of attention to the formulae used to allocate one-fifth of the seats of the House of Representatives—with, as noted above, three major rulings by either COMELEC or the Supreme Court. In recent years, moreover, there have been additional proposals to address the deficiencies of the seat allocation of the Party List Law. The ultimate cause of this contention is a fundamentally flawed PLS, diverging as it does so dramatically from standard PR electoral systems. The three-seat ceiling penalizes those parties that have been able to obtain a higher proportion of the vote. As Muga concludes, "[t]his in effect denies these parties of the seats that [are] rightfully theirs. Hence, the 3-seat cap violates the democratic concept of proportional representation which is one of the principles of social justice." And the lack of a clear minimum electoral threshold means that some parties receiving less than 2 percent of total votes are nonetheless able to obtain seats after the more popular parties have come up against the three-seat ceiling. *The easiest way to resolve the problem, therefore, is not by further tinkering with the PLS formulae but rather by reforming and strengthening the entire system through the adoption of standard PR arrangements that have been tried and tested in other parts of the world.*

ISSUES OF REPRESENTATION

Much of the criticism against the current PLS is targeted at the bastardization of its original objectives of representing the interests of the so-called marginalized sectors of society. Section 5 of Article VI of the 1987 Constitution enumerates these sectors as "labor, peasant, urban poor, indigenous cultural communities, women, youth, and such other sectors as may be provided by law, except the religious sector." The 1995 Party List Law expands the list of sectors to include: "labor, peasant, fisherfolk, urban poor, indigenous cultural communities, elderly, handicapped,

---

4 The Carpio formula uses and modifies what is known as the Hare quota system. As Japanese academic Masataka Kimura explains, the "product of the percentage of votes (the number of votes garnered by each party divided by the total number of votes cast) multiplied by the number of remaining seats is used as the basis of allocation. Interestingly, while only the integer value of the product is used and the fraction is ignored when the product is more than one, those parties whose products are less than one receive a seat until all the remaining seats are allocated" (2013, 73). In other words, remainders are not rounded off to award additional seats, but parties that receive less than the full two percentage points are awarded seats.

women, youth, veterans, overseas workers, and professionals." As a mechanism for sectoral representation, the PLS has failed miserably in enhancing the political participation of marginalized and underrepresented sectors of Philippine society.

From the outset, the framers of the 1987 Constitution were confused about the distinction between sectoral and proportional representation. According to David Wurfel (1997, 20), proportional representation (PR), "implemented through a party-list ballot, is designed to make the number of seats in the legislature proportional to the votes cast—whereas in a single-member district system, the largest party is grossly overrepresented, and minor parties are shut out." As a formula for electoral decision, proportionality means that the share of the total votes cast determine an election. By producing a closer ratio between votes and seats in the legislature, PR systems "intend to reflect as exactly as possible the social forces and political groups in the population" (Nohlen 1984).

On the other hand, sectoral representation can be traced to the corporatist practice of Latin American dictatorships as they appointed cooperative "representatives" from various sectors of society. This was first introduced in the Philippines by the Marcos dictatorship. Ironically, the provision for sectoral representation was assiduously supported by anti-Marcos activists among the Commissioners who drafted the 1987 Constitution. Commissioner Christian Monsod, at the beginning, attempted to clarify the conceptual confusion by stating that "[t]he proposal for the party-list system is not synonymous with that of sectoral representation. Precisely, the party-list system seeks to avoid the dilemma of choice of sectors . . . if this body accepts the party-list system, we do not even have to mention sectors, because . . . there can be sectoral parties within the party-list system" (Wurfel 1997, 22).

Nonetheless, the Constitutional Commission eventually approved the provision for a party list system with a hybrid of sectoral and proportional representation. This constitutional provision became the basis for the passage of the 1995 Party List Law, which perpetuated the confusion earlier found in constitutional deliberations. As Rodriguez and Velasco (1998, 13) observed, "The party-list law is not clear whether it wishes to establish sectoral or proportional representation . . . . By listing sectors it gives the impression that these sectors must be represented, or that all parties, organizations, or coalitions must belong to these sectors. By listing sectors, it has even given the impression that seats will be reserved for sectors listed." This confusion would eventually impact negatively on the implementation and interpretation of the PLS in succeeding elections.

While the implementing law expanded the list of sectors from six to twelve, Wurfel explains, "there are no provisions for refusing to register parties or groups formed around other, unnamed sectors. The only restriction on any sector is that a nominee of the youth sector may not be more than 30 years of age on election day (Section 9). But, of course, there is no age restriction on those who may vote for a youth nominee" (1997, 22).

Eventually, the conceptual confusion and forced hybridization of sectoral and proportional representation resulted in inconsistent implementation by COMELEC in subsequent elections. This was reflected in the incoherent accreditation process utilized by the electoral commission to accredit many non-marginalized sectors (i.e., electric cooperatives, dentists, doctors, security agencies, realtors, publishers, etc.); and to disqualify genuinely marginalized sectors (e.g., those who identify as gay, lesbian, bisexual, and transgender) (Rodriguez 2002; Manalansan 2007).

Another major point of contention is disagreement over the primary objective of representation. Is it to serve as a social justice tool for the marginalized sectors or is it to expand the party system (Tan 2008)? One of the members of the 1986 Constitutional Commission, Rene V. Sarmiento, explicitly stated that the PLS is "a social justice tool and a people empowerment vehicle...a window for the Filipino poor to partake in the affairs of the State (Congress) which is traditionally dominated by parties with well-oiled and funded electoral machineries" (2011, 218).

No less than the Supreme Court was forced to wrestle with these core question about the nature of the PLS. In the landmark case, *Ang Bagong Bayani, et al. v. COMELEC* (2001), Justice Artemio V. Panganiban wrote,

> The party-list system is a social justice tool designed not only to give more law to the great masses of our people who have less in life, but also to enable them to become veritable lawmakers themselves, empowered to participate directly in the enactment of laws designed to benefit them. It intends to make the marginalized and the underrepresented not merely passive recipients of the State's benevolence, but active participants in the mainstream of representative democracy. Thus, allowing all individuals and groups, including those which now dominate district elections, to have the same opportunity to participate in party-list elections would desecrate this lofty objective and mongrelize the social justice mechanism into an atrocious veneer for traditional politics.

For more than a decade, *Ang Bagong Bayani* served to ensure that participation in the PLS was limited to representatives of marginalized and underprivileged sectors. However, the high court again redefined the nature of the PLS in another landmark case, *Atong Paglaum, et al. v. COMELEC* (2013), where Justice Antonio T. Carpio wrote that "the party-list system is not for sectoral parties only, but also for non-sectoral parties." Torres-Pilapil enumerates the differences between *Atong Paglaum* and *Ang Bagong Bayani as follows,*

Whereas *Ang Bagong Bayani* ruled that the party list is exclusively for parties and organizations that represent the marginalized and underrepresented sectors, *Atong Paglaum* ruled that the party list is now also open to national and regional parties and organizations that are not organized along sectoral lines and do not represent any marginalized and underrepresented sectors. Whereas *Ang Bagong Bayani* ruled that political parties that dominated the single-member district elections for the House of Representatives in 1995 are barred from the party list, *Atong Paglaum* ruled that any political party that runs candidates in the single-member district elections can now participate in the party list through its sectoral wing. And whereas *Ang Bagong Bayani* ruled that the nominees themselves must belong to the marginalized and underrepresented sectors they represent, *Atong Paglaum* ruled that for the nominees of sectoral parties, a track record in representing the marginalized and underrepresented sectors is enough (2015, 86).

THE WAY FORWARD

Informed by close to two decades of implementing the Philippine PLS, the following reforms are proposed to address the deficiencies of the current electoral system. It is envisioned that the members of the proposed National Assembly under an amended constitution shall be elected under a parallel mixed electoral system where 60 percent are elected in single-member districts through a first past the post (FPTP) system and 40 percent through a closed-list proportional representation (CLPR) system.

PARALLEL MIXED ELECTORAL SYSTEM

The mixed electoral system provides the best of both the FPTP and CLPR electoral systems. The very substantial FPTP component will not only ensure continuing attention to district-based interest and concerns but also provide a strong sense of continuity with the existing system. It will, moreover, stabilize the party fragmentation (i.e., proliferation of many small parties) usually associated with proportional representation systems.

The proper implementation of the CLPR component can be expected to promote a greater degree of party discipline, as well as a greater focus on party platforms and programs (as opposed to the current system, which focuses to a large degree on pork, patronage, and personalities). In a CLPR system, as explained in Chapter Three, the party both chooses and ranks the candidates. Should candidates fail to adhere to their party's positions once they are in office, they may be either dropped from the subsequent list of candidates or given a much lower ranking. This shift in incentive structures can be expected to help move the Philippines from its current candidate-centric system to a more strongly party-based system—with all of the benefits (for democracy and development) that are enunciated in Chapters One and Two.

In addition, increasing the number of party list seats will provide more opportunities for the representation of marginalized sectors. Regular parties must be encouraged to accommodate sectors (i.e., women, workers, farmers, LGBT, etc.) in its party list nominees. For gender balance, it is also worth exploring the introduction of reserved seats in the nomination of CLPR through a "zipper" system (as explained in Reyes's Chapter Five). *Following Ang Bayani, the CLPR should provide preferential treatment to the economically marginalized and underrepresented sectors including minorities, but also in line with Atong Paglaum, regular political parties can participate only through their sectoral wings. Moreover, sectoral representatives should actually belong to the sector they represent.*

In order to promote program-based and disciplined parties, anti-party switching rules and public financing of parties should be provided in the Constitution. Another innovative proposal is the recognition of political parties as public institutions instead of semi-private organizations. Strict requirements (i.e. membership, chapter organizations, party programs, etc.) for registration of regular parties should be implemented. Following Indonesia (see Chapter Six), this should include a requirement that parties be national in scope. This is critical to ensuring that the political system is oriented to national public goods over local particularistic interests (the importance of which is emphasized in Chapter Two).

WHY CLOSED-LIST RATHER THAN OPEN-LIST PROPORTIONAL REPRESENTATION?

As explained in Chapter Three, there are two major types of proportional representation: open list and closed list. The majority of PR systems in the world are closed, meaning that the order of candidates elected by that list is fixed by the party itself, and voters are not able to express a preference for a particular candidate. A party is empowered to determine the manner by which it presents its candidates to the electorate, and this orients incentives towards the promotion of parties instead of personalities. At the same time, many List PR systems in Western Europe use open lists, in which voters can indicate not just their favored party but their favored candidate within that party (Reynolds et al. 2008). Since Philippine parties are generally weak, and the larger political system already candidate- and personality-centered, it would be better to promote closed-list PR.

The Philippines can learn from the experience of other ASEAN countries. Thailand's adoption of CLPR under their 1997 Constitution stabilized and promoted strong political parties (e.g., Thaksin's Thai Rak Thai, since dismantled through military intervention). In Indonesia, as explained in Chapter Six, the shift from CLPR to OLPR has had very negative consequences—weakening parties in favor of individual candidates. The Philippine PLS has similarities to a CLPR system in that "voters vote for a party and the rank order of its nominees is predetermined by the party" (Kimura 2013, 69). As explained above, however, there are fundamental differences between PLS and standard PR systems—including the lack of proportionality in the former.

In addition, I am urging a doubling in the percentage of seats allocated by party-list mechanisms: from the 20 percent PLS in the current mixed electoral system to 40 percent CLPR in a new mixed system. This will greatly enhance opportunities for political participation of those who are currently marginalized and underrepresented.

SEAT ALLOCATIONS

One of the basic flaws in the current party list system is how seats are allocated. The current system has a "ceiling" in terms of the three-seat cap but doesn't have a "floor" in terms of threshold since the 2009 Supreme Court decision declared the 2 percent threshold on additional seats to be unconstitutional. Generally, a high threshold serves to limit the entry of too many parties. A lower or no threshold, on the other hand, allows for the participation of smaller parties but at the risk of party fragmentation and the entry of extremist parties. Learning from our experience in implementing the party list system, it is imperative that the three-seat cap be removed since it distorts the principle of proportionality. A 2 percent threshold for CLPR seats should be maintained as an entry pass in order to eliminate fly-by-night party-list organizations and to prevent party fragmentation.

DISTRICT MAGNITUDE

District magnitude, which is the number of members to be elected in each electoral district, is one of the crucial determinants of the degree of proportionality in translating votes into seats. Large district magnitude, as explained by Allen Hicken in Chapter Two, "is associated with legislative seats going to many small parties." This can help to encourage a greater degree of proportionality. Small district magnitude, on the other hand, "is associated with relatively fewer and larger political parties winning legislative seats." This produces less proportionality as compared to larger district magnitude, and at the extreme (e.g., a district magnitude of only two seats) tends "to undermine the benefits of PR in terms of representation and legitimacy" (Reynolds et al. 2008, 82). [5]

As districts are made larger, however, the link between elected legislators and their constituents grows weaker. This may be less of a concern in a system that retains a strong role for geographic representation through FPTP (as I am proposing), but there is nevertheless a need to craft the district magnitude for the CLPR system in such a way as to derive the optimal mix of proportionality and representativeness. According to Reynolds et al. (2008, 82), "district magnitudes of between three and seven seats tend to work quite well, and it has been suggested that odd numbers such as three, five and seven work better in practice than even numbers." The possibility of electing CLPR by regions should be seriously studied—albeit with the caveat that parties should (following the example of Indonesia[6]) be strictly regulated to ensure that they are national in scope. A medium district magnitude would enable parties of relatively moderate size to gain seats—while at the same time providing incentives for excessively small parties to merge and coalesce and thus have better chances of translating votes into seats. Ideological and progressive parties can also be mobilized to directly confront and challenge the entrenched political dynasties in the regions. *Regardless of the size of district magnitude, it is critical to follow the example of Indonesia and ensure that parties are strictly regulated to ensure that they are national in scope—and thus oriented to national goals and the provision of national public goods.*

CONCLUSION

Close to two decades since the Philippines implemented its party list system, many lessons have been learned regarding electoral engineering. These lessons can serve as valuable inputs in reforming the electoral system that is to be incorporated into the proposed New Constitution of the Federal Republic of the Philippines. This chapter has highlighted the fundamental flaws of the PLS, most importantly

---

5 Currently, the party list system treats the entire country as a single district. One might therefore expect that it would nurture substantial proportionality. It does not, however, due to the presence of the three-seat ceiling and the unclear electoral threshold. As explained above, these flaws in the PLS very directly violate the principle of proportionality.

6 With the exception of the Indonesian province of Aceh, as explained in Chapter Six.

its lack of proportionality, its failure to promote the political participation of the marginalized sectors, and its contribution to the already substantial weakness of Philippine political parties and to the Philippine party system as a whole.

Despite the flaws of the existing party list system, the goal should not be to abolish it but rather to strengthen it. A new electoral system has enormous potential to change the underlying incentives of politicians and thus to begin to change existing patterns of Philippine politics. The most promising reform, in my view, would be to adopt a new type of mixed electoral system that maintains a substantial role for FPTP but combines it with features of a closed-list proportional representation as practised elsewhere in the world. According to Reynolds et al., "Most countries that have changed electoral systems have done so in the direction of more proportionality, either by adding a PR element to a plurality system (making it a Parallel or MMP system) or by completely replacing their old system with List PR. *The most common switch has been from a plurality/ majority system to a mixed system, and there is not one example of a change in the opposite direction*" (2008, 23; emphasis added).

A future mixed electoral system for the Philippine House of Representatives should, in my view, have the following components. First, 60 percent of seats should continue to be elected via FPTP, and thus ensure a strong basis of geographic representation. Second, the party-list component should be expanded from 20 percent to 40 percent and thus provide more opportunities for the representation of marginalized sectors. Third, the party-list component should be reconfigured into a genuinely proportional system by removing the three-seat cap and enabling political parties to obtain a share of seats that is proportional to the share of votes received. Fourth, in order to avoid the excessive splintering in the number of parties, the 2 percent threshold for first seats should be retained. Fifth, district magnitude (the number of seats elected from each district) will need to be crafted in such a way as to balance considerations of proportionality and representativeness. Sixth and finally, in order to strengthen the capacity of the system to achieve its original goal of empowering those who are currently marginalized and underrepresented, we can draw on creative adaptations of the closed-list proportional representation system as found internationally (including, for example, a "zipper system" that mandates parties to list women and men alternatively in their party list). In sum, CLPR offers enormous potential to change the nature of Philippine political parties and to strengthen the perennially weak Philippine party system. By enhancing party discipline, CLPR puts greater focus on party platforms and programs and thus undercuts many core problems of Philippine politics—namely its focus on pork, patronage, and personalities. Let us hope indeed that such a "change is coming."

Names of candidates have long overshadowed party labels in Philippine election posters and banners. At the entrance to a polling place in Cebu City in 2004, banners are hung in support of individual candidates—including those running for the Philippine Senate and the local city council. These are two of the many Philippine legislative bodies elected via the multi-member plurality system, which by its very nature undermines the value of a party label and encourages candidates to develop personalized networks of support that are independent of party.

Photograph by Paul D. Hutchcroft

CHAPTER TEN
THE MULTI-MEMBER PLURALITY SYSTEM IN THE PHILIPPINES AND ITS IMPLICATIONS

NICO RAVANILLA

INTRODUCTION

Of the over 18,000 posts at stake every election in the Philippines, about 80 percent are decided by the multi-member plurality system (MPS). These include seats for twelve nationally elected senators, twenty-four members of the regional assembly of the Autonomous Region in Muslim Mindanao, 776 provincial board members, and 13,450 city and municipal councilors. The MPS is simply the use of plurality voting in multi-member districts: the candidates with the most votes win, even if they have not managed to secure a majority of the votes.[1] As it applies in the Philippines, MPS gives voters as many votes as there are seats to be filled in their district, as well as the ability to vote for individual candidates regardless of party affiliation.

Notwithstanding the extensive use of MPS in the Philippines, it hardly takes the spotlight in the discourse on the discontent with democracy in the country. The absence of well-functioning political parties, the economic and financial dominance of the major political families, and the particularistic response of elected officials to citizens' demands are, by and large, attributed to "deep" institutions—persistent informal rules that operate at the micro-level (North, 1990). The usual suspects include norms such as the importance of patron-client ties; the central role of the Filipino family in social network structures; and the strength of regional and linguistic affinities (Timberman, 1991). Other problems are viewed as a product of American colonial legacies: the exclusion of the masses and elite hegemony over democratic institutions; the provincial basis of national politics; and a powerful presidency (De Dios 2007; Hutchcroft and Rocamora 2012). Much less attention is given to electoral rules. Yet rules such as the MPS shape the incentives of

---

1 In the political science literature, the MPS is also known as the "block vote." I avoid using the latter term, however, since it tends to have a different meaning in the Philippines (as it is often used to refer to straight-party voting). As explained in Chapter Three, MPS is one of the two major types of plurality systems. When there is one member per district, it is appropriately called a single-member district plurality (SDMP) system, or, alternatively, first past the post (FPTP). When there is more than one member per district, we speak of MPS.

political elites and the function of party-like organizations not only during election campaigns but also while holding office. Institutions, by their very nature, are self-reinforcing and require rather heroic efforts or extraordinary events to be overcome. *Electoral rules are malleable in comparison.* Therefore, bringing electoral rules to the fore of the debate is important because of their potential to improve democratic accountability and undermine Philippine democracy's pernicious institutions.

In this chapter, I bring MPS to the centerstage of the discourse. In particular, I explore how MPS creates a range of incentives for political actors to behave in ways that strengthen or impair democratic accountability. I discuss features specific to each of the elective offices where MPS is used, and analyze how the system a) encourages intra-party competition, b) produces multiple short-lived coalitions, and c) weakens the incentives of politicians to respond to broad constituencies. Given that MPS is the system used in the selection of over 14,000 of the country's some 18,000 elected officials, it is safe to conclude that the deficiencies of MPS translate quite directly into deficiencies of Philippine democracy more generally. I then draw lessons from countries that formerly used versions of MPS and decided to move away from them—in particular, Japan and Thailand—and recommend pathways for reform. I focus on the advantages of retaining the multi-member nature of districts while shifting to closed-list proportional representation (CLPR), and discuss complementary non-electoral reforms that would reinforce the efficacy of redesigning the electoral system.

MULTI-MEMBER PLURALITY SYSTEM IN SENATE ELECTIONS

SENATE ELECTIONS

One of the more attractive features of MPS is that it is straightforward and easy to use. The fact that voters can choose individual candidates becomes especially handy when choosing nationally elected senatorial candidates. There are twenty-four members of the Senate. Senators sit for six-year terms, with half of the seats for reelection every three years, so each voter may vote for up to twelve candidates. Because senators are elected by plurality-at-large voting by the entire national electorate, choosing senatorial candidates is analogous to choosing a presidential candidate, except voters may use as many, or as few, votes as they wish.

IMPLICATIONS OF MPS IN SENATE ELECTIONS

At the same time, one of the implications of the MPS is that it tends to undermine the value of a party label and encourages candidates to develop personalized networks of support that are independent of party (Carey and

Shugart 1995; Hicken 2009). Candidates for the Senate, by necessity, compete with as many as eleven co-partisans and this intraparty competition means that relying primarily on party labels as a campaign tool is a poor strategy (Hicken and Ravanilla 2015). When candidates need to differentiate themselves from members of their own party, it can obviously not be on the basis of a different party platform.

Given intraparty competition, the most successful candidates are those who are able to employ a combination of strategies for developing large, personally tailored national followings. Candidates whose bases of electoral support are their regional/co-ethnic-lingual supporters differentiate themselves by engaging in traditional styles of building a personal vote—providing constituency services, promising material benefits (pork barrel and other forms of patronage), and making personalistic appeals to local leaders in their home regions. Constituency services, material benefits, and personalistic appeals are also very effective means of cultivating votes from the very densely populated National Capital Region (NCR). Incumbents that have served multiple terms in office are most likely to have developed the networks to extend patronage and clientelistic linkages with local vote brokers beyond their home region. This is a strategy commonly undertaken by senators with presidential and vice-presidential ambitions.

However, given the nationwide size of the electorate, relying on regional/ethno-lingual affinities with local brokers and voters is no longer enough to secure seats for many senatorial candidates. Most of them have to rely on other means of mobilizing votes. Table 10.1 summarizes strategies that proved most successful in the past few elections and the winning senatorial candidates who employed them. Although certainly not exhaustive, these strategies include: (1) family ties with prominent historical personalities (typically presidents) with their attendant advantage of name recall; (2) celebrity status based on long-standing media presence (e.g., as actors, television personalities, sports stars, etc.) or on recent high-profile media exposure (e.g., involvement in nationally televised plunder case trials); and (3) ties with the military (including involvement in past military coup attempts). It helps if the candidate is also well-qualified (e.g., a "top-notcher" on the national bar exam), or has served as a former cabinet secretary or held other high-profile government posts.

Another implication of the MPS is that it results in multiple parties fielding candidates. Given that MPS fosters competition among co-partisans, and winning elections is all about building a personalized network of support, candidates have very little incentive to coordinate campaigns and policy stances along party-lines. Political parties are by no means absent during elections, but they are best viewed as merely labels and nothing more. It is therefore no surprise that there are multiple parties represented in any given Senate elections. Table 10.2 lists the parties represented by candidates in Senate elections since 1995. There are a total of thirty-one parties, most of which are short-lived, that have fielded at least one candidate since 1995 (see Table 10.2). Moreover, only one of these parties ever fielded a full slate of candidates—with some fielding only one candidate! During the same period, nearly one-fifth of senatorial candidates chose to give up on party labels altogether and run as independents. With parties having little or no meaning, the organizations that really matter for candidates are the temporary and *ad hoc* teams and coalitions that are formed in the run-up to elections.[2]

TABLE 10.1: 2016 SENATORIAL CANDIDATES AND THEIR BASES OF NATIONAL FOLLOWINGS

Candidate	Family ties with a former president	Son/daughter of prominent (non-president) politician	Celebrity status (self and/or relative)	Regional following	Media exposure	Military ties	High-profile cabinet position
Paolo Benigno "Bam" Aquino IV	X			X			
Gloria Macapagal-Arroyo	X			X			X
Manuel "Mar" Roxas II	X			X			X
Benigno "Noynoy" Aquino III	X			X			
Ferdinand "Bongbong" Marcos Jr.	X			X			
Francis Joseph "Chiz" Escudero		X		X	X		
Grace Poe		X	X		X		
Joseph Victor "JV" Ejercito	X		X	X			
Leila de Lima					X		X
Emmanuel "Manny" Pacquiao			X	X	X		
Miriam Defensor-Santiago				X			X

---

2 Among the candidates who have been elected to the Senate since 1995, only four won without a team/coalition affiliation: Francis Pangilinan and Gregorio Honasan in 2007, Vicente Sotto III in 2010, and Sherwin Gatchalian in 2016.

(Continued)

Candidate	Family ties with a former president	Son/daughter of prominent (non-president) politician	Celebrity status (self and/or relative)	Regional following	Media exposure	Military ties	High-profile cabinet position
Sergio Osmeña III	X			X			
Alfredo Lim			X	X			
Antonio Trillanes					X	X	
Edgardo Angara				X			
Ma. Ana Consuelo "Jamby" Madrigal					X		
John Henry Osmeña	X			X			
Juan Flavier					X		X
Juan Miguel Zubiri		X		X			
Lito Lapid			X	X			
Manuel "Manny" Villar Jr.					X		
Nancy Binay		X		X			
Noli de Castro			X		X		
Ralph Recto		X	X	X			
Risa Hontiveros			X		X		
Juan Edgardo "Sonny" Angara		X		x			
Sherwin "Win" Gatchalian					X		

TABLE 10.2: PARTIES REPRESENTED BY CANDIDATES
FOR THE SENATE ELECTIONS, 1995–2016

Political Party	1995	1998	2001	2004	2007	2010	2013	2016	Total
Independents	4	2	13	6	3	5	5	22	60
Lakas	4	12	5	8	6			2	38
Liberal		2	2	2	2	10	3	8	29
LDP	6	8	7		1		1		23
KBL	1		4	3	7	5		1	21
NPC	9	1			4	2	2	2	20
Nacionalista	1		1		2	7	3	1	15
UNA							8	6	14
Ang Kapatiran					3	7	3		13
KNP				11					11
Aksyon			1	6	1			2	10
Bangon Pilipinas						8	1		9
IBID				9					9
PMP		1		1		5		2	9
Reporma-LM		8		1					9
PDP-LABAN	1	1	1		1	2	1		7
Lakas-KAMPI						6			6
PRP	3		1	1		1			6
KPPP		5							5
DPP							3		3
PDSP	1		1		1				3
UNO					3				3
Akbayan							1	1	2
Makabayan							1	1	2
PMM								2	2
Bagumbayan-VNP					1				1
Bayan Muna						1			1
GAD						1			1
KAMPI					1				1
PIBID			1						1
PGRP					1				1
PROMDI						1			1
Social Justice Society							1		1

TABLE 10.3: PARTIES REPRESENTED BY ELECTED
MEMBERS OF THE SENATE, 1995–2016

Political Party	1995	1998	2001	2004	2007	2010	2013	2016
Lakas	5	8	7	6		3	1	
LDP	14	5	5	2	1	1	1	1
Independent	2	2	5	2	5	4	4	5
Liberal		1	1	4	4	4	4	6
Nacionalista				2	3	5	5	3
NPC	2	2	1		1	2	2	3
PDP-LABAN		1	2	2	1	1	1	2
PMP		1		4	2	2		1
PRP	1	2		1	1	1	1	
UNA							5	2
Lakas-KAMPI					4			
Aksyon		1	1					
Akbayan								1
Bagumbayan-VNP					1			

As candidates organize themselves into teams, the goal is either to affiliate with the administration party to enjoy the benefits of the administration machinery, or to affiliate with other strong candidates whose bases of electoral support would complement rather than erode one's own personal networks of support. As a result, these coalitions do not last beyond a single election, and some candidates simultaneously become members of two (or occasionally even more) rival senatorial slates.

Consequently, multiple parties are represented in the Senate. As shown in Table 10.3, nineteen of the current twenty-four members of the upper house are dispersed across eight parties, with the remaining five declaring themselves to be independent of any party affiliation. This is, quite obviously, a remarkable demonstration of the highly fractured nature of the party system in the Philippines. Moreover, legislative coalitions are commonly formed around the party of the president. Hence, after the 2016 elections, even though PDP-LABAN had only two sitting senators (Aquilino Pimentel III and Emmanuel Pacquiao), the majority party came to be PDP-LABAN by virtue of Pimentel's position (until May 2018) as Senate President. Policy stances are by no means absent but they are highly individualized.

In sum, the MPS in Senate elections generates incentives among candidates to compete against co-partisans for votes, to build personalized networks of support instead of relying on a well-functioning party machinery, and to form temporary and *ad hoc* coalitions to consolidate and streamline each candidate's networks of support. Consequently, multiple parties and independent candidates stand for and win office; party labels are meaningless; there is no true party majority in the Senate; and policy stances are individualized (e.g. votes for important national bills have nothing to do with party affiliation). Thanks to MPS, we can therefore conclude, the party system in the upper house of the Philippine legislature is effectively dysfunctional.

MULTI-MEMBER PLURALITY SYSTEM IN LOCAL ELECTIONS

The Philippines also uses the MPS to elect legislators at the subnational level. Each of the eighty-one provinces of the Philippines elect provincial board members. In addition, each of the 145 cities and 1,489 municipalities elect city and municipal councilors, respectively.

ELECTIONS FOR CITY AND MUNICIPAL COUNCILORS

Municipalities in the Philippines have eight councilors elected at large.[3] Cities, on the other hand, are sub-divided into as many as six districts. Some cities have ten to twelve councilors elected at large, while most other cities have four-, six- and eight-seat districts.

City and municipal councils are also mandated to have (but do not always fill) three seats for ex-officio councilors: the municipal chapter presidents of the *Liga ng mga Barangay* (League of Barangays) and *Pederasyon ng Sangguniang Kabataan* (Federation of Youth Councils) and the Indigenous People's Representative. The Local Government Code of 1991 provides for an additional three sectoral representatives from groups of women or laborers or other specified sector (urban poor, indigenous cultural communities, or disabled persons) or alternatively from another sector that may be identified by the Council. This provision, however, has yet to be implemented with any consistency.

IMPLICATIONS OF MPS IN THE ELECTION OF CITY AND MUNICIPAL COUNCILORS

The MPS in local elections has at least two major implications for outcomes of democracy. First, these multi-seat districts tend to produce multiple parties

---

3 Pateros in Metro Manila is the sole exception. Pateros is divided into two districts, each electing six councilors.

in each district as well as encourage candidates to run as independents. Table 10.4 compares the number of parties represented in the municipal elections, by election year. Statistics in the upper panel show that more party/coalitions are represented in elections for councilor than in elections for mayor and vice-mayor. Moreover, there tend to be more candidates running as independents for council office than for mayor or vice-mayor. The large number of parties represented in elections naturally results in the presence of a large number of parties in post-election local governments (see lower panel of Table 10.4). In just three election years (2001, 2004, and 2007), candidates for city or town mayor ran under a total of 202 party banners while those elected to the post represented a still quite remarkable 101 political parties. With local Philippine mayors thus affiliating themselves across literally dozens of political parties, one sees further evidence—as in the Senate—of a highly fractured party system. This also reflects a very low degree of party coherence or coordination from the national level to subnational levels.

TABLE 10.4: NUMBER OF PARTY/COALITIONS AND INDEPENDENT CANDIDATES BY OFFICE, FOR ELECTION YEARS 2001, 2004, AND 2007

Office	2001	2004*	2007	All Years
	All candidates running for office			
Mayor	41 (633)	129 (660)	91 (604)	202 (1,897)
Vice-Mayor	44 (803)	121 (877)	95 (622)	197 (2,302)
Councilors	56 (10,478)	246 (9,698)	43 (230)**	297 (20,406)
	Post-election officeholders			
Mayor	29 (60)	58 (62)	51 (38)	101 (160)
Vice-Mayor	31 (128)	70 (134)	58 (102)	116 (364)
Councilors	37 (1352)	122 (1,601)	20 (11)**	146 (2,964)

Notes: Numbers in parentheses are the count of independent candidates. *Presidential election. **Based on incomplete data.

In terms of local dynamics, what is especially notable is the particularly large number of party/coalitions in 2004, which is a presidential election year. While further research is required, I suspect that this is because candidates for councilors are mobilized to become supplementary brokers for national candidates. More candidates stand for office and run under different party/coalitions even if they have little chance to win, if only to arbitrage campaign funds from national candidates in exchange for supplying the latter with a ready corps of supporters.

The second major implication of the MPS is that it pits candidates against co-partisans in the same district. Although candidates typically run under the same party label, they often tend to mobilize their own personal networks of support rather than work collectively to get voters to support all of the party team with all of their votes. This intra-party competition exacerbates the meaninglessness of party labels to candidates and voters. This is reflected in the rampant party switching prior to every election, as well as in the split-ticket voting of voters.

Table 10.5 reports the incidence of party switching of candidates for city and municipal councils between election years 2001 and 2004 as well as 2004 and 2007. The numbers indicate that a great majority of candidates for city and municipal councils switch party affiliations (80.47 percent between 2001 and 2004, and 50.81 percent between 2004 and 2007). These numbers are roughly the same as the incidence of party switching among mayoral and vice-mayoral candidates, suggesting that (vertical) realignments between local candidates widely occur.

TABLE 10.5: INCIDENCE OF PARTY SWITCHING OF CANDIDATES FOR CITY AND MUNICIPAL COUNCILS ACROSS ELECTION YEARS 2001, 2004, AND 2007

Office	2001 to 2004	2004 to 2007
Mayor	1,358 / 1,683 (80.69%)	832 / 1,360 (61.18%)
Vice-Mayor	928 / 1,164 (79.73%)	676 / 1,011 (66.86%)
Councilor	10,571 / 13,136 (80.47%)	188/ 370** (50.81%)

Notes: Each entry is presented as a fraction, where the denominator is the number of candidates running for re-election in both years specified in the respective columns, and the numerator is the number of candidates changing party affiliation from one election year to the next. Numbers in parentheses are percentages of party switching from one election to the next.

**Election returns for council elections are missing for most localities, hence the numbers reported here are for a small subset of the full sample.

Tables 10.6a and 10.6b report the number of voters who split their votes between parties represented in a city council election. The data is from a survey of 902 randomly selected voters in Sorsogon City in 2013. Only 157 voters out of 902 report not splitting their votes.[4] In fact, only forty-two voters who used all four of their votes voted for candidates from the same party. This represents less than 5 percent of the sample; all the rest split their votes in various combinations of political parties including independent candidates.

---

4 These 157 voters include those who used four votes toward one party, three votes toward one party, two votes toward one party, and only one vote.

TABLE 10.6a: VOTER PREFERENCES ACROSS PARTIES, PART I

Type of split	District			
	Bacon	East	West	Total
0 - 0 - 0 - 1 - 0	0	1	1	2
0 - 0 - 1 - 0 - 0	14	13	9	36
0 - 0 - 1 - 1 - 0	0	2	5	7
0 - 0 - 2 - 0 - 0	10	5	10	25
0 - 0 - 2 - 0 - 1	0	0	2	2
0 - 0 - 2 - 1 - 0	0	3	2	5
0 - 0 - 3 - 0 - 0	3	4	11	18
0 - 0 - 3 - 0 - 1	0	0	2	2
0 - 0 - 3 - 1 - 0	0	1	9	10
0 - 0 - 4 - 0 - 0	5	5	24	34
0 - 1 - 0 - 0 - 0	2	9	5	16
0 - 1 - 0 - 0 - 1	0	0	2	2
0 - 1 - 0 - 1 - 0	0	1	0	1
0 - 1 - 1 - 0 - 0	8	10	14	32
0 - 1 - 1 - 1 - 0	0	1	5	6
0 - 1 - 1 - 1 - 1	0	0	2	2
0 - 1 - 2 - 0 - 0	5	12	8	25
0 - 1 - 2 - 0 - 1	0	0	1	1
0 - 1 - 2 - 1 - 0	0	6	21	27
0 - 1 - 3 - 0 - 0	4	30	70	104
0 - 2 - 0 - 0 - 0	0	5	3	8
0 - 2 - 0 - 1 - 0	0	1	1	2
0 - 2 - 1 - 0 - 0	3	23	9	35
0 - 2 - 1 - 1 - 0	0	10	4	14
0 - 2 - 2 - 0 - 0	3	47	27	77
0 - 3 - 0 - 0 - 0	0	1	1	2
0 - 3 - 0 - 0 - 1	0	0	1	1
0 - 3 - 0 - 1 - 0	0	3	0	3
0 - 3 - 1 - 0 - 0	1	33	7	41
0 - 4 - 0 - 0 - 0	0	6	2	8

Notes: Data is from self-reports of 902 randomly selected voters in Sorsogon City after the 2013 city council elections. Four parties are represented in these elections. The type of split is coded as split-voting between "Independents - UNA - NPC - NP - LP". So for example, 0-1-1-1-1 means a voter has split his/her vote evenly between UNA, NPC, NP, and LP.

TABLE 10.6b: VOTER PREFERENCES ACROSS PARTIES, PART II

Type of split	District			
	Bacon	East	West	Total
1 - 0 - 0 - 0 - 0	4	0	0	4
1 - 0 - 1 - 0 - 0	11	0	1	12
1 - 0 - 2 - 0 - 0	20	1	2	23
1 - 0 - 2 - 1 - 0	0	1	4	5
1 - 0 - 3 - 0 - 0	38	3	2	43
1 - 1 - 0 - 0 - 0	6	2	1	9
1 - 1 - 1 - 0 - 0	9	1	2	12
1 - 1 - 1 - 1 - 0	0	1	0	1
1 - 1 - 2 - 0 - 0	28	10	8	46
1 - 2 - 0 - 0 - 0	2	1	0	3
1 - 2 - 0 - 0 - 1	0	0	1	1
1 - 2 - 1 - 0 - 0	8	7	1	16
1 - 3 - 0 - 0 - 0	2	1	1	4
2 - 0 - 0 - 0 - 0	3	0	0	3
2 - 0 - 1 - 0 - 0	9	1	0	10
2 - 0 - 2 - 0 - 0	28	0	0	28
2 - 1 - 0 - 0 - 0	3	0	0	3
2 - 1 - 0 - 0 - 1	0	0	1	1
2 - 1 - 1 - 0 - 0	21	0	0	21
2 - 2 - 0 - 0 - 0	5	0	0	5
3 - 0 - 0 - 0 - 0	1	0	0	1
3 - 0 - 1 - 0 - 0	3	0	0	3
3 - 1 - 0 - 0 - 0	2	0	0	2
Refused-to-answer	30	33	35	98
Total	291	294	317	902

The combination of intraparty competition, weak party labels, and relatively small districts encourages council candidates to cultivate and respond to relatively narrow constituencies. Across the ubiquitous practice of vote buying, as is discussed in Chapter Eight, pre-existing, family-based social network structures offer logistical advantages for targeting private inducements. Voters, similarly, use personal ties as heuristics for choosing local candidates, and the most successful candidates are those who have the financial resources for vote buying and those who come from prominent families (Cruz, Labonne and Querubin 2015; Davidson, Hicken and Ravanilla 2016).

Moreover, evidence suggests that dynastic candidates for the local elections and those who are able to build alliances with upper-level candidates (as reflected in the number of party/coalitions they represent) tend to garner higher vote-shares and effectively win seats. Table 10.7 illustrates the advantages that accrue to candidates who are members of political dynasties as well as to candidates who run under multiple party banners. Compared to the average vote-share of a mayoral candidate (34 percent), the average vote-share of candidates from a political dynasty are 3 percent higher at 37 percent, and the average vote-share of candidates representing multiple parties are even higher at 41 percent. In terms of the likelihood of winning elections, the average mayoral candidate has a 34 percent chance of winning, but a mayoral candidate from a political dynasty and those representing multiple parties have an even higher chance of winning at 37 percent and 41 percent, respectively.

TABLE 10.7: CANDIDATE VOTE-SHARES AND
PROBABILITY OF WINNING, BY OFFICE

	Vote-shares			Probability of winning		
	Mayor	Vice-Mayor	Councilor	Mayor	Vice-Mayor	Councilor
Candidate is from a political dynasty	37%	37%	3.9%	0.37	0.37	0.31
Candidate is aligned with multiple parties	41%	40%	4.5%	0.41	0.38	0.38
Average across all candidates	34%	35%	3.8%	0.34	0.34	0.29
Number of observations	12,417	12,462	79,125	12,549	12,578	79,822

Note: Numbers reported are based on coefficient estimates from Ordinary Least Squares regressions of vote-shares (first three columns) and indicator for winning the election (last three columns), and are significant at the 5 percent significance level. Robust standard errors are clustered at the candidate-level and not shown. Outcomes in columns (1) to (3) are vote-shares of candidates, and in columns (4) to (6) an indicator for winning. Dynastic is an indicator for having a candidate with the same family name in the municipality/city, and "aligned with multiple parties" is an indicator for representing more than one party. All regressions include municipality/city and year fixed effects.

PATHWAYS FOR ELECTORAL SYSTEM REDESIGN

The previous sections emphasized how the widespread discontent with Philippine democracy today is very much a function of the electoral rules that impose constraints on the behavior of political actors. Specifically, the multi-member plurality system generates incentives for political actors to behave in ways that undermine democratic accountability and consolidation. Therefore, any reforms or redesign of the electoral system must anticipate how they might alter the behavior of political actors. Before I discuss possible pathways for reform, I briefly survey the experience of Japan and Thailand—two countries that formerly used versions of the MPS and decided to move away from them.

LESSONS FROM JAPAN

Pre-reform. From 1947 through 1993 Japan used a different version of MPS, called the single non-transferable vote (SNTV), to elect the more powerful lower house of the Diet. In this Japanese-style MPS, each voter has only one vote to cast for a single candidate in a multi-candidate race for multiple seats in a district. Posts are filled by the candidates with the most votes. The number of seats ranged from one through six, and most districts had between three and five.

The primary problem with SNTV was that it forced candidates from the same party to compete for votes, much more so than is the case with Philippine-style MPS (where, as explained above, voters can cast as many votes as there are seats in a district). The dominant party throughout this period, the Liberal Democratic Party (LDP), ran multiple candidates in most districts. An LDP candidate who needed a few more votes to gain a seat found it easier to attract voters from other LDP candidates than from one of the opposition parties. This intraparty competition then fostered factionalism inside the LDP (Cox, Rosenbluth and Thies 1999). But the competition that SNTV generated within the LDP was not primarily among ideological camps, as ideological and policy differences became muted; rather, it was competition among camps over constituency service. Since the party in power possesses the advantage in any competition to perform every greater constituency service, SNTV facilitated one-party dominance in the Diet. Combined with this were the concomitant disadvantages that the system posed for opposition parties, which were unable to access the government resources that the ruling LDP could deploy for the benefit of its constituents. The Japan Socialist Party, the largest opposition party, found it increasingly difficult to field multiple candidates. It and other opposition parties fragmented as they competed for the progressive vote.

Consequences of electoral reform. As explained in Chapter Four, the 1994 reforms dramatically changed the Japanese electoral system. In the new system, 300 seats in the lower house of the Diet are now elected via first past the post (in a system, as explained in Chapter Three, that is also known as single-member district plurality, or SMDP). Another 200 members of the Diet are elected via closed-list proportional representation (CLPR) in eleven districts ranging in magnitude from seven to thirty-three seats. There is no compensatory mechanism linking SMDP and CLPR votes. The only connection between the two parts of the system is the double candidacy provision, that a candidate may run both in the geographically based SMDP system and also be included on a CLPR list. Parties may also rank several candidates equally on their lists, allowing the tie to be broken by the SMDP results.

With the SMDP system, political parties now have only one candidate per district. This marks a major change for the LDP. In the past, when more than one candidate sought the LDP nomination, the decision was often left to the voters: let all the candidates run as independents and whoever wins will join the LDP. This option is now much more dangerous. Candidates may be tempted to accept the support of other parties and the winner might not join the LDP, which now has a strong incentive to act in a more coherent way at the local level. For instance, the LDP is making rapid progress toward appointing a single person as the head of the local branch, and thus the prospective nominee for the next election, in every district. There are also indications that the factions have been weakened within LDP, due in large part to the fact that there is no longer as strong a structural basis for intra-party competition.

Theoretically, moving to SMDP should produce incentives for the opposition to coalesce around a single candidate capable of defeating the LDP, but so far the opposition parties continue to be fragmented. This is probably because the incentives toward the consolidation of two-party competition are weakened by the presence of the 200 CLPR seats with only a 2 percent minimum election threshold within regional blocs.[5]

Lastly, the move to SMDP did little to change the incentives of individual candidates to build a personal vote based on constituency service and the disbursement of pork-barrel projects. However, the potential for policy competition among parties has increased.

LESSONS FROM THAILAND

Pre-reform. Prior to 1997, Thailand used a version of MPS to elect the lower House of Representatives. As in the Philippine-style of MPS, voters cast votes for

---

5 In practice, the effective threshold is about 4.3 percent, which is still low enough for smaller parties to have a chance at winning seats (Jou 2009).

candidates regardless of party affiliation, and were allowed to vote for as many candidates as there were seats in a district. They could also vote for as many, or as few, candidates as they wished. Seats were awarded to the top vote-getters on the basis of the plurality rule.

The key difference is that parties in Thailand were required to field a full team of candidates for any district they wished to contest. The country's electoral districts were broken down into one-, two- and three-seat districts, with most districts having more than one seat. Hence, for example, a party was required to field three candidates in a three-seat district.

The MPS in Thailand tended to produce multiple parties in each district, which in turn contributed to the presence of a large number of parties in the House. Consequently, it was very rare for a party to command a majority. Instead governments were made of multi-party coalitions that were generally indecisive and short-lived.

The system also pitted candidates from the same party against one another in the same district. Although each party nominated a team of candidates, they often tended to campaign against each other by building personalized networks of support. As in Japan, this intra-party competition undermined the value of party labels to candidates and voters and contributed to incohesion and factions within parties.

Consequences of electoral reform. In 1997 Thailand adopted a new constitution which paved the way for the replacement of the MPS with a parallel system made up of SMDP and CLPR elements. In this new system, 300 seats in the House of Representatives were now elected via SMDP, and 100 seats from a single nationwide district by CLPR. A party needed to reach a threshold of at least 5 percent of the party-list votes in order to be eligible for seats in this tier. Each party was required to submit a list of candidates for voters to consider, and voters cast two votes, one for a district representative and one for a party list. There was no compensatory mechanism between SMDP and PR votes. Unlike in Japan, double candidacy was not allowed.

An outcome of the move to single-member districts and the 5 percent electoral threshold in the party-list tier was the reduction of the number of parties in Thailand. In the 2001 election for the House of Representatives, the effective number of parties in the legislature fell by half from an average of 6.2 before 1997 to 3.1 (Hicken 2006). For the first time since 1957 a single party, the newly formed Thai Rak Thai party, nearly captured a majority of the seats. It later gained a majority after a smaller party disbanded and joined its ranks.

Adding a national party-list tier and shifting to SMDP also encouraged voters and candidates to focus more on party policy positions regarding national issues. In 2001, for example, political parties, led chiefly by the Thai Rak Thai party, put significant effort into developing coordinated party-centered electoral strategies.

Parties began to differentiate themselves in terms of their policy platforms and in some cases made those differences an important campaign issue. However, the shift towards party-centered strategies was primarily confined to the campaign for party list seats, while contests in the 400 single-member districts generally remained candidate-centered affairs. This is not surprising since single-member districts still generate incentives to cultivate personal support networks, especially when the district size is small and candidates only need to mobilize a small subset of the district electorate to win elections.

REDESIGNING THE ELECTORAL SYSTEM IN THE PHILIPPINES

If there is anything to be learned from the experiences of Japan and Thailand, it is that policy makers need to try to anticipate how electoral reforms will shape politicians' incentives. As they seek to advance their careers, are they likely to keep, modify, or abandon existing strategies?

In Japan, the shift to SMD has largely addressed the problem of intraparty competition and prompted the leadership of the dominant party to be more cohesive in terms of nominating candidates for single seats in every district. The incorporation of CLPR in the reforms also encouraged coordination in terms of policy platforms among members of the party. Factions within LDP began to be undermined, but the reforms did little to encourage smaller opposition parties to coalesce into a single opposition party to defeat LDP, partly because CLPR does not eliminate the incentive of smaller parties to win seats in this tier given the low electoral threshold. Within the new SMDP system, individual candidates continued to promise material benefits to their districts and to make personalistic appeals as this is what delivers the votes.

In Thailand, the shift to SMDP and CLPR succeeded in reducing the number of parties and allowed the Thai Rak Thai to gain a majority in the lower house. The addition of the national party list tier started to encourage voters as well as candidates to focus more on policy positions regarding national issues. However, the shift to a plurality system in the new single-member districts continued to remain as candidate-centered affairs. As in Japan, candidates continued to cultivate personal networks of support even when intraparty competition was no longer a consideration. On the plus side, SMDP has the advantage of ensuring the representation of geographic interests.

SHIFTING TO CLOSED-LIST PR

The lessons for the Philippines from Japan and Thailand both imply that, first, a shift to SMDP for the election of either local legislators or senators (via single-member regional districts) would be ill-advised. Such a shift would surely eliminate intra-party competition. However, it would do little in terms of changing the incentives of individual candidates to build personal networks of support and to employ money politics—especially when candidates know that these strategies are what fundamentally deliver votes.

A second option might be a shift to an open-list PR (OLPR) type of system, in which parties choose the candidates but the voters are able to rank candidates within parties. Relative to the existing MPS (admittedly a very low bar of comparison, given how systematically it produces a highly fractured party system), OLPR could encourage political parties to coordinate policy platforms and positions regarding national issues. But as explained in Chapter Six, the experience of Indonesia cautions very strongly against the adoption of OLPR. There, the shift from CLPR to OLPR led to a shift from a more party-centric system to one that was far more oriented to candidates. In the Philippines, where parties are still at the nascent stage of development, OLPR would be sure to perpetuate the candidate-centric nature of the political system and provide little chance for parties to mature into more stable and coherent organizations.

In light of the above considerations, shifting to closed-list PR while maintaining the multi-member nature of districts might offer some traction and prove successful in improving democratic outcomes in the Philippines. The use of CLPR in the Senate elections would mean that individual candidates are compelled to join a viable political party to have a chance of winning a seat. Because parties would decide the rankings in the slate, its members would now have the incentive to coordinate amongst each other, so that campaign strategies tend to be more party-centered. If there is a significant threshold in place, members of smaller parties, especially the viable candidates, would also have the incentive to join ranks with other parties to form a stronger opposition party that stands a better chance against the ruling party.

The danger to moving to a closed-list PR in Senate elections, however, is that without clear laws governing the conduct of political parties, the system is prone to capture by the "list maker(s)" within the party—those controlling who gets to be included in the party slate and how they are to be ranked. Moreover, for as long as it is costless to switch parties and join temporary and *ad hoc* teams/coalitions, those parties that can effectively consolidate the personalized networks of support of its members would dominate in the elections. The result of such an unfortunate and unintended consequence would be a dominant (but still meaningless) party label composed of powerful individual candidates who continue to rely on their personal networks of support to be included and maintain or improve their rankings within the team/coalition.

Pursuing reforms at the local level by also shifting from MPS to CLPR may help mitigate the formation of meaningless political parties at the national level. A shift to CLPR would mean that local candidates are also now compelled to join a viable political party to have a chance of winning a seat. And as long as the local chief executives (mayors and governors) are up for election at the same time as national politicians, candidates will tend to align with parties that have national followings—further implying a smaller number of political parties.

It is of course very likely the case that, at least in the beginning, such political parties will coordinate campaigns and styles of governance that are largely based on money politics and patron-client relationships. That is, coordination within such political parties may be confined only to the streamlining of retail money politics during elections and patronage when in office, and in the consolidation of each candidate's personalized networks of support. But for as long as there is real competition among a small number of viable national political parties (and not between powerful individuals), such competition has the virtue of bringing out the best in these organizations. It also has the power eventually to undermine the pernicious institutions that rule national and local politics.

To facilitate the development of stable and well-organized parties from these "unified clientelistic machines," nonprofit and international organizations can actively help build party organizational capacity and a leadership team within the party that would outlast the careers of individual members. Entrepreneurs within these political parties can take advantage of social media to build grassroots membership and sustain off-election-cycle accountability through online updates of the activities of the party and its leaders.

No process of political reform is without challenges, and regardless of the type of reform there is always the risk of unintended consequences. This includes electoral system reform. As the Philippines considers a highly ambitious package of political reforms, however, it would do well to recognize that electoral system redesign poses relatively fewer risks of unintended consequences as compared to other reform proposals that are on the table. If the overarching goal is to facilitate democratic accountability and consolidation, develop well-functioning political parties, improve representation, and shift campaign strategies as well as governance styles from personalistic to programmatic, then electoral system reform is a critical first step.

BIBLIOGRAPHY

Abinales, Patricio N., and Donna J. Amoroso. 2017. *State and Society in the Philippines*, 2nd ed. Lanham, MD: Rowan & Littlefield.

Acemoglu, Daron. 2009. *Introduction to Modern Economic Growth*. Princeton: Princeton University Press.

Acemoglu, Daron, and James A. Robinson. 2012. *Why Nations Fail: The Origins of Power, Prosperity and Poverty*. New York: Crown.

Agra, Alberto C. 1997. *The Philippine Party-List System: A List Proportional Representation Scheme of Electing One-Fifth of the Members of the House of Representatives*. Manila: Rex Book Store.

Ang Bagong Bayani-OFW Labor Party et al. v. Commission on Elections et al. Supreme Court of the Philippines, decided 2003. http://sc.judiciary.gov.ph/jurisprudence/2003/jun2003/147589.htm

Aspinall, Edward. 2014. "Parliament and Patronage." *Journal of Democracy* 25(4): 96–110.

Aspinall, Edward, Michael W. Davidson, Allen Hicken, and Meredith L. Weiss. 2016. "Local Machines and Vote Brokerage in the Philippines." *Contemporary Southeast Asia* 38(2): 191–96.

Atong Paglaum, Inc. et al. v. Commission on Elections. Supreme Court of the Philippines, decided 2013. http://sc.judiciary.gov.ph/jurisprudence/2013/april2013/203766.pdf

Balisacan, Arsenio N., and Hal Hill. 2003. "An Introduction to the Key Issues." In *The Philippines Economy: Development, Policies, and Challenges*, edited by Arsenio M. Balisacan and Hal Hill. Oxford University Press.

Barangay Association for National Advancement and Transparency (BANAT) et al. v. Commission on Elections. Supreme Court of the Philippines, decided 2009. http://sc.judiciary.gov.ph/jurisprudence/2009/april2009/179271.htm

Bardhan, Pranab. 1990. "Symposium on the State and Economic Development." *The Journal of Economic Perspectives* 4: 3–7.

_____. 2005. "Institutions Matter, But Which Ones?" *Economics of Transition* 13(3): 499–532.

Bello, Walden. 2005. "Can the Philippines Handle Globalization?" *Business World*, 23 January.

Belmonte, Feliciano et al. 2014. Bangsamoro Basic Law: House of Representatives, 16th Congress. 11 September 2014.

Benoit, Kenneth. 2001. "District Magnitude, Electoral Formula, and the Number of Parties." *European Journal of Political Research* 39: 203–24.

Besley, Timothy, and Maitreesh Ghatak. 2006. "Public Goods and Economic Development." In *Understanding Poverty*, edited by Abhijit Banerjee, Roland Benabou, and Dilip Mookherjee. Oxford: Oxford University Press.

Bjarnegård, Elin. 2009. *Men in Politics: Revisiting Patterns of Gendered Parliamentary Representation in Thailand and Beyond.* Uppsala: Uppsala Universitet.

Boix, Carles. 1999. "Setting the Rules of the Game: The Choice of Electoral Systems in Advanced Democracies." *American Political Science Review* 93: 609–24.

Borromeo-Bulao, Mary Joyce. 2019. "Participatory Governance and Oligarchic Electoral Control: The Case of Naga City." In *Electoral Dynamics in the Philippines: Money Politics, Patronage and Clientelism at the Grassroots*, edited by Allen Hicken, Edward Aspinall, and Meredith Weiss. Singapore: NUS Press.

Buehler, Michael. 2013. "Revisiting the Inclusion-moderation Thesis in the Context of Decentralized Institutions: The Behavior of Indonesia's Prosperous Justice Party in National and Local Politics." *Party Politics* 19(2): 210–29.

Calvo, Ernesto, and María Victoria Murillo. 2004. "Who Delivers? Partisan Clients in the Argentine Electoral Market." *American Journal of Political Science* 48(4): 742–57.

Canes-Wrone, Brandice, and Christian Ponce de Leon. 2014. "Elections, Uncertainty, and Economic Outcomes." http://web.stanford.edu/group/sssl/cgi-bin/wordpress/wp-content/uploads/2013/12/conferencepost.pdf

Carey, John, and Matthew Shugart. 1995. "Incentives to Cultivate a Personal Vote: A Rank Ordering of Electoral Formulas." *Electoral Studies* 14(4): 417–39.

Carter Center. 2016. "Limited Election Observation Mission to the Philippines, June 2016 Statement." https://www.cartercenter.org/resources/pdfs/news/peace_publications/election_reports/philippines-june-2016-election-statement.pdf

Chang, Eric C. C., Mark Andreas Kayser, Drew A. Linzer, and Ronald Rogowski. 2011. *Electoral Systems and the Balance of Consumer-Producer Power.* New York: Cambridge University Press.

Chattharakul, Anyarat. 2010. "Thai Electoral Campaigning: Vote-Canvassing Networks and Hybrid Voting." *Journal of Current Southeast Asian Affairs* 29(4): 67–95.

Colomer, Josep M. 2005. "It's Parties that Choose Electoral Systems (or, Duverger's Laws Upside Down)." *Political Studies* 53: 1–21.

COMELEC-GAD Stakeholders Consultative Planning Conference. 29 June 2016.

Cook, Malcolm, and Lorraine Salazar. 2016. "The Differences Duterte Relied Upon to Win." *ISEAS Perspective* 34: 3.

Cox, Gary W., and Mathew D. McCubbins. 2001. "The Institutional Determinants of Policy Outcomes." In *Presidents, Parliaments, and Policy*, edited by Stephan Haggard and Mathew D. McCubbins. New York: Cambridge University Press.

Crisp, Brian F., and Juan Carlos Rey. 2001. "The Sources of Electoral Reform in Venezuela." In *Mixed Member Electoral Systems: The Best of Both Worlds?* edited by Matthew Soberg Shugart and Martin P. Wattenberg. Oxford: Oxford University Press.

Cruz, Cesi, Julian Labonne, and Pablo Querubin. 2015. "Politician Family Networks and Electoral Outcomes: Evidence from the Philippines." Manuscript, NYU.

Cusack, Thomas R., Torben Iversen, and David Soskice. 2007. "Economic Interests and the Origins of Electoral Systems." *American Political Science Review* 101(3): 373–91.

Dahlerup, Drude. 2009. "Gender Quotas Database." International IDEA and Stockholm University. https://www.idea.int/data-tools/data/gender-quotas/quotas.

Davidson, Michael, Allen Hicken, and Nico Ravanilla. 2016. "Family Networks and Voter Behavior: Evidence from the Philippines." Manuscript, UCSD.

de Dios, Emmanuel. 2007. *The Dynamics of Regional Development: The Philippines in East Asia*. Massachusetts: Edward Elgar Publishing Inc.

de Dios, Emmanuel, and Hadi Salehi Esfahani. 2001. "Centralization, Political Turnover, and Investment in the Philippines." In *Corruption: The Boom and Bust of East Asia*, edited by J. Edgardo Campos. Ateneo de Manila University Press.

de Dios, Emmanuel, and Paul Hutchcroft. 2003. "Political Economy: Examining Current Challenges in Historical Perspective." In *The Philippines Economy: Development, Policies, and Challenges*, edited by Arsenio M. Balisacan and Hal Hill. Oxford University Press.

Denmark, David. 2001. "Choosing MMP in New Zealand: Explaining the 1993 Electoral Reform." In *Mixed Member Electoral Systems: The Best of Both Worlds?* edited by Matthew Soberg Shugart and Martin P. Wattenberg. Oxford University Press.

Dixit, Avinash K. 1994. *Investment Under Uncertainty*. Princeton: Princeton University Press.

Doner, Richard F. 2009. *The Politics of Uneven Development: Thailand's Economic Growth in Comparative Perspective*. New York: Cambridge University Press.

Dressel, Bjoern, and Marcus Mietzner. 2012. "A Tale of Two Courts: the Judicialization of Electoral Politics in Asia." *Governance* 25(3): 391–414.

Dunleavy, Patrick, and Helen Margetts. 1995. "Understanding the Dynamics of Electoral Reform." *International Political Science Review* 16 (1): 9–29.

Farrel, David M. 1997. *Comparing Electoral Systems*. Houndmills, Basingstoke, Hampshire: Macmillan.

Feng, Yi. 2001. "Political Freedom, Political Instability, and Policy Uncertainty: A Study of Political Institutions and Private Investment in Developing Countries." *International Studies Quarterly* 45(2): 271–94.

Gallagher, Michael, and Paul Mitchell, eds. 2005. *The Politics of Electoral Systems*. Oxford: Oxford University Press.

Garcia, Moises S. Jr. 1997. "Meeting the Optimists." *Kasarinlan* 13(2): 31–64.

Gary W. Cox, Frances McCall Rosenbluth, and Michael F. Thies. 1999. "Electoral Reform and the Fate of Factions: The Case of Japan's Liberal Democratic Party." *British Journal of Political Science* 29(1): 33–56.

Geddes, Barbara. 1995. "The Politics of Economic Liberalization." *Latin American Research Review* 30(2): 195–214.

Gerring, John. 2003. "Minor Parties in Plurality Electoral Systems." *Party Politics* 11(1): 79–107.

Gimpelson, Vladimir, and Daniel Treisman. 2002. "Fiscal Games and Public Employment." *World Politics* 54: 145–83.

Goodwin-Gill, Guy S. *Codes of Conduct for Elections*. Geneva: Inter-Parliamentary Union.

Grofman, Bernard, and Arend Lijphart. 2003. *Electoral Laws and their Political Consequences*. New York: Agathon Press.

Grzymala-Busse, Anna. 2008. "Beyond Clientelism: Incumbent State Capture and State Formation." *Comparative Political Studies* 41(4/5): 638–73.

Gutierrez, Ibarra III, and Walden Bello. Women's Participation and Representation in Political Parties Act of 2013: House of Representatives, 16th Congress.

Hadiz, Vedi R. 2010. *Localising Power in Post-Authoritarian Indonesia: A Southeast Asia Perspective*. Stanford: Stanford University Press.

Hallerberg, Mark, and Patrik Marier. 2004. "Executive Authority, the Personal Vote, and Budget Discipline in Latin American and Caribbean Countries." *American Journal of Political Science* 48(3): 571–87.

Hankla, Charles R. 2006a. "Party Strength and International Trade: A Cross-National Analysis." *Comparative Political Studies* 39: 1133–56.

_____. 2006b. "Party Linkages and Economic Policy: An Examination of Indira Gandhi's India." *Business and Politics* 8(3): 1–29.

Henisz, Witold J. 2002. *Politics and International Investment: Measuring Risk and Protecting Profits*. London: Edward Elgar Publishers Ltd.

Hibbs, Douglas. 1977. "Political Parties and Macroeconomic Policy." *American Political Science Review* 71: 1467–87.

Hicken, Allen, and Erik Martinez Kuhonta. 2011. "Shadows from the Past: Party System Institutionalization in Asia." *Comparative Political Studies* 55(5): 572–97.

Hicken, Allen, and Erik Martinez Kuhonta. 2014. "Rethinking Party System Institutionalization in Asia." In *Party and Party System Institutionalization in Asia: Democracies, Autocracies and the Shadows of the Past*, edited by Allen Hicken and Erik Martinez Kuhonta. New York: Cambridge University Press.

Hicken, Allen, and Joel Simmons. 2008. "The Personal Vote and the Efficacy of Education Spending." *American Journal of Political Science* 52(1): 109–24.

Hicken, Allen, and Nico Ravanilla. 2015. "Electoral Pressures and the Incentive to 'Bring Home the Pork': The Case of Philippine Senators." Manuscript, University of Michigan.

Hicken, Allen, Edward Aspinall, and Meredith Weiss, eds. 2019. *Electoral Dynamics in the Philippines: Money Politics, Patronage and Clientelism at the Grassroots*. Singapore: NUS Press.

Hicken, Allen. 2006. "Party Fabrication: Constitutional Reform and the Rise of Thai Rak Thai." *Journal of East Asian Studies* 6(3): 381–407.

_____. 2007. "The 2007 Thai Constitution: A Return to Politics Past." *Crossroads* 19(1): 128–59.

_____. 2008. "Developing Democracies in Southeast Asia: Theorizing the Role of Parties and Elections." In *Southeast Asia in Political Science: Theory, Region, and*

Qualitative Analysis, edited by Erik Kuhonta, Dan Slater, and Tuong Vu. Stanford: Stanford University Press.

————. 2009. *Building Party Systems in Developing Democracies*. New York: Cambridge University Press.

————. 2011. "Clientelism." *Annual Review of Political Science* 14: 289–310.

————. 2014. "Party and Party System Institutionalization in the Philippines." In *Party and Party System Institutionalization in Asia: Democracies, Autocracies and the Shadows of the Past*, edited by Allen Hicken and Erik Martinez Kuhonta. New York: Cambridge University Press.

————. 2016. "Party Systems and the Politics of Development." In *Handbook on the Politics of Development*, edited by Carol Lancaster and Nicolas van de Walle. Oxford University Press.

Hill, Hal. 1997. "Towards a Political Economy Explanation of Rapid Growth in ASEAN: A Survey and Analysis." *ASEAN Economic Bulletin* 14(2): 131–49.

Hillman, Ben. 2012. "Power-sharing and Political Party Engineering in Conflict-prone Societies: The Indonesian Experiment in Aceh." *Conflict, Security and Development* 12(2): 149–69.

Holmes, Ronald D. 2016. "Can the Gains be Sustained? Assessing the First Five Years of the Aquino Administration." In *Mindanao: The Long Journey to Peace and Prosperity*, edited by Paul D. Hutchcroft. Manila: Anvil.

————. 2019. "The Centrality of Pork Amidst Weak Institutions: Presidents and the Persistence of Particularism in Post-Marcos Philippines (1986–2016). Ph.D. dissertation, Department of Political and Social Change, The Australian National University.

Holmes, Ronald D. 2019. "The Myth of the Machine." In *Electoral Dynamics in the Philippines: Machines and Money Politics at the Grassroots*, edited by Allen Hicken, Edward Aspinall, and Meredith Weiss. Singapore: NUS Press.

Hukumonline. 2002. "Pemilihan secara Langsung Dapat Dianggap sebagai Kudeta" [Direct Elections can be Considered a Coup D'etat]. http://www.hukumonline.com/berita/baca/hol5218/pemilihan-secara-langsung-dapat-dianggap-sebagai-kudeta. Accessed 1 August 2016

Huntington, Samuel P. 1968. *Political Order in Changing Societies*. New Haven: Yale University Press.

Hutchcroft, Paul, and Joel Rocamora. 2003. "Strong Demands and Weak Institutions: The Origins and Evolution of the Democratic Deficit in the Philippines." *Journal of East Asian Studies* 3(2): 259–92.

Hutchcroft, Paul D., and Joel Rocamora. 2012. "Patronage-Based Parties and Democratic Deficit in the Philippines: Origins, Evolution, and the Imperatives of Reform." In *Routledge Handbook of Southeast Asian Politics*, edited by Richard Robinson. London, United Kingdom: Routledge.

Hutchcroft, Paul D. 1998. *Booty Capitalism: The Politics of Banking in the Philippines*. Ithaca, N.Y.: Cornell University Press.

————. 2000a. "Obstructive Corruption: The Politics of Privilege in the Philippines." In *Rents, Rent-Seeking and Economic Development: Theory and Evidence in Asia*, edited by Mushtaq H. Khan and K. S. Jomo. Cambridge: Cambridge University Press.

————. 2000b. "Colonial Masters, National Politicos, and Provincial Lords: Central Authority and Local Autonomy in the American Philippines, 1900–1913." *Journal of Asian Studies* 59(2): 277–306.

————. 2008. "The Arroyo Imbroglio." *Journal of Democracy* 19(1): 141–55.

————. 2014a. "Dreams of Redemption: Localist Strategies of Political Reform in the Philippines." In *Social Difference and Constitutionalism in Pan-Asia*, edited by Susan H. Williams. New York: Cambridge University Press.

————. 2014b. "Linking Capital and Countryside: Patronage and Clientelism in Japan, Thailand, and the Philippines." In *Clientelism, Social Policy, and the Quality of Democracy*, edited by Diego Abente Brun and Larry Diamond. Baltimore, MD: Johns Hopkins University Press.

————. 2017. "Federalism in Context: Laying the Foundations for a Problem-Driven Process of Political Reform." In *Debate on Federal Philippines: A Citizen's Handbook*, edited by Ronald U. Mendoza. Quezon City: Ateneo de Manila University Press.

Hutchcroft, Paul D., and Erik Martinez Kuhonta. 2018. "Upending the 'Rules of the Game': Toward Greater Clarity in the Conceptualization of Institutions," a paper presented at the 2018 annual meeting of the American Political Science Association, Boston, Massachusetts, 31 August.

Hutchinson, Jane. 2001. "Crisis and Change in the Philippines." In *The Political Economy of Southeast Asia*, edited by Garry Rodan, Kevin Hewison, and Richard Robison. Oxford: Oxford University Press.

Imbeau, Louis M., François Pétry, and Moktar Lamari. 2001. "Left-Right Party Ideology and Government Policies: A Meta-Analysis." *European Journal of Political Research* 40(1): 1–29.

Inter-Parliamentary Union. 2016. "Women in National Parliaments." http://www.ipu.org/wmn-e/world.htm

Iverson, Torben, and David Soskice. 2006. "Electoral Institutions and the Politics of Coalitions: Why Some Democracies Redistribute More than Others." *American Political Science Review* 100(2): 165–81.

Jensen, Nathan. 2008. "Political Risk, Democratic Institutions, and Foreign Direct Investment." *The Journal of Politics* 70(4): 1040–52.

Jones, Mark P. 2005. "The Role of Parties and Party Systems in the Policymaking Process." Paper presented at the workshop on "State Reform, Public Policies, and Policymaking Processes," Inter-American Development Bank, Washington, D.C., 28 February–2 March.

Jou, Willy. 2009. "Electoral Reform and Party System Development in Japan and Taiwan: A Comparative Study." *Asian Survey* 49(5): 759–85.

Kang, Wensheng, Kiseok Lee, and Ronald A. Ratti. 2014. "Economic Policy Uncertainty and Firm-Level Investment." *Journal of Macroeconomics* 39: 42–53.

Katz, Richard. 2001. "Reforming the Italian Electoral Law, 1993." In *Mixed Member Electoral Systems: The Best of Both Worlds?* edited by Matthew Soberg Shugart and Martin P. Wattenberg. Oxford University Press.

Keefer, Philip. 2006. "Programmatic Parties: Where Do They Come From and Do They Matter." Paper prepared for the American Political Science Association Annual Meeting, 2006.

_____. 2007. "Clientelism, Credibility, and the Policy Choices of Young Democracies." *American Journal of Political* Science 51(4): 804–21.

_____. 2011. "Collective Action, Political Parties, and Pro-Development Public Policy." *Asian Development Review* 28(1): 94–118.

Kemp, Simon. 2017. "Digital in 2017: Global Overview," We Are Social. https://wearesocial.com/special-reports/digital-in-2017-global-overview

Kimura, Masataka. 2013. "Toward a More Workable Party-List System: Addressing Problems of Sectoral and Proportional Representation." *Philippine Political Science Journal* 34(1): 62–82.

Krennerich, Michael. 2009. "Impact of Electoral Systems on Women's Representation in Politics." *Report: European Commission for Democracy Through Law.* 23 February.

Kuhonta, Erik Martinez. 2008. "The Paradox of Thailand's 1997 'People's Constitution': Be Careful What You Wish For." *Asian Survey* 48: 373–92.

Ladra, Esmeralda. 2016. "Election-related Sex Disaggregated Data." Manila: unpublished manuscript.

Landé, Carl. 1965. *Leaders, Factions, and Parties: The Structure of Philippine Politics.* New Haven: Yale University Southeast Asian Studies.

Lim, Joseph Y., and Clarence G. Pascual. 2001. "The Detrimental Role of Biased Policies: Framework and Case Studies." *The Political Economy of Corruption: Studies in Transparency and Accountable Governance* No. 3. Transparent and Accountable Governance (TAG) Project, Manila.

Lin, Jih-wen. 2006. "Electoral Systems Today: The Politics of Reform in Japan and Taiwan," *Journal of Democracy* 17(2): 118–31.

Lindberg, Staffan, ed. 2009. *Democratization by Elections: A New Mode of Transition.* Baltimore, MD: Johns Hopkins University Press.

MacIntyre, Andrew J. 2002. *The Power of Institutions: Political Architecture and Governance.* Cornell: Cornell University Press.

Mainwaring, Scott, and Mariano Torcal. 2006. "Party System Institutionalization and Party System Theory After the Third Wave of Democratization." In *Handbook of Political Parties*, edited by Richard S. Katz and William J. Crotty. London: Sage.

Mainwaring, Scott, and Matthew Soberg Shugart. 1997. "Conclusion: Presidentialism and the Party System." In *Presidentialism and Democracy in Latin America*, edited by Scott Mainwaring and Matthew Soberg Shugart. New York: Cambridge University Press.

Mainwaring, Scott. 1999. *Rethinking Party Systems in the Third Wave of Democratization: The Case of Brazil*. Stanford: Stanford University Press.

Manacsa, Rodelio Cruz, and Alexander C. Tan. 2005. "Manufacturing Parties: Re-examining the Transient Nature of Philippine Political Parties." *Party Politics* 11(6): 748–65.

Mananlansan, Ely H. Jr. 2007. "The Philippine Party List System: Opportunities, Limitations and Prospects." In *Oligarchic Politics: Elections and Party-List System in the Philippines*, edited by Bobby M. Tuazon. Quezon City: Center for People Empowerment in Governance.

Massicotte, Louis, and André Blais. 1999. "Mixed Electoral Systems: A Conceptual and Empirical Survey." *Electoral Studies* 18: 341–66.

Matland, Richard E. 1993. "Institutional Variables Affecting Female Representation in National Legislatures: The Case of Norway." *Journal of Politics*, 55(3): 737–55.

Mayorga, Rene Antonio. 2001. "Electoral Reform in Bolivia: Origins of the Mixed-Member Proportional System." In *Mixed Member Electoral Systems: The Best of Both Worlds?* edited by Matthew Soberg Shugart and Martin P. Wattenberg. Oxford University Press.

McGillivray, Fiona. 1997. "Party Discipline as a Determinant of The Endogenous Formation Of Tariffs." *American Journal of Political Science* 41(2): 584–607.

Mietzner, Marcus. 2006. "Local Democracy." *Inside Indonesia 85*. http://www.insideindonesia.org/local-democracy

_____. 2013. *Money, Power, and Ideology: Political Parties in Post-Authoritarian Indonesia*. Honolulu, Singapore and Copenhagen: Hawaii University Press, NUS Press and NIAS Press.

Minnesota Advocates for Human Rights. 1996. *Report: Summary of Beijing Declaration and Platform for Action*. https://www.theadvocatesforhumanrights.org/uploads/beijing_declaration_1996.PDF

Montinola, Gabriella R. "Parties and Accountability in the Philippines." *Journal of Democracy* 10 (1999): 126–40.

Muga, Felix P. II. 2007a. "On Stakeholder-Based Allocation Method: A Fair Allocation of Power in Philippine Party-List System." In *Oligarchic Politics: Elections and Party-List System in the Philippines*, edited by Bobby M. Tuazon. Quezon City: Center for People Empowerment in Governance.

_____. 2007b. "The Negation of the Party-List System Law on the Principle of Proportional Representation." In *Oligarchic Politics: Elections and Party-List System in the Philippines*, edited by Bobby M. Tuazon. Quezon City: Center for People Empowerment in Governance.

_____. 2011. "The Carpio Formula and the Philippine Party-List System." In *12 Years of the Party List System: Marginalizing People's Representation*, edited by Bobby M. Tuazon. Quezon City: Center for People Empowerment in Governance.

National Electoral Reform Summit on the 2016 Elections "Unities." Cebu, December 5–6, 2015.

Nielson, Daniel L. 2003. "Supplying Trade Reform Political Institutions and Liberalization in Middle-Income Presidential Democracies." *American Political Science Review* 47(3): 470–91.

Noble, Greg W. 2010. "The Decline of Particularism in Japanese Politics," *Journal of East Asian Studies* 10(2): 239–67.

Nohlen, Dieter. 1984. *Elections and Electoral Systems*. Bonn: Friedrich Ebert Stiftung.

North, Douglass C. 1990. *Institutions, Institutional Change, and Economic Performance*. New York: University Press.

———. 1997. "Some Fundamental Puzzles in Economic History/Development." *Santa Fe Institute Studies in the Sciences of Complexity-Proceedings* 27: 223–38. Addison-Wesley Publishing Co.

North, Douglass. 1990. *Institutions, Institutional Change, and Economic Performance*. Cambridge, United Kingdom: Cambridge University Press.

O'Dwyer, Conor. 2006. *Runaway State-Building: Patronage Politics and Democratic Development*. Maryland: John Hopkins Press.

Olson, Mancur. 1982. *The Rise And Decline Of Nations: Economic Growth, Stagflation, And Social Rigidities*. New Haven, CT: Yale University Press.

———. 1993. "Dictatorship, Democracy, and Development." *American Political Science Review* 87(3): 567–76.

———. 2000. *Power And Prosperity: Outgrowing Communist and Capitalist Dictatorships*. New York: Basic Books.

Pangalangan, Raul C. 2011. "The Party-List Experiment: Three Challenges to Reformers." In *12 Years of the Party List System: Marginalizing People's Representation*, edited by Bobby M. Tuazon. Quezon City: Center for People Empowerment in Governance.

Persson, Torsten, and Guido Tabellini. 2003. *The Economic Effects of Constitutions*. MIT Press.

Philippine Commission on Women. 2010. *Magna Carta of Women*. [Republic Act 9710 and Implementing Rules and Regulations.] https://pcw.gov.ph/sites/default/files/documents/laws/republic_act_9710.pdf

Philippine Congress. 1995. Republic Act 7941. http://www.chanrobles.com/republicactno7941.htm

Presidential Museum and Library, Republic of the Philippines. "Elections of 1992." http://malacanang.gov.ph/74718-elections-of-1992/.

———. "Elections of 1998." http://malacanang.gov.ph/74722-elections-of-1998/.

———. "Elections of 2004." http://malacanang.gov.ph/74726-elections-of-2004/.

———. "Elections of 2010." http://malacanang.gov.ph/74730-elections-of-2010/.

———. "Elections of 2016." http://malacanang.gov.ph/77204-elections-of-2016

Quimpo, Nathan Gilbert. 2005. "The Left, Elections, and the Political Party System in the Philippines." *Critical Asian Studies* 37: 1–29.

Rahat, Gideon. 2001. "The Politics of Reform in Israel: How the Israeli Mixed System Came to Be." In *Mixed Member Electoral Systems: The Best of Both Worlds?* edited by Matthew Soberg Shugart and Martin P. Wattenberg. Oxford University Press.

Randall, Vicky, and Lars Svåsand. 2002. "Party Institutionalization in New Democracies." *Party Politics* 8(1): 5–29.

Reed, Steven R., and Michael F. Thies. 2001. "The Causes of Electoral Reform in Japan." In *Mixed Member Electoral Systems: The Best of Both Worlds?* edited by Matthew Soberg Shugart and Martin P. Wattenberg. Oxford University Press.

Reilly, Benjamin, and Ramon C. Casiple. 2016. "Single Ticket: How about Voting for President and VP Together." Rappler, 23 March 2016. https://www.rappler.com/nation/politics/elections/2016/126795-single-ticket-president-vice-president.

Reilly, Benjamin, and Reyes, Socorro L. 2016. "Zipper System: How to Get More Women Elected". Rappler, 18 April 2016. https://www.rappler.com/nation/politics/elections/2016/129938-zipper-system-get-more-women-elected-congress

Reilly, Benjamin. 2001. *Democracy in Divided Societies: Electoral Engineering for Conflict Management.* Cambridge University Press.

———. 2006. *Democracy and Diversity: Political Engineering in the Asia-Pacific.* Oxford: Oxford University Press.

———. 2007. "Democratization and Electoral Reform in the Asia-Pacific Region: Is there an 'Asian Model' of Democracy?" *Comparative Political Studies* 40(11): 1350–71.

———. 2011. "Centripetalism." In *The Routledge Handbook of Ethnic Conflict,* edited by Karl Cordell and Stefan Wolff. London and New York: Routledge.

———. 2015. "Electoral Systems." In *Routledge Handbook of Southeast Asian Democratization,* edited by William Case. London and New York: Routledge.

———. 2016. "PH Party List: Making it More Representative." Rappler, 1 April 2016. https://www.rappler.com/nation/politics/elections/2016/127800-philippines-party-list-more-representative

Remmer, Karen L. 2008. "The Politics of Institutional Change: Electoral Reform in Latin America: 1978–2002." *Party Politics* 14(1): 5–30.

Ressa, Maria A. 2016. "Propaganda War: Weaponizing the Internet." Rappler, 3 October 2016. https://www.rappler.com/nation/148007-propaganda-war-weaponizing-internet

Reyes, Socorro L. 2016. "Gender-Sensitive Code of Conduct for Candidates and Political Parties." Manila: unpublished manuscript.

Reynolds, Andrew, Ben Reilly, and Andrew Ellis. 2005. *Electoral System Design: The New International IDEA Handbook.* Stockholm: International Institute for Democracy and Electoral Assistance.

Rich, Roland. 2012. *Parties and Parliaments in Southeast Asia: Non-Partisan Chambers in Indonesia, the Philippines and Thailand.* London and New York: Routledge.

Rivera, Temario. 2007. "The Crisis of Philippine Electoral Democracy." In *Oligarchic Politics: Elections and Party-List System in the Philippines,* edited by Bobby M. Tuazon. Quezon City: Center for People Empowerment in Governance.

———. 2012. "In Search of Credible Elections and Parties: The Philippine Paradox." In *Chasing the Wind: Assessing Philippine Democracy,* edited by Felipe B.

Miranda, Malaya C. Ronas, and Ronald D. Holmes. Quezon City: Commission on Human Rights, Philippines.

Roberts, Kenneth M. 2002. "Party-Society Linkages and Democratic Representation in Latin America." *Canadian Journal of Latin American and Caribbean Studies* 27(53): 9–34.

Rock, Michael. 2013. "East Asia's Democratic Developmental States and Economic Growth." *Journal of East Asian Studies* 13(1): 1–34.

Rodan, Garry. 2005. "Westminster in Singapore: Now You See it, Now You Don't." In *Westminster Legacies: Democracy and Responsible Government in Asia and the Pacific*, edited by Haig Patapan, John Wanna and Patrick Weller. Sydney: UNSW Press.

Rodriguez, Agustin Martin G. 2002. *The Winding Road to Representation: The Philippine Party-List Experience*. Quezon City: Ateneo School of Government/ Friedrich Ebert Stiftung.

Rodriguez, Agustin Martin G., and Djorina Velasco. 1998. *Democracy Rising? The Trials and Triumphs of the 1998 Party-List Elections*. Quezon City: Institute of Politics and Governance/Friedrich Ebert Stiftung.

Rodrik, Dani. 1989. "Credibility of Trade Reform: A Policy Maker's Guide." *World Economy* 12(1): 1–16.

_____. 1991. "Policy Uncertainty and Private Investment in Developing Countries." *Journal of Development Economics* 36(2): 229–42.

_____. 2007. *One Economics, Many Recipes: Globalization, Institutions, and Economic Growth*. Princeton: Princeton University Press.

Rubaidi. 2016. "East Java: New Clientelism and the Fading of Aliran Politics". In *Electoral Dynamics in Indonesia: Money Politics, Patronage and Clientelism at the Grassroots*, edited by Edward Aspinall and Mada Sukmajati. Singapore: National University of Singapore Press.

Santos, Soliman M. 1997. "The Philippines Tries the Party-List System (A Progressive Approach)." *Kasarinlan* 13(2): 5–18.

Sarmiento, Rene V. 2011. "The Party-List System: A Social Justice Tool." In *12 Years of the Party List System: Marginalizing People's Representation,* edited by Bobby M. Tuazon. Quezon City: Center for People Empowerment in Governance.

Schaffer, Charles. 2007. *Elections for Sale : The Causes and Consequences of Vote Buying*. Quezon City: Ateneo De Manila University Press.

Scheiner, Ethan. 2008. "Does Electoral System Reform Work? Electoral System Lessons from Reforms of the 1990s." *Annual Review of Political Science* 11: 161–81.

Selway, J. S. 2011. "Electoral Reform and Public Policy Outcomes in Thailand: The Politics of the 30 Baht Health Scheme." *World Politics* 63(1): 165–202.

_____. 2015. *Coalitions of the Well-Being*. Cambridge University Press.

Shugart, Matthew S. and Martin P. Wattenberg, eds. 2001. *Mixed-Member Electoral Systems: the Best of Both Worlds?* New York: Oxford University Press.

Shugart, Matthew Soberg, and Martin P. Wattenberg. 2001. "Mixed Electoral Systems: A Definition and Typology." In *Mixed Member Electoral Systems: The Best of Both Worlds?* edited by Matthew Soberg Shugart and Martin P. Wattenberg. Oxford University Press.

Shugart, Matthew Soberg, E. Moreno, and L. E. Fajardo. 2007. "Deepening Democracy Through Renovating Political Practices: The Struggle for Electoral Reform in Columbia." In *Peace, Democracy, and Human Rights in Columbia*, edited by C. Welna and G. Gallon. Notre Dame University Press.

Shugart, Matthew Soberg. 2001. "Electoral 'Efficiency' and the Move to Mixed-member Systems." *Electoral Studies* 20(2): 173–93.

_____. 2008. "Inherent and Contingent Factors in Reform Initiation in Plurality Systems." In *To Keep or To Change First Past the Post*, edited by Andre Blais. Oxford University Press.

Stokes, Susan. 1999. "Political Parties and Democracy." *Annual Review of Political Science* 2: 243–67.

Tan, Paige Johnson. 2002. "Anti-Party Reaction in Indonesia: Causes and Implications." *Contemporary Southeast Asia* 24(3): 484–50.

Taylor, Robert H. 1996. "Introduction." In *The Politics of Elections in Southeast Asia*, edited by R. H. Taylor. Cambridge: Woodrow Wilson Center and Cambridge University Press.

Thames, Frank C., and Martin S. Edwards. 2006. "Differentiating Mixed-Member Electoral Systems: Mixed Member Majoritarian and Mixed-Member Proportional Representation System and Government Expenditures." *Comparative Political Studies* 39(7): 905–27.

Timberman, David G. 1991. *A Changeless Land: Continuity and Change in Philippine Politics*. Armonk, New York: M.E. Sharpe.

Tommasi, Mariano. 2006. "The Institutional Foundations of Public Policy." *Economia* 6(2): 1–36.

Torres-Pilapil, Crisline. 2015. "The Origins of the Party List System in the 1986 Constitutional Commission." *Social Science Diliman* 11(1): 85–125.

Tsebelis, George. 1995. "Decision Making in Political Systems: Veto Players in Presidentialism, Parliamentarism, Multicameralism, and Multipartyism." *British Journal of Political Science* 25: 289–325.

_____. 2002. *Veto Players: How Political Institutions Work*. Princeton University Press.

Tuazon, Bobby M. 2007. "The Future of Oligarchic Politics and the Party-List System." In *Oligarchic Politics: Elections and Party-List System in the Philippines*, edited by Bobby M. Tuazon. Quezon City: Center for People Empowerment in Governance.

Tuazon, Bobby M., ed. 2011. *12 Years of the Party List System: Marginalizing People's Representation*. Quezon City: Center for People Empowerment in Governance.

Tucay, Marjohara. 2016. "Should the Party-List System Go?" Rappler, 8 August 2016. https://www.rappler.com/views/imho/142311-should-party-list-system-go

Ufen, Andreas. 2006. "Political Parties in Post-Suharto Indonesia: Between politik aliran and 'Philippinisation.'" GIGA Working Papers No. 37. Hamburg: German Institute of Global and Area Studies.

UN General Assembly, 66th Session. Resolution on Women and Political Participation. 19 December 2011.

Van Cott, Donna Lee. 2000. "Party System Development and Indigenous Populations in Latin America: The Bolivian Case." *Party Politics* 6(2): 155–74.

van de Walle, Nicolas, and Andres Rius. 2005. "Political Institutions and Economic Policy Reform." In *Understanding Market Reforms. Volume1: Philosophy, Politics and Stakeholders*, edited by José María Fanelli and Gary McMahon. Palgrave-MacMillan.

Veteran Federation Party, et al. v. Commission on Elections. Supreme Court of the Philippines, decided 2000. http://sc.judiciary.gov.ph/jurisprudence/2000/oct2000/136781.htm

Vitug, Marites Dañguilan. 2016. "The Scrum: Roxas, Binay, and the Political Machine." *Rappler*, 20 April 2016. http://www.rappler.com/nation/politics/elections/2016/129982-roxas-binay-political-machine.

Women's Environment and Development Organization. 2008. "Getting the Balance Right in National Parliaments." https://wedo.org/50-50-getting-the-balance-right-in-national-parliaments/

Wu, Yu-Shan. 2007. "Semi-Presidentialism—Easy to Choose, Difficult to Operate: The Case of Taiwan." In *Semi-Presidentialism Outside Europe*, edited by Robert Elgie and Sophia Moestrup. London: Routledge.

Wurfel, David. 1988. *Filipino Politics: Development and Decay*. Ithaca: Cornell University Press.

———. 1997. "The Party-List Elections: Sectoral or National? Success or Failure?" *Kasarinlan* 13(2): 19–30.

CONTRIBUTORS

EDWARD ASPINALL is a professor in the Department of Political and Social Change, part of the Coral Bell School of Asia-Pacific Affairs in the Australian National University. He is a specialist in the politics of Southeast Asia, especially Indonesia, and most of his research has been on democratization, ethnic politics and civil society in Indonesia, the separatist conflict and peace process in Aceh, and money politics in Southeast Asia. A co-authored book on vote buying and related forms of clientelistic politics in Indonesia is forthcoming with Cornell University Press.

RAMON C. CASIPLE, a political reform advocate and a political analyst, is the executive director of the non-governmental organization in the Philippines, the Institute for Political and Electoral Reform (IPER). He is a fellow in the Federalism Institute of the ruling party, the Partido Demokratiko Pilipino-Lakas ng Bayan (PDP-LABAN). He recently was author of the chapter "Political Reforms and Federalism" in the book *The Quest for a Federal Republic of the Philippines,* edited by the Federalism Institute (Manila: 2017).

ALLEN HICKEN is professor of political science at the University of Michigan. He studies political parties, institutions, political economy, and policy making in developing countries, with a focus on the Philippines and Thailand. He is the co-editor of *Electoral Dynamics in the Philippines: Money Politics, Patronage and Clientelism at the Grassroots*, forthcoming from NUS Press.

PAUL D. HUTCHCROFT, a scholar of comparative and Southeast Asian politics who has written extensively on Philippine politics and political economy, is a professor of political and social change in the Coral Bell School of Asia Pacific Affairs at the Australian National University. In recent work, he is editor of *Mindanao: The Long Journey to Peace and Prosperity* (Manila: Anvil Press, 2016).

NICO RAVANILLA is an assistant professor at the University of California San Diego's School of Global Policy & Strategy. His work spans the political economy of development, governance and policy analysis, with expertise on Southeast Asia, in particular, the Philippines.

BENJAMIN REILLY, a professor at the University of Western Australia, is a political scientist who specializes in democratization and electoral reform in the Indo-Pacific region. He was formerly dean of the Sir Walter Murdoch School at Murdoch University, and head of the Policy and Governance Program and director of the Centre for Democratic Institutions at the Australian National University. Prior to the 2016 Philippine elections, he wrote a series of informational articles (with accompanying videos) published by the online news source Rappler.

SOCORRO L. REYES, a feminist political analyst and women's rights advocate who has written extensively on women's political representation and participation, headed up the Asia-Pacific and Arab States division of UNIFEM (now UN Women) in New York from 2005 to 2011. She is currently Regional Gender and Governance Adviser of the Center for Legislative Development, and is the author of "Gender Assessment of National Law-Making Mechanisms and Processes in Selected Southeast Asian Countries: A CEDAW Perspective" (Bangkok: UN Women, 2012).

JULIO C. TEEHANKEE, an educator, researcher, and political consultant with wide experience in electoral and political party related activities, is professor of political science and international studies at De La Salle University. Teehankee served as chair of the Subcommittee on Political Reforms of the Consultative Committee to Review the 1987 Constitution that was convened by President Rodrigo Duterte in early 2018. He has published extensively on Philippine elections and party politics, and his latest publication is "Regional Dimensions of the 2016 General Elections in the Philippines: Emerging Contours of Federalism," *Regional and Federal Studies* 28 (2018).

MEREDITH L. WEISS, professor of political science at the Rockefeller College of Public Affairs & Policy at the University at Albany, State University of New York, has published widely on political mobilization and contention, the politics of identity and development, and electoral politics in Southeast Asia, with particular focus on Malaysia and Singapore. A forthcoming book explores the resilience of electoral-authoritarian politics in Malaysia and Singapore.

INDEX

Abdurrahman Wahid, 96
act motivation, 68
alternative vote system (AV), 45–46
Ang Bagong Bayani, et al. v. COMELEC
   (2001), 162–163
Aquino, Benigno Jr, 113
Aquino, Benigno S. III, 8, 115, 120
Aquino, Corazon C., 8, 113
Asia, electoral reform in, 56
Asian Financial Crisis, 71
Atong Paglaum, et al. v. COMELEC (2013),
   162–163

ballot structure, 27, 28–29
Bangsomoro Basic Law, 90
Banharn Silpa-archa, 70
barangay captains, 135
Beijing Platform for Action 1995, 78
block vote, 45 fn 2
Bolivia, 64

Cambodia, 50
campaign finances, 123, 124, 137
   donations, 138, 143
   expenditures, 127–128
   Indonesia, 144
   team expenses, 135
campaign machinery, local, 141, 144
campaign structure, 135
campaign teams, Philippines, 135
   monitoring loyalty, 135
   and patronage, 104–105
   pre-election activities, 136
campaign teams, Indonesia, 100, 101–102
candidate support to voters, 145
candidate-centric (centered) systems, 14–15,
   16, 23
   and clientelism, 37

consequences of, 40
   election of executives, 11 l
   lack of long-term focus, 36
   and national policies, 35
   party discipline, 37
   reversal risk, 33
   Thailand, 70
candidate-centric elections, Indonesia,
   99–101, 103
Carpio formula, 158, 159–160, 160 fn4
catalytic event, 60, 63–66, 72–73
   1987 Constitution, 66
Chile, 82
clientelism, 37
   Indonesia, 97, *see also* vote buying
closed-list proportional representation, 4, 24,
   47, 147, 163–164, 167
   in ASEAN countries, 165
   as future direction for Philippines, 186
   and gender equality, 47–48
   Indonesia, 97
   Japan, 183
   local level, 187
   party cohesion, 32
   with party list system, 151–152
   public goods delivery, 52
   reasons for use, 164–165
   women's representation, 77, 82
club goods, 133
collective gifts, 105
COMELEC, 123, 127, 146, 162
   Gender and Disability Committee, 88
Commission on Audit (COA) (Philippines),
   127
Communist Party of the Philippines, 112
compensatory mixed electoral systems
   (mixed-member proportional systems,
   MMP), 48, 48 fn6, 154

Consortium on Electoral Reforms (CER), 118, 119
Consortium on Political Party Reforms (CPPR), 119
Constitution, 1973 (Philippines), 8, 112
Constitution, 1987 (Philippines), 66 national list in, 49
    party list system, 151
    term limits in, 114
    and weak political parties, 10
Constitutional Convention, 1971, 7
Constitutional Convention, 1986, 8
Constitutional Court (Indonesia), 99
Constitutional Drafting Assembly (Thailand), 70–71
constitutional revision, 8
    Duterte administration, 129–130
Consultative Committee to Review the 1987 Constitution, 2, 8, 73, 74, 129–130
    draft constitution, 9 (fn10) federalism, 9
Convention on the Elimination of All Forms of Discrimination Against Women (CEDAW), 78–79, 88
Costa Rica, 83

delegative institutions, 68–69, 71, 73–74
    New Zealand, 69
    Thailand, 70
    Venezuela, 69–70
democracy and political parties, 116–117
democratic accountability, electoral rules, 169–170
democratic transition, 66
development outcomes, 20
disproportionality, 154
district magnitude, 5, 27, 28, 46–47 and proportionality, 165–166
    and women's representation, 77, 82–83
Duterte, Rodrigo, 73, 116
    and constitutional revision, 8, 129 and PDP-LABAN, 142
dynastic candidates, 147, 180–181

East Timor, 50
EDSA "People Power" Revolution, 1986, 113

election campaigns, Indonesia, 100–101, 102, 103
election campaigns, 141–143
election payments, 136, *see also* vote buying, vote brokers, campaign teams
elections 1992 (Philippines), 113–114
electoral administration, 5
electoral districts, Thailand, 184
electoral formula, 27
electoral reform proposals, 57
electoral rules, 169–170
electoral system diversity, Southeast Asia, 49
electoral system redesign (or reform), 2, 3, 10, 20, 59
    act motivation, 68
    advantages of, 22, 23
    Asia, 56
    Bolivia, 64
    catalytic event, 63–66
    conditions for, 60
    coordination with other reforms, 54
    delegative institutions, 68–69
    executive elections, 4, 5
    Great Britain, 64–65
    incumbent preferences, 67
    Italy, 63, 64
    Japan, 63, 65–66
    New Zealand, 63. 64–65
    outcome motivation, 67–68
    tension between different institutional reforms, 55
    Thailand, 53, 63
    SMDP and OPLR shortcomings, 186
    Venezuela, 63, 69–70
electoral systems, 3, 7, 27, 43, 152
    district magnitude, 5
    implementation risk, 33
    incentives, 53
    intraparty and interparty dimensions, 61–62
    number of parties, 32
    and party system, 153
    and politics of development, 38
    reversal risk, 33

systemic failure, 62
types of, 7, 44
Electoral Systems Redesign for Development
project, 19–22
electoral threshold, minimum, 160
electronic voting, 135
employment, as patronage, 139
Estrada, Joseph, 8
executive elections, 4
Indonesia, 95–96, 97–98
and party cohesion, 39
separate, 11, 113

factionalization, 39
federalism, 2, 8, 22
and electoral reforms, 57
and party development, 130
and political stability, 9
and women's representation, 90
first past the post (FPTP), 3, 45, 53, 151, *see
also* single-member district plurality
formula of decision, 152

gender equality, 24, 77
in closed-list proportional representation,
47–48
within political parties, 87–88
Gender Parity Law, 2000 (France), 86
gender quota, 78, 84, 85–86, 147
Gender Sensitive Code of Conduct
for Candidates and Political Parties
(Philippines), 88
gifts, as patronage, 105
Great Britain, 64–65

House Bill 3655, *see* Political Party
Development Act, 2008
hyper-particularism (hyper-personalism), 62,
70, 72
hyper-partisanship, 62
hyper-representation, Thailand, 70
hyper-representativeness, 62

Iglesia ni Cristo, 143
implementation risk, 33, 34
incumbent preferences, 67, 71, 73,
independent candidates, 172, 177
Indonesia, 99
Indonesia, electoral system, 93, 94–95,
96–97, 99, 106–107
direct elections, of executive, 97–98
indirect elections, of executive, 95–96
open-list proportional representation
system, 50, 54, 55
Indonesia, election campaigns, 100–101
campaign expenditure, 144
Indonesia, patronage politics 104–106, 108
candidate support to voters, 56, 144, 145
clientelism, 97
vote buying, 104–106
Indonesia, political parties, 51–52, 140
instant runoff voting, *see* alternative vote
institutionalization, of political parties, 51
institutionalization, of politics, 5
integration, in party list system, 157–160
Interim Batasan Pambansa (IBP), 112–113
interparty dimension, 62
intraparty competition, in MPS, 10, 178,
182
intraparty dimension, 62
Ireland, 82
Islamic parties, Indonesia, 95, 103
Israel, 64
Italy, 63, 64

Japan Socialist Party, 182
Japan, electoral system, 63, 183, 185
catalyst for reform, 65–66
multi-member plurality system, 182–183

Kilusang Bagong Lipunan (KBL), 112

Lakas ng Bayan (LABAN), 112–113
legal threshold, women's representation, 83
legislated (or mandated) quotas, 84, 85
Liberal Democratic Party (Japan), 65, 182,
183
Liberal Party (Philippines), 141, 142

lider, campaign teams, 135, 145
Liga ng mga Barangay, 176
list proportional representation, and women's representation, 81–82
local elections, 176–177, 187, 180–181, *see also* local politics
Local Government Code, 1991, 134–135, 176
local party machines, 140–141, 142, 144–145
  incumbent advantage, 145–146
  non-party networks, 143
  patronage practices, 146

Macapagal-Arroyo, Gloria, 114–115
  and constitutional revision, 8
  and Political Party Development Bill, 118
Magna Carta of Women, 2009 (Philippines), 78, 79, 88
majoritarian systems, 45, 46, 152, 153, *see also* plurality and majoritarian systems
Malaysia, electoral system, 50–51
candidate support to voters, 144, 145
  political parties, 140
mandated quotas, 84, 86
Marcos-era politics, 112–113
Marcos, Ferdinand E., 8
marginalized groups and sectors, 24, 49, 156, 164
  in party list system, 151, 160
martial law (Philippines), 112
mass media, in campaign finances, 124
Megawati Surkarnoputri, 94, 96, 98
mixed electoral systems, 4, 28, 151, 153–154, 167
  Cambodia, 50
  Indonesia, 50
  Philippines, 49
  Singapore, 50
  Thailand, 49–50
  types of, 48
mixed-member majoritarian (MMM) systems, *see* parallel mixed electoral systems
mixed-member proportional (MMP) systems, *see* compensatory mixed electoral systems

motivation, for electoral system reform, 60
multi-member districts, 82
multi-member electorates, 46
multi-member plurality system (MPS), 3, 11, 38, 45, 169
  incentives in, 170
  intraparty competition, 10, 178
  Japan, 182–183
  multiple parties in, 171
  and party weakness, 39
  Senate elections, 170–171
  subnational elections, 176–177
  Thailand, 183–184
multi-party system, 94–95, 153
Myanmar, electoral system, 50–51, 53

National Assembly, proposed (Philippines), 163
national policies, 31, 34–35
  and candidate-centered system, 40
  and clientelism, 37
  and regionally based parties, 35–36
  party-centric vs candidate-centric systems, 37
  see also national goods, 30 (fn3)
New People's Army, 140
New Zealand, 63, 64–65, 69
Nominated Members of Parliament (Singapore), 50
non-compensatory system, *see* parallel mixed electoral systems

objective of representation, 152–153
open-list proportional representation, 4, 47
  election campaigns, 103
  Indonesia, 99–100, 108
  and marginalized groups, 49
  and patronage, 106
  shortcomings, 186
outcome motivation, 67–68

Panganiban formula, 158
parallel mixed electoral systems (mixed-member majoritarian systems, MMP), 48, 69, 154, 163

Thailand, 184
New Zealand, 69
parliamentarism, 6
parliamentary system, 22
Partai Demokrasi Indonesia (PDI-P), 94
Partai Nasional Indonesia (PNI), 94
Partido Demokratiko Pilipino (PDP), 113
party institutionalization, 32
Party List Law, 1995, 113, 158, 161
party list organizations, number of, 158
party list seats, in proposed National
    Assembly, 164
party list system (PLS), 4, 11, 39, 72, 113
    differences to standard proportional
      representation, 155
    effect of court rulings, 54–55
    integration issues, 157–160
    measures for reform, 163–164
    and national policies, 31
    reform of, 151–152
    representation issues, 160–161
    seat allocation, 158–159
    shortcomings of, 151, 156–157
    vote threshold, 156
    women's representation, 81
party magnitude and women's representation,
    82–83
party registration, Indonesia, 95, 107
party registration, 164
party switching, 39, 107, 130
    measures for reform, 164
party-centered politics, 62
party-centered systems, and national policies,
    24, 35, 36, 37
patronage politics, 13, 37, 134
    donations to organizations, 143
    Indonesia, 104–106, 108
    at local level, 146
    and Political Party Development Bill, 118
    role of campaign teams, 136
    vote buying or support, 144 *see also*
      clientelism
patronage, and weak parties, 14
patronage, types of , 139, 140
patron-client model, Philippines, 144

Pederasyon ng Sangguniang Kabataan, 176
People's Consultative Assembly (MPR)
    (Indonesia), 96
People's Representative Council (DPR)
    (Indonesia), 94–95
personalistic politics, 61, *see also* clientelism
Philippine Political Party Conference, 2002,
    118
pluralitarianism, 62, 72
plurality systems, 3, 45
    formula of decision, 152
    objective of representation, 153
plurality and majoritarian systems (winner-
    takes-all), 27–28, 61
    and party cohesion, 32
policy environments, and economic
    development, 29, 30
political parties, large number of, 14–15, 23,
    32, 171–172
political parties, 13, 39, 114
    and democracy, 116–117
    and gender equality, 87–88
    local, 140–141
    regulation of, 51–52
    in Senate, 175
    state subsidy, 125–126
Political Party Development Bill for proposed
    Political Party Development Act, 117–118,
    119
    campaign contributions, 124
    campaign expenditures, 127
    Duterte administration, 129
    provisions, 121
    state subsidy for political parties, 125
    turncoatism, 121–122
Political Party Reform workshop, 2012,
    119–120
poll watchers, 138
poorer voters, 56
populist leaders, 66, 73 fn5
Prabowo Subianto, 98
Presidential Commission on Reform of the
    State, 1984 (Venezuela), 70
presidential elections, 2004, 115, 177
presidential elections, 1998, 114

presidential elections, 2010, 115–116
presidential elections, 2016, 116
presidentialism, 6
presidents, post-Marcos, 8
proportional representation (PR) systems, 3, 4, 27, 28, 46
  in 1987 Constitution, 161
  differences to party list system, 155
  formula of decision, 152
  Indonesia, 95
  in mixed electoral systems, 48
  technical process, 46 fn4
  types of, 47
  vision of, 61
  and women's representation, 77
proportionality, and district magnitude, 165–166
proportionality, in party list system, 158, 161
public goods delivery, 52, 56

Ramos, Fidel V., 8
regionally based parties, and national policies, 35–36
representation in party list system, 160–161
representational structures, 2, 6
reserved seats, 84
retail politics, 144, *see also* vote buying
reversal risk, 33
Royal Commission on the Electoral System, 1980 (New Zealand), 69

scholarships, as patronage, 139
seat allocation, in party list system, 158–159
sectoral representation, 161, *see also*
  marginalized sectors
  Ang Bagong Bayani, et al. v. COMELEC (2001), 162
  Atong Paglaum, et al. v. COMELEC (2013), 163
semi-presidentialism, 6
Senate elections, 175, 186
  multi-member plurality system, 170–171
  personalistic campaigns, 171
Singapore, 50

single non-transferable vote (SNTV) (Japan), 182
single transferable vote (STV), 47 fn5
single-member district plurality (SMDP), 3, 28, 38, 45, 151
  Japan, 183
  Malaysia and Myanmar, 50–51
  shortcomings of, 186
  Thailand, 184
  women's representation, 81
  see also first past the post
social media, in campaigns, 142–143, 148
Southeast Asia electoral reform, 51, 54
  lack of cohesion, 55
state subsidy, political parties, 125–126
  audit, 127–128
  monitoring, 127
Statement of Contributions and Expenditures (SOCE), 123, 124
Stinky Trick (Israel), 64
subnational elections, 176–177, *see also* local elections
subnational levels of government, 7
subnational politics, 140–141
success teams, *see* campaign teams
Sukarno, 94
Susilo Bambang Yudhoyono, 98
Sweden, 83
systemic failure, of electoral system, 60–61, 72

Task Force on Campaign Finance (COMELEC), 123
term limits, 39
Thai Rak Thai party (Thailand), 53, 184
Thailand, 33, 34, 70, 185
  1997 Constitution and electoral reform, 51
  delegative institutions, 70
  electoral districts, 184
  health reforms, 56
  mixed electoral system, 49–50
  multi-member plurality system, 183–184
  post-1987 public goods delivery, 52–53
  single member districts and political party development, 55

thinking and working politically (TWP), 20
three-seat cap, 165 *see also* party list system: seat allocation
threshold rules , 107, 184
Tricycle Operators and Drivers Associations, 143
Tunisia, 82
turncoatism, political, 121–122
two-party system, 153
two-round system (TRS), 5, 45–46
    Indonesia, 98 fn1

United Democratic Opposition (UNIDO), 113
United Nations General Assembly Resolution of 2011, 78
utang na loob, 145

Venecia, Jose de, 118, 119
Venezuela, 63, 69–70
voluntary party quotas, 84–85, 86, 87
vote brokers, 136, 101–102
vote buying, 133, 134
    bloc payments, 139
    cultural acceptance of, 144-145
    and electronic voting, 135
    goods and services, 139
    Indonesia, 96, 104-106
    limitations of term, 143–144
    Local Government Code, 1991, 135
    non-incumbents, 139
    polling day, 138
    role of campaign teams, 136–137
vote selling, 138
vote shares, 181
vote splitting, 178
vote squatting, 136
vote threshold, 156
voter mobilization, Indonesia, 103, 171
voter turnout, 14

winner-takes-all, *see* plurality and majoritarian systems
Women and Gender and Development Programs, 79

Women Participation and Representation in Political Parties Act, 2013 (Philippines), 79
women's representation, 12, 77
    Bangsomoro Basic Law, 90
    Chile, 82
    district magnitude, 82–83
    and dynastic system, 147
    frameworks, 78–79
    legal threshold, 83
    in list proportional representation, 81–82
    party magnitude, 82–83
    structural factors, 87–88, 90
    top 15 parliaments, 80, 82

Yudhoyono, Susilo Banbang, 56

zipper system, 24, 47, 81–82, 90, 147
    see also gender equality

TABLE 7.1 TIMELINE OF POLITICAL PARTY DEVELOPMENT BILL

Congressional Year	House /Senate Bill Number	Title and Progress of Bills	Principal Author(s)
12th Congress (2001–2004)	**House Bill 3665**	**"The Political Party Development Act of 2003"**	Representative Jose De Venecia Jr.
	Senate Bill 2442	**"The Political Party Development Act of 2003"**	Senator Edgardo Angara
13th Congress (2004–2007)	**House Bill 5877** (Substituting HBs 190 and HB 224) As per committee report 2024	**"The Political Party Development Act of 2007"** or its full title: "An Act Strengthening the Political Party System, Appropriating Funds Therefor, and for Other Purposes" *Passed on 3rd reading*	Representative Jose De Venecia Jr.
	Senate Bill 1051	**"The Political Party Development Act of 2004"** or its full title: "An Act Strengthening the Political Party System, Appropriating Funds Therefor, and for Other Purposes"	Senator Edgardo Angara
	Senate Bill 1329	**Campaign Finance Reform and Party Development Act** "An Act Instituting Campaign Finance Reform and Strengthening the Political Party System and Providing Funds Therefor"	Senator Ralph Recto
14th Congress (2007–2010)	**House Bill 3655** (Substituting HBs 124, 1677, 2054, 2128, & 2268)	**"The Political Party Development Act of 2007"** or its full title: "An Act Strengthening the Political Party System, Appropriating Funds Therefor, and for Other Purposes" *Passed on 3rd reading but subsequently recalled to*	Representatives Juan Edgardo Angara, Jose de Venecia Jr., Rufus Rodriguez, and Teodoro Locsin Jr.

	Senate Bill 587	**"The Political Party Development Act of 2007"** or its full title: "An Act Strengthening the Political Party System, Appropriating Funds Therefor, and for Other Purposes"	Senator Jinggoy Ejercito Estrada
	Senate Bill 227	**"The Political Party Development Act of 2007"** or its long form: "An Act Strengthening the Political Party System, Appropriating Funds Therefor, and for Other Purposes"	Senator Loren Legarda
	Senate Bill 67	**"The Political Party Development Act of 2007"** or its full title: "An Act Strengthening the Political Party System, Appropriating Funds Therefor, and for Other Purposes"	Senator Edgardo Angara
	Senate Bill 147	**An Act defining and Punishing Political Turncoatism and Opportunism**	Senator J. Richard Gordon
15th Congress (2010–2013)	**House Bill 6551** (Substitute bill for HB 49 and 403) per committee report	**"The Political Party Development Act of 2012"** or its full title: "An Act Strengthening the Political Party System, Appropriating Funds Therefor, and for Other Purposes" *Passed on 3rd reading*	Representative Rufus Rodriguez
	Senate Bill 3214 (Substitute bill for SB 51 and SB 607) per committee report	**"Political Party System"** or its full title "An Act Strengthening the Political Party System, Appropriating Funds Therefor, and for Other Purposes"	Senators Edgardo Angara, Miriam Defensor-Santiago, Jinggoy Ejercito Estrada, and Franklin Drilon

	Senate Bill 51	**"The Political Party Development Act of 2010"** or its long form: "An Act Strengthening the Political Party System, Appropriating Funds Therefor, and for Other Purposes"	Senator Edgardo J. Angara
	Senate Bill 607	**"The Political Party Development Act of 2010"** or its full title: "An Act Strengthening the Political Party System, Appropriating Funds Therefor, and for Other Purposes"	Senator Jinggoy Ejercito Estrada
16th Congress (2013–2016)	**House Bill 3987** (Substitute bill for HBs 3242, 2362, 389, and 309)	**"The Political Party Development Act of 2014"** or its full title: "An Act Strengthening the Political Party System, Appropriating Funds Therefor, and for Other Purposes"	Representative Gloria Macapagal-Arroyo
	Senate Bill 1099	**"The Political Party Development Act of 2013"** or its full title: "An Act Strengthening the Political Party System, Appropriating Funds Therefor, and for Other Purposes"	Senator Joseph Victor G. Ejercito
	Senate Bill 2635	**"The Political Party Development Act of 2015"** or its full title: "An Act Strengthening the Political Party System, Appropriating Funds Therefor, and for Other Purposes"	Senator Jinggoy Ejercito Estrada
17th Congress (2016–2018)	**House Bill 522**	"An Act Strengthening the Political Party System and Appropriating Funds Therefor"	Representative Fredenil Castro, Jr.
	House Bill 697	"An Act Strengthening the Political Party System and Appropriating Funds Therefor"	Representative Gloria Macapagal-Arroyo

House Bill 1695	"An Act Strengthening the Political Party System and Appropriating Funds Therefor"	Representative Maximo Rodriguez, Jr.
House Bill 7088	"An Act Strengthening the Political Party System and Appropriating Funds Therefor and for Other Purposes"	Representative Gary Alejano
Senate Bill 226	**"Political Party System Act"** or its full title "An Act Strengthening the Political Party System"	Senator Franklin Drilon
Senate Bill 455	**"Political Party System Development Act of 2016"** or its full title "An Act Strengthening the Political Party System, Appropriating Funds Therefor, and for Other Purposes"	Senator Antonio Trillanes, Jr.
Senate Bill 885	**"Political Party Development Act of 2016"** or its full title "An Act Strengthening the Political Party System, Appropriating Funds Therefor, and for Other Purposes"	Senator Joseph Victor Ejercito
Senate Bill 1696	**"Women Participation and Representation in Political Parties Act of 2018"** or its full title "An Act Promoting Women Participation and Equitable Representation In and by Political Parties, Giving Incentives Therefor, Creating the Women In Political Parties Empowerment Fund, and For Other Purposes"	Senator Risa Hontiveros

CPSIA information can be obtained
at www.ICGtesting.com
Printed in the USA
JSHW021759210120
3659JS00001B/2